EDUCATION AND NEW TECHNOLOGIES

When should children begin their digital diet? Does the use of new technology hinder or enhance children's literacy development? Do new technologies give children new abilities or undermine their skills and identities? Are learners safe in modern online educational spaces?

Kieron Sheehy and Andrew Holliman have assembled expert contributors from around the world to discuss these questions and have divided the book into three parts:

- early engagement with new technologies: decisions, dangers and data
- new technology: supporting all learners or divisive tools
- global and cultural reflections on educational technology.

Education and New Technologies focuses on aspects of education where the use of twenty-first-century technologies has been particularly controversial, contemplating the possible educational benefits alongside potential negative impacts on learners. Topics covered include:

- e-books and their influence on literacy skills
- games-based learning
- the impact of new technologies on abilities and disabilities
- learning analytics and the use of large-scale learner data
- cyberbullying
- intelligent technologies and the connected learner.

A twenty-first-century book for twenty-first-century concerns, *Education and New Technologies* presents up-to-date research and clear, engaging insight about the relationship between technology and how we learn.

Kieron Sheehy is Professor of Education in Innovation Pedagogies in the Faculty of Wellbeing, Education & Language Studies, The Open University, UK, specialising in inclusion, pedagogy and new technologies. He is Editor of the *Current Debates in Educational Psychology* series.

Andrew Holliman is a Senior Lecturer in the Faculty of Health and Life Sciences, Coventry University, UK, specialising in the study of children's literacy learning. He recently edited *The Routledge International Companion to Educational Psychology* and is also Associate Editor for the *Journal of Research in Reading*.

EDUCATION AND NEW TECHNOLOGIES

Perils and Promises for Learners

Edited by Kieron Sheehy and Andrew Holliman

Routledge
Taylor & Francis Group

LONDON AND NEW YORK

First published 2018
by Routledge
2 Park Square, Milton Park, Abingdon, Oxon OX14 4RN

and by Routledge
711 Third Avenue, New York, NY 10017

Routledge is an imprint of the Taylor & Francis Group, an informa business

© 2018 selection and editorial matter, Kieron Sheehy and Andrew
Holliman; individual chapters, the contributors

British Library Cataloguing in Publication Data
A catalogue record for this book is available from the British Library

Library of Congress Cataloging in Publication Data
A catalog record for this book has been requested

ISBN: 978-1-138-18493-0 (hbk)
ISBN: 978-1-138-18494-7 (pbk)
ISBN: 978-1-315-64485-1 (ebk)

Typeset in Bembo
by Deanta Global Publishing Services, Chennai, India

This book is dedicated to Andrew's *little men* (children), Alexander and Leo – you make your Mum and Dad so proud every single day.

It is also dedicated to the Craniofacial Support charity 'Headlines' (www.headlines.org.uk) and to the Oxford Craniofacial Unit at John Radcliffe Hospital.

CONTENTS

FIGURES

TABLES

CONTRIBUTORS

Mirit Barzillai, PhD, is an Associate Researcher at the Edmond J. Safra Brain Research Center for the Study of Learning Disabilities at the University of Haifa, IL. Her work focuses on reading development and remediation across different media.

Charlotte Brownlow, PhD, is an Associate Professor in the School of Psychology and Counselling, The University of Southern Queensland, Australia. Her research interests focus on understandings of diversity and difference and the impacts that constructions of these have on the crafting of individual identities, particularly for individuals identifying as being on the autism spectrum.

Lucie Corcoran, PhD, is a Psychologist and Researcher based in Dublin, Ireland. Having graduated from University College Dublin with a BA in Psychology, Lucie attained an MA by research on the psychology of bullying and cyberbullying in the Dun Laoghaire Institute of Art, Design and Technology. Lucie completed her PhD in Trinity College Dublin, with research focusing on bullying, cyberbullying and cyber aggression, in relation to psychological aspects such as mental health, empathy and coping styles. Lucie has a particular interest in the application of psychology to educational and healthcare settings in order to maximize schoolchildren's educational attainment and health and well-being.

Rebecca Ferguson, PhD, is a Senior Lecturer in the Institute of Educational Technology, The Open University. She is an executive member of the Society for Learning Analytics Research, and has taken a leading role in many international learning analytics events, including several associated with her work on the European Learning Analytics Community Exchange (LACE). Recently, she led the LAEP project, which helped European policy-makers to set out an agenda for the use of learning analytics.

Clifford Omodele Fyle, PhD, is Assistant Professor in Instructional and Learning Technologies, Sultan Qaboos University, Oman. He has conducted research in the areas of learning styles, instructional design and technology-enhanced education. He also has significant practical experience as an instructional and educational designer for a number of higher educational institutions that include Florida State University, Savannah College of Art and Design and the University of Leicester, and has conducted a number of external evaluations for distance and elearning programmes catering to developing world learners.

Andrew Holliman, PhD, is a Senior Lecturer in Developmental Psychology, Coventry University. He is also a Senior Fellow of the Higher Education Academy (SFHEA) and holds an MA in Teaching and Learning in Higher and Professional Education from the Institute of Education, University College London. His research focus is the development of children's reading and the role of speech rhythm (or prosodic) sensitivity in this development. More recently, he has begun to focus on university teaching and learning, and the relationship between motivation, engagement and achievement.

Wayne Holmes, PhD, is a Research Lecturer in the Institute of Educational Technology (IET), The Open University, UK. He has been involved in education, educational technologies and education research for more than 25 years, receiving his PhD in Education (Learning and Technology) from the University of Oxford. His research interests are in the learning sciences, artificial intelligence in education (AIED) and adaptive digital learning environments.

Natalia Kucirkova, PhD, is a Senior Research Fellow, the University College London. Her research concerns innovative ways of supporting children's book reading, digital literacy and exploring the role of personalisation in the early years. Her publications have appeared in *Communication Disorders Quarterly*, *First Language, Computers & Education* or *Cambridge Journal of Education*. She has been commended for her engagement with teachers and parents at a national and international level.

Duo Liu, PhD, is an Associate Professor in the Department of Special Education and Counselling, the Education University of Hong Kong. He obtained his PhD from the Department of Psychology, the Chinese University of Hong Kong. His current research interests focus on cognitive development and related problems, especially on language and literacy development and difficulties.

Miriam McBreen is a PhD candidate in the Human Development programme, McGill University, currently working under the supervision of Dr Savage. She has an MA in Cognitive Science from the University of Copenhagen. The focus of her research is on motivational and engagement factors in struggling readers, and tailoring interventions to persistent non-responders.

Conor Mc Guckin, PhD, is an Assistant Professor in Educational Psychology in the School of Education, Trinity College Dublin. Conor is a Chartered Psychologist (CPsychol) with The British Psychological Society and The Psychological Society of Ireland, and a Chartered Scientist (CSci) with The Science Council. He is also an Associate Fellow of both The British Psychological Society (AFBPsS) and The Psychological Society of Ireland (AFPsSI). His research interests are in the area of psychology applied to educational policy and processes, educational psychology, bully/victim problems among children and adults, special educational needs, disability and rare disease.

Anne Mangen, PhD, is Professor of Literacy at the Reading Centre, University of Stavanger, Norway. Mangen conducts empirical research on the effects of digitization on cognitive and emotional aspects of reading, comparing the reading of different kinds of texts on paper and on screens and measuring the effect of technical and material affordances of the interface on, for instance, reading comprehension or narrative engagement.

Aishwarya Nair is a PhD candidate working under Dr Savage's supervision in the Faculty of Education, McGill University. She obtained her Master's degree in Applied Psychology from the University of Delhi, India. She has previously worked in the high school learning supports division focusing on collaborative learning in maths classrooms. Her research interests include maths learning, maths pedagogy and inclusive education.

Jenny Radesky, MD, is an Assistant Professor of Pediatrics in the Division of Developmental Behavioral Pediatrics, the University of Michigan Medical School. Her research and clinical work focuses on early childhood self-regulation, parent–child relationships, disadvantaged populations and their intersections with digital media use. She is a lead author of the 2016 American Academy of Pediatrics policy statement on digital media use in early childhood.

Robert Savage, PhD, is Professor at University College London, Institute of Education. He obtained his degrees from Oxford and Cambridge Universities and his PhD from the University of London in 1998. He has published nearly 100 research articles in international journals on children's literacy. He has most recently published research on school-based assessment and preventative early intervention projects for reading and spelling problems using educational technologies.

Maggi Savin-Baden, PhD, is Professor of Education at the University of Worcester. She has researched and evaluated staff and student experiences of learning for over 20 years and gained funding in this area (Leverhulme Trust, JISC, Higher Education Academy, MoD). She has a strong publication record of over 50 research publications and 15 books which reflect her research interests on the impact of innovative learning, digital fluency, cyber-influence and research methods.

Kieron Sheehy, PhD, is Professor of Education (Innovation Pedagogies), The Open University, UK. He has a particular interest in addressing issues for those who might be stigmatized and excluded within educational systems. This has encompassed examining the relationship between new technologies and the notion of learning difficulties, developing practical pedagogies for inclusive classrooms and researching the relationship between epistemological beliefs and educational practices.

Donna-Marie Thompson, MPsychClin., is a Psychologist with extensive experience working with people with disabilities and mental illness in academic, forensic and health contexts. She has an interest in applying evidence-based psychological theory towards solving practical problems of the human experience, and has developed and disseminated a peer-mentored group programme for university students with autism spectrum conditions.

Jennifer M. Thomson, PhD, is a Reader in Language and Literacy in the Department of Human Communication Sciences, University of Sheffield, UK. Her research focuses on struggling readers and the affordances and challenges that digital technology offers this population.

Gregor Wolbring, PhD, is an Associate Professor in Community Rehabilitation and Disability Studies in the Department of Community Health Sciences, the University of Calgary, working on issues such as governance of ability expectations, STEM, social situation of disabled people and education. He has published 98 academic articles and 20 book chapters since 2010. He has received four research teaching awards since 2011 and the Queen Elizabeth II Diamond Jubilee Medal in recognition of his work, which was cited as 'tireless and of benefit to the greater community' in 2013.

Eileen Wood, PhD, is a full-time Faculty Member in the Psychology Department, Wilfrid Laurier University. She obtained an MA at the University of Western Ontario and her PhD from Simon Fraser University. Her primary research interests involve examining how children, youth and adults (young through old) acquire and retain information especially in educational contexts. These include investigating instructional strategies that facilitate learning and memory and the impact of new technologies as instructional tools.

Zhengye Xu is a PhD student in the Department of Special Education and Counselling, the Education University of Hong Kong. Her current research focus is on Chinese children's literacy development and its relationship with embodied cognition.

Peter Zentel, PhD, is Professor in Education, the University of Education in Heidelberg, Germany, whose work focuses on people with moderate to severe learning disabilities. His main research interest is in ICT and learning disabilities including technology-based empirical research methods. In this context he is investigating the suitability of Eye-Tracking-Devices for this target group. Additionally, he is conducting a research project on foster care for children with special needs.

ACKNOWLEDGEMENTS

We would like to thank Andrew Martin for inviting us to host a symposium on 'The Promises and Perils of Technology in Educational Contexts' at the 28th International Congress of Applied Psychology (Division 5: Educational, Instructional, and School Psychology) in Paris, July 2014. This seminar directly inspired our publication. We would also like to give special thanks to all those who were involved in the review of this work, including those students of psychology who provided student reviews of individual chapters: Katherine Boaden, Agnieszka Czarnecka, Lea Evers, Polly Hicks, Melissa Gray, Bindu Kizhakethil, Maggie Leese, Elizabeth Marsh, Hannah Nash, Mirabel Pelton, James Rowland, Kate Torrens and Szilvia Toth.

NEW TECHNOLOGIES AND A WORLD OF DIFFERENCES

Introducing the perils and promises for learners

Kieron Sheehy and Andrew Holliman

Welcome to *Education and New Technologies: Perils and Promises for Learners*.

It is unarguable that new technologies are creating profound changes within society. These technologies are becoming so integral to our lives and cultures that we might often fail to notice the changes that they have brought. One way of reflecting on the changes that have occurred is to conduct a thought experiment in which we try to see the world through the eye of someone from the relatively recent past.

A time traveller, let us call her Mary, from Europe in 1927 would be amazed by the things she would encounter in the early twenty-first century. Mary would find technologies can speak and guide people as they drive to their destinations, or label stars and planes as they move across the sky; and digital assistants that respond to varied verbal or written requests, turn on household devices, answer our questions, read our 'mail', augment our perceptions of the world, and offer a vast array of diversions and amusements. She would be amazed by how easily an unimaginably vast amount of information is routinely accessed, searched and transferred around the world using everyday technologies. Mary would quickly become aware that the people she meets in this new century are becoming connected to technologically mediated information for almost all their waking hours (and some sleepers might even be measuring the quality of their sleep through 24/7 health trackers). She would see how this connection begins in early childhood. For example, in the UK 33% of 3–4-year-olds and 92% of 12–15-year-olds (Ofcom 2013) access the Internet and across Europe the likelihood of children owning a smartphone increases by 58% for each year they grow older (Mascheroni and Ólafsson 2015). This access to technologically mediated experiences is increasing year on year as smartphones, tablets and other devices become evermore ubiquitous, so that 'mobile communication has become a taken for granted condition of young people's everyday lives' (Mascheroni and Ólafsson 2015: 3). Although children's access to smart technologies reflects and intersects with their social and economic situations, Mary could still conclude that children's access to virtual spaces and online interactions is becoming part of daily experiences, and expectations, on a global level. Parents need answers to questions that would have been unknown in Mary's time. For example, when should young children begin to use these new technologies, are these technologies beneficial to children's development or are they harmful virtual pacifiers and electronic babysitters (Haughton, Aiken and Cheevers 2015), and are the social lives of children (and adults) damaged through 'digital addiction' (Kucirkova, Littleton and Kyparissiadis 2017)? The use of digital connected technologies appears to bring benefits but also to create potential problems.

In learning about the modern world, Mary would realise that much of the news and information she receives is actually scraped and generated by software, perhaps delivered by chatbots, rather than human beings. In experiencing modern social interactions, she would understand that our lives are increasingly enacted within technological spaces and shaped by the affordances of the social media and communication software that is being used. In relation to work and employment, Mary would be able to visit factories, warehouses and farms, where robots have replaced human labour or where technologically mediated jobs exist that could not have been imagined or understood in her own time. It would be obvious to our time traveller that 'modern lives' have been technologically transformed, or at least made more efficient in many respects, and that at the start of the new century human activities are very different from those in her own time.

However, if Mary visited a school she would probably feel very much at home, recognising many familiar structures and practices. The buildings would serve largely the same function, and she would find classroom spaces which have the form of desks, chairs and classroom (albeit perhaps electronic white) boards. The reading, handwriting and arithmetic activities the children carry out would be entirely comprehensible to her. The dizzying array of online and technologically mediated experiences which she would have encountered elsewhere would seem less obvious in modern settings explicitly designated for educational activities. This raises the question of why these institutions might appear to be slower in reflecting newer social practices, and whether this apparent lack of innovation could actually be protecting learners from technologies that might impair their learning experiences and development, or place them at personal risk. A clear illustration of this issue is the debate concerning smartphones and the effects of texting on the development of literacy skills. This example indicates how heated the 'perils and promises' debate can become, even for such an apparently everyday and seemingly innocuous practice.

There has been a concern amongst many educators and parents that the popularity of text messaging has been responsible for a marked deterioration in literacy abilities (Paton 2011). This is a longstanding issue, reflected across the years in popular newspaper headings:

- 'I h8 txt msgs: How texting is wrecking our language' (Humphrys 2007: Para 1, *Daily Mail*).
- 'TXT BAD 4 UR BRAIN? Text messaging can dent your reading abilities, say scientists' (Waugh 2012: Para 1, *Daily Mail*).

In contrast to these warnings and declarations of opposition are the results of research studies that suggest a much more positive picture. For example, controlled and longitudinal research (Wood, Kemp, Waldron and Hart 2014) indicates that the use of textese slang (on smartphones) might have, at worst, a neutral effect on literacy and can actually benefit children's spelling attainment. When early research in this area was reported in the media, it was often framed as being in marked contrast to established common-sense beliefs and practice, for example:

- 'findings fly in the face of long-held views of parents and teachers who believe text messaging damages children's ability to write properly' (Anon. 2011: Para 3, *Daily Mail*).

News media reports of a positive impact of text usage on aspects of literacy development often evoked vociferous comments from educators and the general public. For example:

- 'you wouldn't be saying that if you'd tried to mark written work littered with "text speak" because they have no idea how to write properly' (Anon. 2011: Comments, *Daily Mail*).
- 'Yeah and they'll soon be needing ops on the NHS for rsi conditions in their late teens. Anything to avoid learning to read and write by reading books and being taught to write. What a stupid article!' (Anon. 2011: Comments, *Daily Mail*).
- 'Total rubbish ! the decline is there and will get worse, texting will only speed up the decline. The parents are not wrong they see it daily from their children not from some cockeyed research over 10 years!!' (Anon. 2011: Comments, *Daily Mail*).

It is against this social backdrop that the educational uses of technologies are being judged, and perhaps this backdrop might influence how or why new technologies are implemented (or not) in society's 'designated' learning environments. Since these heated early public debates, the research evidence has grown and a body of evidence now suggests that texting has a positive impact on spelling, that a learner's amount of texting correlates with their overall language skills and that use of textese is positively related to children's grammar performance (Alvermann and Harrison 2016; van Dijk *et al.* 2016). Although the textese debate may be partly resolved, in terms of research, this does not mean that new technologies are necessarily becoming perceived as offering or providing positive benefits for all learners.

Understanding the perils and promises of new technologies is a complex real-life issue, which makes it difficult for those who are concerned with supporting learners, and indeed learners themselves, to make informed decisions about how best to use them. For example, let us look at smartphones again. These devices have become so popular in the last decade that it feels wrong to describe them being a 'new' technology, and they only appear to be new when discussed within an educational context. They are essentially powerful pocket computers, capable of running a wide array of software. It might seem obvious therefore that giving learners access to their own pocket computers would reap educational benefits. However, there is a widespread belief that the presence of mobile phones in schools damages learners' academic achievements, and consequently many schools ban their use. In contrast to the textese debate, there is some support for this belief. Researchers sampled the academic performance of over 130,000 teenagers in UK schools before and after the introduction of a smartphone ban (Beland and Murphy 2016). They found a significant improvement in student performance in schools once smartphones were banned, with bans having the most benefit for previously low-achieving students and none for previously high-achieving students. Beland and Murphy argue that this effect occurs because of students' differential ability to be distracted from their studies by smartphones. In considering the results of studies such as this, it is important to consider how the effects of the technology are evaluated. For example, the tests on which the smartphone usage is evaluated can be handwritten pencil and paper summative assessments of largely memorised content. Mary might be familiar with the format of these long-established forms of examinations. Could it be that new technologies which might help learners are being assessed through, or being used in service of, outmoded educational practices? This is not a new idea. The educational visionary Seymour Papert used a parable to explain his argument concerning the ways in which the merits of computing technologies were being assessed in educational settings:

> The parable is about a brilliant engineer around 1800 who invented the jet engine. Since he was dedicated to improving transportation, he took his invention to the people most involved with transportation, namely the makers of stagecoaches. He said, 'Look, I've got this thing. Find out how to use it.' So the makers of stagecoaches looked at it and they said, 'Well, let's tie it on to a stagecoach and see if it helps the horses.' So they tied the jet engine on the stagecoach and of course it shattered the stagecoach to pieces. So that wasn't any good … However, somebody got a brilliant idea, 'We'll make a tiny little jet engine. And we will put that on the stagecoach, and it won't shatter it to pieces. Besides, its price is affordable.' In fact, very careful statistics managed to show that this did have a minor effect on the performance of the horses … I hate to say it, but I think that this is a very accurate portrayal of what is being done with computers in schools.
>
> *(Papert 1996: Paras 3–5)*

Though it was written over two decades ago, one could propose that this argument still holds true and may help explain the divide between many learners' experiences of technologies in their formal education and their social and work lives.

The current situation is that educators and learners are living in an increasingly technologically mediated world. Yet judging the relative perils and promises of new technologies for learning is not an easy task. As illustrated in the examples of texting and mobile phones, there are controversies that result from widely accepted 'common-sense' views on the dangers that such technologies might bring, research evidence that is nuanced in terms of indicating possible benefits for learners in different situations, different ages and abilities, or where the ways in which technologies are being assessed and implemented undermine or mask the affordances that they offer. In these circumstances it can be a challenging task to gain a clear picture of the relative perils and promises that new technologies bring for learners.

This book has been designed to shed light on these issues, and to help readers to gain a clearer understanding of the pitfalls and benefits that exist. In order to do this we have selected specific aspects of learners' experiences which have been identified as controversial and/or where the impact of new technologies is believed to be profound. The chapter authors are experts within their diverse fields, and we have consciously embraced international perspectives and adopted a variety of styles in terms of presentation, writing, composition and tone, which enables the reader to engage with the personality of the authors through their explanations and discussions.

The chapter authors address major issues in understanding the ways in which technologies impact upon learners. Across the chapters the topics are examined at various levels of analysis, encompassing culture, learner identity and development, and specific curricula. Each author raises key questions and provokes critical enquiry about some of the newest possibilities in education. They illustrate how technological developments can be harnessed to support learning and also identify risks associated with these new practices. The book is divided into three themed parts. It has been carefully designed to be read sequentially, although some readers may prefer to dip in and out of different chapters. By drawing on researchers from different areas, the book seeks to offer insights and conclusions about the nature of opportunities and risks that exist, and how these might be managed for the benefit of future learners.

PART I: Early engagement with new technologies: Decisions, dangers and data

This part is concerned with issues that have importance in relation to the development of learners, in an area where accessible research data is often lacking, and in creating frameworks that can support evidence-informed decisions. There is a deliberate emphasis on literacy skills as this emerges as a key concern from both government reviews and public forums, and is an issue where the use of new technologies can evoke conflicting opinions.

Young children are interacting with digital technologies through play, and international concerns (see Clark *et al*. 2015) have been raised about the impact this is having on their early development. Repeated calls have been made for guidance regarding when and how young children should use new technologies. For example, there has been much hyperbole concerning the negative impact of too much 'screen time', but the research evidence underpinning such concerns are seldom examined, nor do they acknowledge sufficiently the influence of children's social context. In Chapter 1, *Natalia Kucirkova and Jenny Radesky* provide this in their contextualised and research-based examination of children between 0–2 years of age. They consider the question of whether screen technologies are able to support early creativity and learning or if they actively interact with children's development and fundamental social interactions. Drawing on this discussion they construct a framework for educators, parents and policy-makers to guide proactive decisions about their infants' use of media and technologies.

We have already indicated the often-heated debate that surrounds the impact of new technologies on the development of literacy skills. Within this area, the rise of e-books is believed to have a significant impact. Research within this field allows us to understand the ways in which changing the medium through which stories and information are presented, and the possibilities offered by digital enhancements to simple text influences learners' attitudes to reading and the development of their literacy skills. As in the preceding chapter, *Mirit Barzillai, Jennifer Thomson and Anne Mangen* acknowledge the importance of the social context of learning and examine research evidence to create a nuanced critical understanding of the benefits and pitfalls that e-books, with their 'bells and whistles', offer learners of different ages and in different situations.

Research into the ways new technologies influence the development of literacy skills is overwhelmingly 'Western-centric' and often fails to reflect the scale, and importance, of Chinese language usage worldwide; for example, in 2016 there were over 900 million Chinese (Mandarin) speakers in contrast to approximately 350 million English language speakers (Nations Online 2017). It is therefore essential that a text that examines the impact of new technologies on literacy development acknowledges this reality and, for example, discusses the interplay between logographic Chinese script, alphabetic keyboards and how the Chinese language is learnt. This issue is therefore addressed within Chapter 3, where *Duo Liu and Zhengye Xu* provide a critical examination of the development of Chinese children's literacy abilities when mediated through both computers and traditional handwriting. The importance given to literacy development internationally, and the commercial opportunities that this offers, had led to the creation of numerous applications in which pedagogies, of different forms, are built into literacy teaching software. Educators and parents are therefore faced with the difficult question of making choices about which of these different approaches would work for particular situations and children. In Chapter 4, *Robert Savage, Aishwarya Nair, Miriam McBreen and Eileen Wood* look at the pedagogical aspects, and outcomes, of web-based literacy technologies. This chapter creates a helpful framework for judging 'what works' in a situation where formal controlled evaluations are often not accessible to teachers and parents. In particular, the authors consider what evidence-based design might look like and the quality of instruction that web-based approaches to literacy can offer. The issue of quality is assessed with regard to outcomes, comparison with face-to face teaching, and the extent to which the risks of creating poor learning experiences can be mitigated. There is a trend in which intelligent tutoring systems, with pedagogy controlled by the software rather than a human, are becoming increasing available and promoted as educational solutions. This, combined with the possibilities offered by mobile learning technologies, challenges existing classroom practices and teachers' traditional roles. *Savage* and colleagues review these issues and draw conclusions about the importance, or not, of human mediation in these new environments in relation to supporting learners effectively.

PART II: New technology: Supporting all learners or divisive tools

New technologies are often believed to be able to transform the learning experiences of people who have physical or sensory impairments or learning disabilities (McKnight and Davies 2012). For example, these learners will increasingly make use of assistive technologies, and the UN Convention on the rights of persons with disabilities position these new technologies as significant ways in which barriers to independence can be removed and participation in decision-making can be enabled or enhanced (Wright, Sheehy, Parsons and Abbott 2011).

However, technologies are not a universal panacea for social issues, and it is necessary to critically examine their use in relation to social diversity and educational need, and the ways in which they transform or actively create or reproduce barriers for learners. These issues are often relevant to all learners, but are exemplified and highlighted in discussion of learners with impairments or learning disabilities. Part II considers the relationship between these learners and new technologies, and discusses the perils and promises that emerge, from three different perspectives. In Chapter 5, *Peter Zentel* looks at digital assistive technologies and educational need. He gives a historical overview to develop a way of examining the extent to which these technologies offer benefits for different groups of learners and the ways in which their inclusion in society, and learning opportunities, are enabled or held back by these technologies. The chapter that follows this focuses on the learner's social world and how their identities are shaped and constructed within cyber and physical environments. Social and online media are ubiquitous sources of information about difference and diversity issues. The narratives and discourses that they create impact upon how learners are regarded and the experiences they consequently have. *Charlotte Brownlow and Donna-Marie Thompson* discuss how autism is conceptualised and constructed within online and face-to-face environments in relation to professional dialogues. They develop a perspective that considers autism from an abilities framework (one where the presumption is of competence rather than impairment) and the need to involve people with autism through participatory research approaches. This view complements that of the subsequent chapter. Here, in Chapter 7, *Gregor Wolbring* introduces the concept of 'ability expectations' as a lens through which the education system can be examined, and as a way of facilitating innovative ways of thinking about learning activities and their purposes. He problematises the notion of ability and ability frameworks, and considers the ways in which technologies create ability expectations of learners. These expectations influence the knowledge and skills that learners are taught, and also which groups in society are taught them. The interplay between technologies, knowledge, and the construction and enhancement of learners' abilities/disabilities is seen as being dynamic and evolving as new technologies such as nanotechnologies arise. The chapter argues that awareness and governance of ability expectations is an important social and educational issue.

PART III: Global and cultural reflections on educational technology

Educational technology's global and persistent reach gives learners new forms of connectedness. This has a profound impact on learners' cultural experiences, their personal safety and privacy, and potentially their biology. In our earlier 'thought experiment' we felt that our time traveller would notice the ways in which people are being linked to technologies for most of their waking hours. In Chapter 8, *Maggi Savin-Baden* considers what learning in the digital age means when people are 'digitally tethered' to different devices that provide them with information about the world but also collect information about their own lives and actions. This mediation of information can be through sophisticated virtual pedagogical agents, through educationally focused apps, or within virtual worlds and online games. *Maggi Savin-Baden* looks at the impact these agents and virtual spaces can have on learners. She is clear that we should not assume that digital technologies necessarily bring positive developments and recommends that we should be critically aware of the ways in which being always connected can shape and change our notions of what being a learner might be.

A significant feature in a world of connected learners is that data about their learning can be readily harvested and used as evidence to improve teaching and learning. The ways in which these evidence-based changes can occur is informed by the new field of 'learning analytics', and this is the focus of Chapter 9. Here, *Rebecca Ferguson* examines the interaction between big data, online learning and national concerns, and examines the practical and ethical issues that arise when data ownership and curation become valuable educational and commercial commodities. This illustrates that one way in which new technologies are able to have such a powerful influence is because they are able to work on a very large scale. Learners may be unaware of the learning analytics that are shaping their experiences behind the scenes, but many will be aware of, and learning from, Massive Open Online Courses (MOOCs). These free courses are accessed by many thousands of learners around the world, and have been seen both as a disruptive force for traditional educational practices and also a way of offering educational opportunities for developing countries. In Chapter 10, *Clifford Omodele Fyle* discusses the extent to which MOOCs might be able to address the worldwide shortage of teachers. He critically examines the appropriateness of using this distance learning approach for different aspects of teacher education, how one might deal with quality assurance and issues of developing massive-scale pedagogies that have relevance to local cultures and contexts.

One of the most popular 'non-educational' uses of new technologies has been in the development of games. These games are played every day by many millions of children and adults. The appeal of these experiences, combined with a belief that successful learning can occur through games, has led many educators to develop games for learners (Sheehy, Ferguson and Clough 2014). Indeed, as *Wayne Holmes* (Chapter 11) explains, it has even been suggested that digital games will become the way in which everybody learns. This argument arises because new technologies are able to create engaging and authentic learning experiences, and because repeated national reviews indicate the benefits to learners of this approach. *Wayne Holmes* considers the situation of digital games-based learning and assesses why the repeated predictions of their imminent welcome and adoption within the education system has yet to materialise. A feature of many new technologies is that they enable social interaction either as their specific purpose, as in social media, or within collaborative games, or via back channels associated with games or digital spaces (Sheehy and Littleton 2010). This is a positive feature for learning, but it may also bring the risk of negative social experiences, including cyber-bullying and contact with strangers (Livingstone and Smith 2014). These issues, which have been the subject of considerable public concern for parents, educators and policy-makers, are the focus of the final chapter in this text (Chapter 12). An often overlooked, yet significant, aspect of this situation is the coping skills and resilience of children and young people as they learn to navigate through these online interactions. *Conor Mc Guckin and Lucie Corcoran* critically consider this aspect in their discussions of the research evidence concerning cyber aggression and identify the effective development of prevention and intervention strategies. As in other chapters, acknowledging the complex interplay between digital and real-world experiences is shown to be essential in understanding the perils and promises that new technologies create for learners.

The book presents the voices of international authors and their perspectives on new learning possibilities, tools and environments. We hope these voices illustrate why this is an exciting time within the broad sphere of education, with rapid developments in technology that have the potential to change the ways in which learners interact with their worlds. Several of the chapters create evidence-informed frameworks, and we hope that these will support readers in developing their own use of new technologies within their teaching and learning. Other chapters give insights into how technologies have a profound influence on learner identity, and learners' sense of who they are and their abilities within the world.

Before beginning to read this book, it is worth reflecting on the notion that the perils and promises that are identified by the authors represent perspectives from this particular point in history, and these perspectives can change. For example, Socrates was concerned, over 2,000 years ago, about the effects of the [then] new technology of being able to write ideas down and so store them, and the impact it would have on learners:

> [writing will] create forgetfulness in the learners' souls, because they will not use their memories; they will trust to the external written characters and not remember of themselves.
>
> *(Socrates, cited in Plato 2008: 65)*

> [*learners*] will be hearers of many things and will have learned nothing; they will appear to be omniscient and will generally know nothing; they will be tiresome company, having the show of wisdom without the reality.
>
> *(Socrates, cited in Plato 2008: 65)*

Yet today we see learning to read and write as a fundamental skill, with equitable access to it promoted universally. The knowledge and skills that this technological advance created, and gave access to, gradually moved from the preserve of the few and transformed the everyday lives of the many.

It is difficult to predict the long-term risks and benefits of the technologies that are encompassed by this book. Some may simply enable the efficient repetition or re-representation of materials or activities that the learner might engage with equally well without the technology. The educational content and objective remain untouched but the process is automated in some way (Bradshaw, Twining and Walsh 2012). More commonly described within this book are technologies that support the creation of new curriculum content and where the learner's experience is potentially transformed as a result of the technology. It is in these experiences where the possible benefits and risks are in the greatest need of research-based examination. We hope that this book provides this lens for the reader, and supports an enjoyable critical engagement with this a diverse and exciting field.

References

Alvermann, D. E., and Harrison, C. (2016) 'Are computers, smartphones, and the internet a boon or a barrier for the weaker reader?', *Journal of Adolescent and Adult Literacy*, 60(2): 221–225.

Anon. (2011) *Children who regularly text message have BETTER English than those who don't (even if thy use txt spk)*. Available online from: http://www.dailymail.co.uk/news/article-1353658/Children-regularly-text-message-BETTER-English-dont-thy-use-txt-spk.html#ixzz4dZTV0LRl [16 May 2017].

Beland, L. P., and Murphy, R. (2016) 'III Communication: Technology, distraction & student performance', *Labour Economics*, 41: 61–76.

Bradshaw, P., Twining, P., and Walsh, C. (2012) 'The vital program: Transforming ICT professional development', *American Journal of Distance Education*, 26: 37–41.

Clark, H., et al. (2015) *A report by the all-party parliamentary group on a fit and healthy childhood.* Available online from: https://adrianvoce.files.wordpress.com/2015/10/play-report-final-designed.pdf [16 May 2017].

van Dijk, C. N., van Witteloostuijn, M., Vasić, N., Avrutin, S., Blom, E., and Laakso, M.-L. (2016) 'The influence of texting language on grammar and executive functions in primary school children', *PLOS ONE*, 11(3): e0152409.

Haughton, C., Aiken, M., and Cheevers, C. (2015) 'Cyber babies: The impact of emerging technology on the developing infant', *Psychology Research*, 5: 504–518.

Humphrys, J. (2007) *I h8 txt msgs: How texting is wrecking our language.* Available online from: http://www.dailymail.co.uk/news/article-483511/I-h8-txt-msgs-How-texting-wrecking-language.html#ixzz4dZLm2jwE [16 May 2017].

Kucirkova, N., Littleton, K., and Kyparissiadis, A. (2017) 'The influence of children's gender and age on children's use of digital media at home', *British Journal of Educational Technology*, doi: 10.1111/bjet.12543.

Livingstone, S., and Smith, P. K. (2014) 'Annual research review: Harms experienced by child users of online and mobile technologies: The nature, prevalence and management of sexual and aggressive risks in the digital age', *Journal of Child Psychology and Psychiatry and Allied Disciplines*, 55(6): 635–654.

McKnight, L., and Davies, C. (2012) Current perspectives on assistive learning technologies. 2012 review of research and challenges within the field, Kellogg College Centre for Research into Assistive Learning Technologies.

Mascheroni, G., and Ólafsson, K. (2015) 'The mobile Internet: Access, use, opportunities and divides among European children', *New Media & Society*, 1–23.

Nations Online (2017) *Most widely spoken language.* Available online from: http://www.nationsonline.org/oneworld/most_spoken_languages.htm [16 May 2017].

Ofcom (2013) *The Ofcom Broadcasting Code*, Available online from: www.ofcom.org.uk [16 May 2017].

Papert, S. (1996) *Looking at technology through school-colored spectacles*, Available online from: http://www.papert.org/articles/LookingatTechnologyThroughSchool.html [16 May 2017].

Paton, G. (2011) *Text messaging 'improves children's spelling skills'* Available online from: http://www.telegraph.co.uk/education/educationnews/8272502/Text-messaging-improves-childrens-spelling-skills.html [16 May 2017].

Plato (2008) The Project Gutenberg EBook of Phaedrus. Available online from: http://rhetoricblog.com/wp-content/uploads/2014/11/Phaedrus.pdf [16 May 2017].

Sheehy, K., and Littleton, T. (2010) 'The business of child protection in educational virtual worlds', in K. Sheehy, R. Ferguson, and G. Clough (eds.) *Virtual worlds: Controversies at the frontier of education*, Hauppauge, NY: Nova Science Publishers (pp. 53–66).

Sheehy, K., Ferguson, R., and Clough, G. (2014). *Augmented education: Bringing real and virtual learning together*, London: Springer.

Waugh, R. (2012) TXT BAD 4 UR BRAIN? *Text messaging can dent your reading abilities, say scientists.* Available online from: http://www.dailymail.co.uk/sciencetech/article-2102554/TXT-BAD-4-UR-BRAIN-Text-messaging-dent-reading-abilities-say-scientists.html#ixzz4hF9lM0Dv.

Wood, C., Kemp, N., Waldron, S., and Hart, L. (2014) 'Grammatical understanding, literacy and text messaging in school children and undergraduate students: A concurrent analysis', *Computers and Education*, 70: 281–290.

Wright, J. A., Sheehy, K., Parsons, S., and Abbott, C. (2011) *Guidelines for research into the effectiveness of Assistive Technologies (AT)*. Available online from: www.kcl.ac.uk/sspp/departments/education/research/crestem/steg/recentproj/assistivetech.aspx [24 May 2017].

PART I

Early engagement with new technologies

Decisions, dangers and data

1

DIGITAL MEDIA AND YOUNG CHILDREN'S LEARNING

How early is too early and why? Review of research on 0–2-year-olds

Natalia Kucirkova and Jenny Radesky

Introduction

Children's ages and developmental stages play an important role in how beneficial or harmful exposure to screen media might be. In this chapter, we focus on typically developing children aged 0–2 years, referred to as infants from hereafter, and four types of digital media: video, TV, tablets and electronic toys.

For infants, anxieties around digital media use are most pronounced and vividly demonstrated in research and policy-making discussions. While concerns around children's use of technology are not new (e.g. TV has been called the 'boob tube' since the 1970s, and Postman [1982] worried that it would rob children of their childhood), concerns have been heightened as the use of newer technologies (such as smartphones and tablets) by infants has been increasing steadily over the past five years. As an illustration, in the United States in 2011, only 10 per cent of children under 2 years of age had ever used a mobile device (Common Sense Media and Rideout 2011). This increased to 38 per cent of 0–2-year-olds in 2013 (Common Sense Media and Rideout 2013). A smaller study conducted in a low-income urban paediatric clinic in 2015 showed that almost all (97 per cent) of 0–4-year-olds had used a mobile device, three-quarters owned their own device, and most young children were primarily using mobile devices for entertainment, not educational, purposes (Kabali *et al.* 2015). When last examined, 0–2-year-olds were estimated to use an average of 1 hour and 15 minutes of screen media per day (Wartella *et al.* 2013), despite professional guidelines that children under 18 months avoid media use (American Academy of Pediatrics [AAP] 2016).

While we acknowledge that many questions in relation to new technologies remain unanswered, we also perceive an urgency to provide parents and educators with guiding principles. Considering the rapid uptake of digital media by families in the Minority World (such as the UK, Australia, USA and Canada), it is important to draw together the current available evidence on the affordances and limitations of digital media for infants and reflect on how to best support parents and educators in their decision-making around their use.

To frame this reflection in a broader exploration of the cognitive and socio-emotional development of infants, we first review the evidence on how infants learn more generally, followed by the key theoretical conceptualisations of children's learning.

How do children learn?

There are various ways to describe how children learn; and given the idiosyncratic nature of development for each child, there are probably as many ways as there are children in the world. Developmental milestones, which are used clinically to screen for developmental delays and help parents understand what behaviours to expect and how to best support their children's developmental trajectory, are one framework for considering how infants might interact with media. Milestones are not fixed points in time; they often overlap with each other and occur in parallel. Some children develop milestones at different times, different children develop in different patterns, and individual differences can be accentuated in different contexts. We revisit key developmental stages selectively, paying special attention to those milestones which are relevant for the chapter's discussion of the influence of new technologies on young children's development and for identifying the current research gaps.

0–3 months

Children between 0–3 months are in the process of developing their auditory abilities, which means that they react to loud noises, often with a distress response such as spreading out their arms or crying. They typically respond to close sounds, and develop their distance hearing abilities later on. Infants of 0–3 months develop motor strength and coordination principally in their trunk and neck, while distal extremity coordination (e.g. voluntary grasp and release of objects) has not yet matured. They attend to faces and eyes and can imitate basic facial expressions.

Children at this age would therefore process very little from screen technologies because of their immature auditory and visual processing. Cross-sectional associations between screen media use and excessive crying have been reported (Thompson *et al.* 2013), suggesting that audio-visual stimulation from media may contribute to irritability and children's desire for attention from others, instead of a screen. On the other hand, parents of fussy infants may be putting them in front of digital media in an effort to calm them down. Future research should consider how the presence of features particularly salient for this age group might influence irritability, self-regulation and social co-regulation, particularly for infants with a low sensory threshold or high sensory reactivity. For instance, many infant apps include mirrors and high-definition images of colourful characters, but it is not known whether these features support or confuse children's understanding of self and others – a crucial development in these early months. There are also many technologies developed for this age group that include audio recordings of voiceovers and music, but it is not known whether these audio features influence children's earliest stages of auditory processing.

4–6 months

At this age, motor coordination and strength mature so that infants can start to use their hands to voluntarily grasp objects, bring their feet to mouth when lying on the back or sit unsupported. Children's hearing skills progress as well, and they are now able to enjoy listening to familiar sounds and create babbling noises with different sound qualities (e.g. volume, pitch and rate). They explore with touch and taste (or hand and mouth). They do not recognise that an image in the mirror is a reflection – they would reach out to it and experiment how it responds. They are fascinated with and enjoy exploring simple cause-and-effect toys and objects, such as rattles and other noisemakers (see Davies 2010).

These abilities mean that children would enjoy exploring simple cause and effect responses on the screen (e.g. tapping an area of a touchscreen and seeing how it changes colour or produces a sound), but they would not be expected to have the motor control to recreate this effect over and over. Future research needs to establish whether apps and technologies which elicit the cause-and-effect response in children support their development of causality in other 3-dimensional play. Babies at this age enjoy the sensory experience and interact more with their own body (e.g. chewing their own hands or feet), so they would explore digital devices in a largely sensorimotor manner. It would be interesting to find out whether children's physical manipulation of technology can develop their emerging understanding of space, or whether displacement of 3-dimensional play by watching videos (i.e. 2-dimensional experiences) has a net detrimental influence on visual–spatial abilities.

7–9 months

Children aged 7–9 months enjoy responding to sounds, objects and people around them with imitation and their own sounds. Children of this age babble and respond to family members' names and familiar pictures. They love producing their own sounds, such as clapping and cooing, and playing games with a surprise effect (such as peek-a-boo, which takes advantage of their emerging understanding of object permanence).

There are many apps that record and play back to children the sounds they can make, such as gurgling, laughing and babbling. However, as children at this age do not appear to understand audio- or video-recorded language the same way they do spoken speech (see Doupe and Kuhl 1999; Kuhl et al. 2006), they would not be expected to learn from, or understand, such apps. Child-directed in-person speech is the most important facet of language development at this age. Future research is necessary to determine whether the presence of child-directed and child-reflective speech in children's software helps their language development or displaces parent–child verbal interaction, as other interactive media have been shown to do (as discussed below). What we do not know is whether children benefit from such interaction at repeated exposure or whether the novelty effect is the crucial means for learning.

10–12 months

A 1-year-old child can use their entire body to respond to music, including moving to rhythm and dancing. One-year-olds can also attend to new words and look for new and familiar objects when asked. First words also emerge during this time. Popular activities with this age group are often centred on the exploration of songs and pictures of their family and friends and personal experiences in various contexts. Children love to look at family pictures over and over, pronounce the names of the people they recognise and point to them with their finger. They now better understand that people in pictures do not have to be present physically for sounds and images of their faces – this understanding is often reflected in their ability to look for objects even when these are hidden and they have to find them. However, children of this age do not have fully developed symbolic thinking and memory flexibility, which makes it more difficult for them to make a transfer of knowledge from 2D to 3D objects (see Barr 2013). We therefore recommend that future studies examine children's understanding of object permanence, understanding of commonly used symbols in commercial apps, and the role of 2D pictures in children's understanding of self and others.

12–24 months

Children aged between 1 and 2 years of age enjoy simple stories, rhymes and songs. They often respond to them by imitating the sounds and words. Therefore a very popular activity with this age group often is songs and story apps, with which children enjoy pointing to objects and naming them, as well as exploring new textures and shapes. As yet, there is very little known about the impact of repeated, technology-mediated experience of stories, rhymes and songs on children's language development. Future research is needed to elucidate how children's emerging understanding of mathematical concepts can be influenced by specifically designed apps and electronic toys, independent of parent re-teaching known to be crucial for this age group to learn from digital media.

There are many important milestones to be mastered in this crucial period of child development. As for those which are most relevant to the use of media with this age group, 18–24-month-olds start to develop symbolic thinking, understanding of cause, effect and sequence, and use much more verbal and nonverbal communication with caregivers during toy play. If we consider the many skills and abilities developed at this age (Davies 2010), it is clear that more research is needed regarding how much 18–24-month-olds can learn independently from well-designed touchscreen media, how they interact verbally and nonverbally with others around them while using technologies and whether they are able to generalise this knowledge to their surroundings.

In addition, 12–24-month-olds begin the process of individuation from their caregivers, which is accompanied by an increase in negativism, tantrums and self-directed behaviour (Steinberg *et al.* 2010). Parents usually experience a higher degree of parenting stress during this time. Only one study (Radesky *et al.* 2016) has examined how parents use mobile devices to calm difficult infants/toddlers or keep them quiet. In this study, 144 caregivers were surveyed about their toddler's development, parenting practices and their child's media use practices. Toddlers rated as having social-emotional difficulties were 2.7 times more likely to be given a mobile device to calm down when upset, and 3.6 times more likely to be given a device to keep peace and quiet in the house. However, more research is needed to examine whether this alters toddlers' social–emotional trajectory.

Developmental milestones can tell us what infants can achieve at approximate ages; what they cannot tell us is what is actually happening in terms of the mechanism of learning, i.e. how do babies learn and acquire new knowledge? The discussion of potential benefits and limitations of infants' learning with digital media necessitates a theoretical explication of the nature of children's learning. There is a range of theories and possibilities in this area and we spotlight two key learning theories, which have historically dominated the child development literature.

How do babies learn? Research and theories

Infants learn by surprise and testing hypotheses

An exciting theory about children's learning is based on the premise that children are born with rich expectations about the world and learn when some of these expectations are violated. They also engage in exploratory behaviours to test and defy their expectations.

In the 1980s and 1990s, this notion was revolutionary: before, the accepted wisdom was that infants do not go beyond the here-and-now sensations in their thinking. In a number of studies, researchers at the John Hopkins University have shown how children's knowledge of the world around them can ignite and further drive their learning. In a carefully designed experiment, Stahl and Feigenson (2015) examined whether children as young as 11 months would use their surprise at unexpected events as motivation to learn about and explore the events. Examples of unexpected events in such experiments often draw on the basic laws of physics; for example, researchers may show babies small car toys which do not drop on the floor but instead can float in the air or roll through walls. When Stahl and Feigenson (2015) showed 110 infants some examples of such expectancy-defying events, they saw that babies stared at them for a longer time. Moreover, the babies were more motivated to explore the objects (touching them, putting them into their mouth, shaking them) and were also better at retaining new information associated with objects which violated their expectations (and common sense).

It is still a mystery how the mechanisms of learning work through surprise. One theory is that there is greater brain activity following a surprise reaction, which could explain babies' ability to create relationships between concepts (see Baillargeon *et al.* 2016). Another possibility is that babies learn by testing hypotheses and statistical probability. Gopnik *et al.* (see also Bedny *et al.* 2014; Jara-Ettinger *et al.* 2015; Meltzoff and Gopnik 2013) have carried out a number of experiments showing that children can figure out cause and effect and use probability calculations to discover new and surprising facts about the world. Their findings show that children spontaneously and naturally engage in cause-and-effect testing in their play, and in that way, they test hypotheses, compute several scenarios, falsify and verify information, and explore open-ended questions about them – just like scientists do.

In their investigations of children's learning from media, these theories are more likely to foreground the importance of children's own engagement with the technology. The socio-cultural perspective, on the other hand, foregrounds the mediation of technology use with a parent or another child.

Babies learn through guided interaction with others

In 1950, Knowles suggested guided interaction as the ideal adult–child or teacher–student relationship for children's learning. Children do not acquire new information through a simple one-way process of content transmission from the object or environment to their brain. Rather, this learning is always situated and mediated by others who guide their understanding. Knowles developed guided interaction into a theory of adult learning building on the earlier writings of Kapp in 1833. In this century, Lydia Plowman (1992) used the theory in the context of children's learning with digital media (TV, computers and electronic toys) to conceptualise the various ways in which pre-schoolers learn with technologies at home and in school. Although Plowman's seminal study did not focus on infants and toddlers, the studies provide a relevant conceptual language. Drawing on a series of case studies of pre-schoolers' use of digital media, Plowman and Stephen (2007) argue that guided interaction has two components: proximal and distal. Examples of distal (or indirect) interaction include planning, monitoring, providing resources, ensuring access and help, setting up activities, or ensuring access to ICT. On the other hand, proximal (direct interaction) involves demonstrating, enjoying, explaining, instructing, managing, modelling, prompting, and providing support and feedback (Plowman and Stephen 2007). For these researchers it is primarily through social interaction that children's learning can occur, and the importance of social mediation does not come second as it perhaps would from the previous perspective, but is given primacy.

Reflecting on these two main theoretical approaches and their historical importance in advancing the child development research, we recommend that future research on children's development mediated by the use of technology considers, or at least clearly outlines, the adopted theoretical approach. Much contemporary research on children's use of technology is guided by urgency and practical concern, which is problematic. Research which is theory- rather than practice-driven can generate conclusions that are generalisable and applicable across contexts. This is particularly important in a field where practices and tools mediating these are in a state of rapid change and development.

Current guidance in relation to technologies and under 2s

The American Academy of Pediatrics (AAP 2016) has advised parents to avoid media use in children under 18-24 months because it was argued that current research shows children under this age do not benefit from interactions with technology. It was also argued that time allocated to video screens provides no educational benefits and leaves less room for activities than does for example interacting with other people and playing. The new guidelines, accounting for the abundance of new digital media such as smartphones and tablets, emphasise co-viewing with young children and the importance of high-quality content (e.g. *CBeebies* in the UK or *Sesame Street* in the USA).

How can parents reconcile the existing body of evidence linking screen media use to more negative developmental and health outcomes (AAP 2016), with the hope that interactive technologies might be more educational and with the fact that increasingly more children are using digital toys, touchscreens and TV on a daily basis? In this chapter, we formulate a conceptual framework of key stages, which could inform parents', educators' and policy-makers' decisions around children's (0–2-year-olds) use of technologies. This framework is not intended to replace official guidance; it merely provides some thinking tools facilitating the decision-making around this important topic.

How do infants learn from digital media?

In the remainder of this chapter, we review the available research evidence specifically in relation to four types of screens and technologies to which infants are frequently exposed: videos, TV, touchscreens and electronic toys. We purposefully separate video studies from TV studies because of the different lines of research in this area. Video studies typically study children's responses to pre-recorded materials under laboratory conditions, while TV research tends to focus on children's programmes aired on national TV and watched in the home. Under touchscreens we included studies that focus on children's use of touch-manipulable screens such as tablets and smartphones and all activities available for these technologies, apart from TV watching.

Videos

Early research with videos showed that children younger than 30 months do not learn from screen media as well as they do from in-person interactions, even with child-appropriate educational content (Anderson and Pempek 2005). This so-called video deficit is thought to stem from infants' and toddlers' immature attentional controls, memory flexibility and symbolic thinking, which prevent them from understanding content (including novel words or visual–spatial reasoning) presented on 2-dimensional screens (Barr 2013). Several studies support this notion, for example, Troseth and DeLoache (1998) and Anderson and Pempek (2005). Despite the vast array of videos marketed to infants as 'educational', such as the now disproven *Baby Einstein* series, laboratory studies suggest that children under 2 years actually struggle to make sense of screen media, and need help from interactive adults in order to do so. For example, Richert *et al.* (2010) found that when word-learning videos are co-viewed by infants and parents, 16-month-olds could learn new words taught on the videos much better than if they watched the videos alone.

The age of the infant matters significantly when considering learning from video presentations. For example, Deloache *et al.* (2010) compared word learning of 12–18-month-old children in a video and non-video condition. The latter was mediated by adults and was shown to be the most effective condition to teach children new words. Despite parents' beliefs that their baby learns from the popular video used in this study, the findings demonstrated that younger infants did not learn from video exposure without re-teaching from their parents. On the other hand, a study by Krcmar et al. (2007) showed that while children older than 22 months can identify new words when taught through a television programme, children under the age of 22 months were not able to identify new words presented on a television screen.

More recent research has shown that, under particular conditions, children between 15 and 24 months of age can learn from repeated viewing of video without adult help. Dayanand *et al.* (2016) showed that 15-month-olds could learn the meaning of sign language symbols after 3 weeks of watching a commercially available video four times per week. However, infants in the comparison arm (in which parents taught them signs from a book) retained their knowledge of sign language for longer in this study, suggesting that socially mediated learning may have different storage in memory than video-mediated learning. Parasocial relationships with video characters may also augment learning: Calvert *et al.* (2014) showed that after 3 months of playing with a personalised interactive toy, 21-month-olds could learn how to stack cups from a video demonstration by this same toy, suggesting that building an emotional bond with an on-screen character improves learning potential.

More recent studies, however, are showing that this 'video deficit' can be overcome with videochatting, which offers contingent interactions with others via a screen medium. Roseberry *et al.* (2014) examined how 36 24–30-month-olds learn new words in three conditions: live interaction training, socially contingent video training over video chat and non-contingent video training. It was only in the socially contingent video training condition that children were able to effectively learn new words. It is important to note that these children were 2 years and older. More recent work has shown that infants as young as 16 months can show shared visual attention with others via videochat, and are able to sustain interactions on Skype more readily with parent support (McClure *et al.* in press).

The conclusion from the above studies has been that children under the age of 2 years cannot transfer information presented on a 2D screen to their 3D environments effectively, and that they learn much more readily from real-life interactions. The few studies to show independent learning of new skills from video in children under 2 years necessitated rarefied conditions or repeated viewing, which is not typically reproducible in naturalistic settings. While it might be argued that an educational video is better for child development than a non-interactive parent, or one with low literacy or teaching skills, this has not been borne out in population-based research; Tomopoulos *et al.* (2010) found that low-income toddlers whose mothers did not interact with them during video viewing had poorer language development overall.

TV and educational TV programmes

While many of the above experimental designs involved randomising children to repeatedly watching videos focusing on specific content, studies of naturalistic TV viewing in children have had less positive findings. In a correlational design, Zimmerman *et al.* (2007) administered a survey asking parents of 8–24-month-olds about the content and frequency of TV watched at home. They correlated these data with standardized parent-report language measures and found that infants 8–17 months had smaller vocabulary sizes if they watched more TV. There was no apparent association between the amount of TV watching and vocabulary size for children aged 17 months and older. Given that the study was correlational, it cannot be concluded that TV watching was reducing children's vocabulary, as many other factors (including parenting and other factors in the home environment) might be at play. The study does, however, highlight the close association between the amount of time a child spends watching TV and their vocabulary growth.

Lisa Guernsey's framework of 3Cs – content, context and individual child (Guernsey 2012) – reminds us that in any evaluation of benefits and limitations of technology on children's learning, the content of the video programme matters. Longitudinal studies suggest that high-quality content is protective of child developmental outcomes. For example, Nathanson *et al.* (2014) found that the earlier the age that children began regularly watching TV, the higher their risk of executive functioning problems as pre-schoolers; however, high-quality content (e.g. *Sesame Street* shows, which have been crafted under the guidance of developmental experts and avoid fast-paced editing) protected against this risk. This study supports earlier work on content: Linebarger and Walker (2005) compared data reported of parents of children aged between 3 and 6 months, in relation to the programme, content, intended audience of TV watched with children's vocabulary knowledge, and expressive language skills. They found that some programmes (*Dora the Explorer, Blue's Clues, Arthur, Clifford* or Dragon Tales) were actually supportive of children's language scores, while others (e.g. *Teletubbies*) were associated with lower expressive language outcomes. As with all other resources, in addition to the actual content of programming, parents' presence during TV watching and their verbal support can determine whether an infant will, or will not, learn from media. With pre-school-ers, parent co-viewing (i.e. watching the TV together with the child) has been advocated by a number of organisations, including Joan Ganz Coney Centre, USA.

Touchscreens

While TV watching on a TV is typically a unidirectional experience – a baby watches a programme without interacting with it – educational programmes and games designed for touchscreens require children's active input. Touchscreens are designed for finger-and touch-manipulation, which does not require teaching, as was the case with a PC mouse. With a range of in-built features (such as micro-phone, camera and touchpad), the possibilities for a child's interaction with moving images and sounds are unprecedented.

Published evidence regarding learning from touchscreens is still sparse, but recent work by Kirkorian *et al.* (2016) has shown that the video deficit can be eliminated in 24-month-olds (e.g. to learn a novel word or solve a puzzle) if the app is designed in such a way that it scaffolds the child's choices. It is important to note that apps used in this lab-based experiment were specially designed teaching videos that the child could forward by tapping on certain highlighted areas. Such design is quite different from commercially available 'educational' apps, which have been shown to have low educational potential, target only rote academic skills, are not based on established curricula and have almost no input from developmental specialists or educators (Guernsey and Levine 2015). The field of children's apps is growing and new programmes are being designed and introduced to the market at a rapid rate. At the time of writing we can say with confidence that the apps which can be useful for infants are those which can be used as prompts for parent–child communication (e.g. browsing pictures), connecting families and building bonds (e.g. Skype with a grandparent or parent not physically available).

Children's electronic toys/objects

In a recent study, Zosh *et al.* (2015) compared parent–child interaction when shar-ing electronic versus traditional shape sorters. The researchers transcribed the verbal feedback provided by the parent and the toy itself when they interacted with the shape sorter and found that there was significantly less rich language (in terms of the spatial vocabulary and mathematics concepts) introduced by parents in the elec-tronic toy condition. Although children in this study were slightly older (3-year-olds), the study highlights what similar studies with children's digital books have found: parent–child interaction and parents' talk are impoverished when they use digitally enhanced books.

For example, Parish-Morris *et al.* (2013) examined and compared parent–child interaction with 165 children in three conditions: Electronic console (EC) books,

CD-rom books and e-book apps. They found that the more these different kinds of digital books contained enhanced features (e.g. pre-recorded sounds), the less beneficial they were for the parent's use of high-quality language (dialogic reading strategies) and the child's learning (story comprehension). Again, children in this study were 3-year-olds but it is likely that similar differences in parent–child interaction would occur with electronic toy play with younger children, as another study recently demonstrated (Sosa 2016). Sosa (2016) conducted a controlled experiment with 26 parent–infant dyads. The children (10–16-month-olds) were observed playing with their parents and three different toy sets: electronic toys, traditional toys and books. The analysis focused on the overall numbers of words produced by the parent, by the child and mutual conversational turns (per minute per each toy/condition). The results showed that with electronic toys, both adults and children produced fewer words, and there were also fewer conversation turns when compared to parent–child play with traditional toys and books. In other words, traditional books and toys can inspire conversations of higher quality than those with enhanced electronic features. There is therefore insufficient evidence to suggest that children under the age of 2 years playing with an adult should be exposed to digital instead of traditional toys. At the time of writing, studies which would compare children's solitary play with digital versus traditional toys are not available. However, it has been posited that solitary digital play does not allow the sensorimotor exploration important to parietal lobe development and later visual–spatial abilities, which block play, for example, allows (Verdine *et al.* 2014).

While these studies focused on the ways in which children could learn from digital media, there is also evidence of potential risks of technologies on children's development, notably in relation to excessive use.

Limitations of excessive use of digital media for infants

Several potential risks of excessive media use in early childhood have been established. Population-based studies have shown associations of excessive TV viewing in infants with cognitive (e.g. Schmidt *et al.* 2009; Tomopoulos *et al.* 2010), language (e.g. Duch *et al.* 2013; Zimmerman *et al.* 2007) and social/emotional delays (Conners-Burrow *et al.* 2011; Hinkley *et al.* 2014; Tomopoulos *et al.* 2007). Possible mechanisms include effects of adult-oriented content, decreases in parent–child interaction and play when the TV is on (Christakis *et al.* 2009), and overall higher family chaos in high media use households.

In addition, due to the effects of food advertising and sedentary lifestyle, high levels of media use are associated with obesity and cardiovascular disease later in childhood (Bel-Serrat *et al.* 2013). For example, a recent study in 2-year-olds demonstrated that body mass index was linked to the amount of media exposure (as measured by every hour per week, see Wen *et al.* 2014).

In addition, the presence of TV or mobile devices in the bedroom is associated with fewer minutes of sleep per night, a finding that is stronger among racial/ethnic minority children (Cespedes *et al.* 2014). Mechanisms are thought to include later bedtimes after evening media use (McDonald *et al.* 2014), arousing effects of violent content (Garrison and Christakis 2012) and suppression of the sleep-inducing hormone, melatonin, by blue light emitted from screens (Higuchi *et al.* 2003).

In sum, the current literature focuses strongly on learning discrete skills from screen media – often in laboratory-based settings – or on the developmental and health risks associated with children's reported media use in the home. Considering the complex nature of children's development, it is likely that several areas of infant/toddler development are not represented in the literature. We therefore approach the gaps in literature in clinical and theoretical terms of infant/toddler development. To frame the discussion, we use the developmental milestones, which provide an approximate timetable and range of skills children gradually develop as they mature.

Framework to guide practical interpretation of research evidence

The first key decision stage relates to establishing whether children use the technology independently or with an adult/older peer. In our review, we outlined how parents' active presence can mitigate against the video deficit effects in 15–30-month-olds, albeit the learning benefits of parent co-viewing of educational media most strongly manifest at the pre-school age. Other studies examined the video deficit effects, and current evidence is that the adult's physical and virtual presence can mitigate against video deficit, but the child's age is important. Roseberry *et al.* (2009) examined how ninety-six 30–42-month-old children learn verbs from video watching with and without the support of adults (live video interaction). They found that the child's age matters: while younger study participants could only learn new verbs when the videos were accompanied by adult interaction, older study participants could learn the new vocabulary from videos alone. Strouse and Troseth (2014) hypothesise that parents' presence can mitigate against the video deficit, while Dayanim and Namy (2015) stress that this can be even greater if the learning stimuli are not spoken words but signs, such as for example the American Sign Language signs. Considering the importance of guided interaction for all kinds of learning and the emerging evidence on parents' supporting role with interactive media use (e.g. Hassinger-Das *et al.* 2016), it is crucial to consider the nature of the interaction: infants will learn considerably more from unidirectional (i.e. videos, TV) or interactive touchscreens/videochat when the activity is scaffolded by a caregiver.

Second, consider the type of technology used by the child: is it an electronic toy specifically developed for children or a parent's smartphone lent to the child? It used to be the case that a screen could be used synonymously with TV as there were not many other screens with which young children would interact. Today, however, the word screen can encompass a wide variety of digital devices, including PCs, Leapsters, Kindles, iPads, smartphones and others. When talking about the effects of 'screens' on young children's development, we need to be clear about which device we have in mind, as well as which features of this device (e.g. its portability; its possibility to connect to the Internet; possibility to personalise or customise the content). In our review, we considered three different kinds of screens (videos, TV and touchscreens) and electronic toys. Current evidence suggests that the device or platform is as important as the design of the interactive interface. Although it could be argued that mobile devices are more likely to be used independently rather than shared (Wartella *et al.* 2013), it is also important that the specific app being used scaffolds a child's choice rather than distracts with bells and whistles (Hirsh-Pasek *et al.* 2015).

Third, consider the content of the activity – is it appropriate for your child? Content is one of the 3Cs we mentioned earlier – content, context and individual child (Guernsey 2012) – and is crucially important when thinking about the effects a particular technology might have on a child's learning. The quality of the digital content influences what and how much children learn during the interaction. For children's apps available for smartphones and tablets, the UK's literacy charity National Literacy Trust developed an 'app guide', which lists apps recommended by experts to support children's reading for pleasure (http://literacyapps.literacytrust. org.uk/). Other organisations, for instance the Common Sense Media in the USA, regularly review apps for a number of learning benefits, including key language skills relevant for the youngest users (www.commonsensemedia.org).

The content of the activity is closely linked to the skills the child can gain from using the technology. In assessing the 'added value' of a technology for the child's development, it is best if teachers and parents reflect on the ways children learn and the key milestones they need to master as they mature. Again, the type of the technology used and whether its content and design are appropriate for the developmental level of the child will strongly influence the skills and knowledge children can gain.

Finally, it is important for caregivers and adults making media use decisions for infants to think about their own use of technologies and how that might influence your perception of how your child learns and interacts with technology. Currently, many caregivers feel pulled by two opposing public discourses: one which suggests that technologies can improve if not transform children's play, creativity and learning; and a contrasting discourse, which suggests that technologies can damage children's development and be detrimental to their relationships with others and holistic growth. The extent to which one or the other discourse dominates a parent's decision-making is a function of personal theories, beliefs, previous experiences and values of how infants should be raised (as well as the popular media, which often take advantage of this polarised topic). We therefore recommend that caregivers reflect upon their family's culture of technology use as a whole, so that they can make proactive decisions about allowing infant media use only if it supports their parenting values and goals regarding what they want their child to learn.

This leads us to the following cycle of questions and evidence-checking (see Figure 1.1).

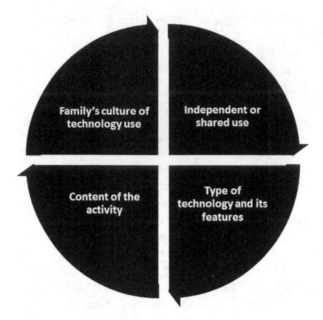

FIGURE 1.1 Key considerations when evaluating the benefits and limitations of infants' use of digital media.

Future directions

Some important considerations for future research based on our literature review therefore include these four key points:

When evaluating the benefits and limitations of digital media for infants:

1 Reflect on your own personal theories, beliefs, previous experiences and values of how infants should be raised and how technology might influence them.
2 Consider whether the technologies are used by the child on their own or with an adult.
3 Think about the content of the activity – what is the specific app/digital game/activity the child is engaging with?
4 In addition to the content of the activity, think about the type of technology (video, TV, electronic toys or tablets) the child is using, the particular features of this technology and the context in which it is used.

Conclusion

The aim of this chapter was to ensure that readers are aware of the various possibilities of children's learning when evaluating the question of whether technology is, or is not, appropriate to support the earliest stages of children's learning and development. Our review confirms the conclusion drawn by the Academy of Paediatrics in 2016: currently, we do not have sufficient evidence to recommend the independent use of digital media for children under the age of two. Early introduction of screen media is associated with several adverse developmental and health outcomes, but supportive parent interaction around media and high-quality content can reduce some of these risks. Yet, we also know from several survey and observation studies that toddlers and infants regularly interact with tablets, their parents' smartphones or electronic toys designed for them. The technologies therefore are likely interacting with their developmental trajectory, and we need more research to help us understand how.

All technologies are a moving target; designers and technology developers are refining their products based on the users' feedback and uptake. Our framework provides not only a guide to caregiver decision-making about media use in infants, but also a general approach for understanding, interpreting and generating new research evidence on this important topic. The framework is not hierarchical – each element matters and is interconnected with the other elements. What is crucial for practitioners, childminders, parents and policymakers is the importance of others in mediating children's technology use, which is why we include it as the key first question to ask when thinking about technology's impact on infants/toddlers.

In conclusion, with our socio-cultural orientation towards child development, we highlight that for a holistic, optimal and long-lasting learning to occur, no technology can replace positive human interaction. This is especially true for the development of children's first knowledge of the world and their skills to fully function in it.

References

American Academy of Pediatrics Council on Communication and Media (AAP) (2016) 'Media and young minds', *Pediatrics, epub ahead of print*.

Anderson, D. R., and Pempek, T. A. (2005) 'Television and very young children', *American Behavioral Scientist*, 48(5): 505–522.

Baillargeon, R., Scott, R. M., and Bian, L. (2016) 'Psychological reasoning in infancy', *Annual Review of Psychology*, 67: 159–186.

Barr, R. (2013) 'Memory constraints on infant learning from picture books, television, and touchscreens', *Child Development Perspectives*, 7(4): 205–210.

Bedny, M., Dravida, S., and Saxe, R. (2014) 'Shindigs, brunches, and rodeos: The neural basis of event words', *Cognitive, Affective, & Behavioral Neuroscience*, 14(3): 891-901.

Bel-Serrat, S., Mouratidou, T., Santaliestra-Pasías, A. M., Iacoviello, L., Kourides, Y. A., Marild, S., and Vanaelst, B. (2013) 'Clustering of multiple lifestyle behaviours and its association to cardiovascular risk factors in children: the IDEFICS study', *European Journal of Clinical Nutrition*, 67(8): 848–854.

Calvert, S. L., Richards, M. N., and Kent, C. C. (2014) 'Personalized interactive characters for toddlers' learning of seriation from a video presentation', *Journal of Applied Developmental Psychology*, 35(3): 148–155.

Cespedes, E. M., Gillman, M. W., Kleinman, K., Rifas-Shiman, S. L., Redline, S., and Taveras, E. M. (2014) 'Television viewing, bedroom television, and sleep duration from infancy to mid-childhood', *Pediatrics*, 133(5): 1163–1171.

Christakis, D. A., Gilkerson, J., Richards, J. A., Zimmerman, F. J., Garrison, M. M., Xu, D., and Yapanel, U. (2009) 'Audible television and decreased adult words, infant vocalizations, and conversational turns: A population-based study', *Archives of Pediatrics & Adolescent Medicine*, 163(6): 554–558.

Common Sense Media, and Rideout, V. (2011) *Zero to eight: Children's media use in America*. Common Sense Media.

Common Sense Media, and Rideout, V. (2013) *Zero to eight: Children's media use in America*. Common Sense Media.

Conners-Burrow, N. A., McKelvey, L. M., and Fussell, J. J. (2011) 'Social outcomes associated with media viewing habits of low-income preschool children', *Early Education and Development*, 22: 256–273.

Davies, D. (2010) *Child development: A practitioner's guide*, New York: Guilford Press.

Dayanim, S., and Namy, L. L. (2015) 'Infants learn baby signs from video', *Child Development*, 86(3): 800–811.

DeLoache, J. S., Chiong, C., Sherman, K., Islam, N., Vanderborght, M., Troseth, G. L., and O'Doherty, K. (2010) 'Do babies learn from baby media?', *Psychological Science*, 21(11): 1570–1574.

Doupe, A. J., and Kuhl, P. K. (1999) 'Birdsong and human speech: common themes and mechanisms', *Annual Review of Neuroscience*, 22(1): 567–631.

Duch, H., Fisher, E. M., Ensari, I., Font, M., Harrington, A., Taromino, C., and Rodriguez, C. (2013) 'Association of screen time use and language development in Hispanic toddlers: A cross-sectional and longitudinal study', *Clinical Pediatrics*, 52(9): 857–865.

Garrison, M. M., and Christakis, D. A. (2012) 'The impact of a healthy media use intervention on sleep in preschool children', *Pediatrics*, 130(3): 492–499.

Guernsey, L. (2012) *Screen time: How electronic media from baby videos to educational software affects your young child*, New York: Basic Books.

Guernsey, L., and Levine, M. H. (2015) *Tap click read: Growing readers in a world of screens*, San Francisco, CA: Jossey-Bass.

Hassinger-Das, B., Mahajan, N., Metz, R., Ramsook, K. A., Margulis, K., Hirsh-Pasek, K., Golinkoff, R. M., and Parish-Morris, J. (2016, April) 'Shared book-reading in the digital age: Examining differences in traditional and tablet books', in J. E. Kim and J. Anderson (Chairs), *Young children's literacy practices with digital books at home and school: International evidence*. Symposium conducted at the annual meeting of the American Educational Research Association, Washington, D.C.

Higuchi, S., Motohashi, Y., Liu, Y., Ahara, M., and Kaneko, Y. (2003) 'Effects of VDT tasks with a bright display at night on melatonin, core temperature, heart rate, and sleepiness', *Journal of Applied Physiology*, 94(5): 1773–1776.

Hinkley, T., Verbestel, V., Ahrens, W., Lissner, L., Molnár, D., Moreno, L. A., and Veidebaum, T. (2014) 'Early childhood electronic media use as a predictor of poorer well-being: a prospective cohort study', *JAMA Pediatrics*, 168(5): 485–492.

Hirsh-Pasek, K., Zosh, J. M., Golinkoff, R. M., Gray, J. H., Robb, M. B., and Kaufman, J. (2015) 'Putting education in "educational" apps: lessons from the science of learning', *Psychological Science in the Public Interest*, 16(1): 3–34.

Jara-Ettinger, J., Gweon, H., Tenenbaum, J. B., and Schulz, L. E. (2015) 'Children's understanding of the costs and rewards underlying rational action', *Cognition*, 140: 14–23.

Kabali, H. K., Irigoyen, M. M., Nunez-Davis, R., Budacki, J. G., Mohanty, S. H., Leister, K. P., and Bonner, R. L. (2015) 'Exposure and use of mobile media devices by young children', *Pediatrics*, 136(6): 1044–1050.

Kirkorian, H. L., Choi, K., and Pempek, T. A. (2016) 'Toddlers' word learning from contingent and noncontingent video on touch screens', *Child Development*, 87(2): 405–413.

Knowles, M. (1950) *Informal adult education*. Chicago: Associated Press.

Krcmar, M., Grela, B., and Lin, K. (2007) 'Can toddlers learn vocabulary from television? An experimental approach', *Media Psychology*, 10(1): 41–63.

Kuhl, P. K., Stevens, E., Hayashi, A., Deguchi, T., Kiritani, S., and Iverson, P. (2006) 'Infants show a facilitation effect for native language phonetic perception between 6 and 12 months', *Developmental Science*, 9(2): 13–21.

Linebarger, D. L., and Walker, D. (2005) 'Infants' and toddlers' television viewing and language outcomes', *American Behavioral Scientist*, 48(5): 624–645.

McClure, E. R., Chentsova-Dutton, Y. E., Barr, R. F., Holochwost, S. J., and Parrott, W. G. (2017) 'Look at that! Skype and joint visual attention development among babies and toddlers', *Child Development* (submitted).

McDonald, L., Wardle, J., Llewellyn, C. H., van Jaarsveld, C. H., and Fisher, A. (2014) 'Predictors of shorter sleep in early childhood', *Sleep Medicine*, 15(5): 536–540.

Meltzoff, A. N., and Gopnik, A. (2013) 'Learning about the mind from evidence: Children's development of intuitive theories of perception and personality', in S. Baron-Cohen, H. Tager-Flausber, and M. Lombardo (eds.) *Understanding other minds* (3rd ed), Oxford, England: Oxford University Press (19–34).

Nathanson, A. I., Aladé, F., Sharp, M. L., Rasmussen, E. E., and Christy, K. (2014) 'The relation between television exposure and executive function among preschoolers', *Developmental Psychology*, 50(5): 1497–1506.

Parish-Morris, J., Mahajan, N., Hirsh-Pasek, K., Golinkoff, R. M., and Collins, M. F. (2013) 'Once upon a time: Parent–child dialogue and storybook reading in the electronic era', *Mind, Brain, and Education*, 7(3): 200–211.

Plowman, L. (1992) An ethnographic approach to analysing navigation and task structure in interactive multimedia: Some design issues for group use. *People and Computers*, VII: 271-271.

Plowman, L., and Stephen, C. (2007) 'Guided interaction in pre-school settings', *Journal of Computer Assisted Learning*, 23(1): 14–26.

Postman N. (1982) *The disappearance of childhood*, New York: Vintage Books, revised ed. 1994.

Radesky, J. S., Peacock-Chambers, E., Zuckerman, B., and Silverstein, M. (2016) 'Use of mobile technology to calm upset children: Associations with social-emotional development', *JAMA Pediatrics*, 170(4): 397–399.

Richert, R. A., Robb, M. B., Fender, J. G., and Wartella, E. (2010) 'Word learning from baby videos', *Archives of Pediatrics & Adolescent Medicine*, 164(5): 432–437.

Roseberry, S., Hirsh-Pasek, K., Parish-Morris, J., and Golinkoff, R. M. (2009) 'Live action: Can young children learn verbs from video?', *Child Development*, 80(5): 1360–1375.

Roseberry, S., Hirsh-Pasek, K., and Golinkoff, R. M. (2014) 'Skype me! Socially contingent interactions help toddlers learn language', *Child Development*, 85(3): 956–970.

Schmidt, M. E., Rich, M., Rifas-Shiman, S. L., Oken, E., and Taveras, E. M. (2009) 'Television viewing in infancy and child cognition at 3 years of age in a US cohort', *Pediatrics*, 123(3): 370–375.

Sosa, A. V. (2016) 'Association of the type of toy used during play with the quantity and quality of parent–infant communication', *JAMA Pediatrics*, 170(2): 132–137.

Stahl, A. E., and Feigenson, L. (2015) 'Observing the unexpected enhances infants' learning and exploration', *Science*, 348: 91–94.

Steinberg, L., Vandell, D. L., and Bornstein, M. H. (2010) *Development: Infancy through adolescence*, Wadsworth: Nelson Education.

Strouse, G. A., and Troseth, G. L. (2014) 'Supporting toddlers' transfer of word learning from video', *Cognitive Development*, 30: 47–64.

Thompson, A. L., Adair, L. S., and Bentley, M. E. (2013) 'Maternal characteristics and perception of temperament associated with infant TV exposure', *Pediatrics*, 131(2): 390–397.

Tomopoulos, S., Dreyer, B. P., Valdez, P., Flynn, V., Foley, G., Berkule, S. B., and Mendelsohn, A. L. (2007) 'Media content and externalizing behaviors in Latino toddlers', *Ambulatory Pediatrics*, 7(3): 232–238.

Tomopoulos, S., Dreyer, B. P., Berkule, S., Fierman, A. H., Brockmeyer, C., and Mendelsohn, A. L. (2010) 'Infant media exposure and toddler development', *Archives of Pediatrics & Adolescent Medicine*, 164(12): 1105–1111.

Troseth, G. L., and DeLoache, J. S. (1998) 'The medium can obscure the message: Young children's understanding of video', *Child Development*, 69(4): 950–965.

Verdine, B. N., Golinkoff, R. M., Hirsh-Pasek, K., Newcombe, N. S., Filipowicz, A. T., and Chang, A. (2014) 'Deconstructing building blocks: Preschoolers' spatial assembly performance relates to early mathematical skills', *Child Development*, 85(3): 1062–1076.

Wartella, E., Rideout, V., Lauricella, A. R., and Connell, S. (2013) 'Parenting in the age of digital technology', *Report for the Center on Media and Human Development School of Communication Northwestern University*.

Wen, L. M., Baur, L. A., Rissel, C., Xu, H., and Simpson, J. M. (2014) 'Correlates of body mass index and overweight and obesity of children aged 2 years: Findings from the healthy beginnings trial', *Obesity*, 22(7): 1723–1730.

Zimmerman, F. J., Christakis, D. A., and Meltzoff, A. N. (2007) 'Associations between media viewing and language development in children under age 2 years', *Journal of Pediatrics*, 151: 364–368.

Zosh, J. M., Verdine, B. N., Filipowicz, A., Golinkoff, R. M., Hirsh–Pasek, K., and Newcombe, N. S. (2015) 'Talking shape: Parental language with electronic versus traditional shape sorters', *Mind, Brain, and Education*, 9(3): 136–144.

2

THE INFLUENCE OF E-BOOKS ON LANGUAGE AND LITERACY DEVELOPMENT

Mirit Barzillai, Jennifer M. Thomson and Anne Mangen

Introduction

For the young child just discovering the written word, shared storybook reading can be a transportative time of coming together with a loved one to unlock a world of experiences and emotions. A number of studies underscore the significance of shared storybook reading for the development of children's language and literacy skills (see for instance Bus 2001; Bus *et al.* 1995; Mol and Bus 2011; Scarborough and Dobrich 1994). Moreover, mere access to physical books at home has been shown to correlate with literacy development (Krashen 2013). For instance, Evans *et al.* (2010) found that children growing up in homes with many books get three years more schooling than children from bookless homes, and gain exposure to vocabulary, as well as 'broad horizons of history and geography, familiarity with good writing, understanding of the importance of evidence in argument' (Evans *et al.* 2010: 190). With digital technologies rapidly replacing printed books in study as well as leisure reading, researchers and parents are anxious to understand the influence of technology, and particularly e-books, on the reading development of children. A recent report from the UK (Kucirkova and Littleton 2016) revealed parents' growing concern that e-books will negatively affect children's attention and lead to a loss of interest in print books. Some even worried that e-books would inhibit learning and harm their children's brain development (ibid.). While some of these concerns may seem overstated, they reflect a genuine worry that young children acquiring language and literacy skills are particularly vulnerable to the impact of digital media, and underscore the need to shed light on several pressing questions: how does the medium on which storybooks are shared influence the development of children's language and literacy skills? Will e-books and digital enhancements prove beneficial or detrimental for aspects of reading or profiles of readers?

The present chapter contributes to this effort by providing an overview of relevant research on the affordances of e-books as compared to print books, and how these may influence children's early literacy development. We focus on the ways technological affordances affect the interactions and language surrounding shared storybook reading and shape children's developing attitudes towards reading. We further explore the potential of digital books to support literacy growth among readers of different profiles and skill levels. The chapter concludes with a consideration of the benefits and pitfalls of e-books for developing young readers.

Hardware and software affordances of e-books, and the conundrum of immersion and interactivity

Ever since the appearance of desktop computers, digital technologies have been used in reading activities with children, in both educational and family settings. The emergence of touch-screen tablets (e.g. the iPad) and other portable devices, such as e-readers (like the Kindle) and smartphones prompted a surge of interest in the use of digital technologies in early literacy. This increased popularity can be linked to both ergonomic affordances of the tablet hardware as well as to software affordances – characteristics and possibilities pertaining to the integration and display of interactive multimedia content. Understanding hardware (i.e. ergonomic) and software (i.e. content-related; audiovisual) affordances of tablets is thus necessary for any discussion on the usefulness and potential of e-books for children's literacy development.

The move from desktop computers to tablet technologies was a major improvement in hardware, especially with respect to children (see Romeo *et al.* 2003, for example). Where desktop computers and laptops require the use of an external input device (typically, a computer mouse and a keyboard), touch-screen tablets minimize the need for challenging hand-eye coordination. Hence, the tactile tablet user interface appears more intuitive and transparent, making touch-screen technologies more developmentally appropriate for younger children (Couse and Chen 2010; Merchant 2015). Tablets are also lightweight and portable, and they provide ergonomic affordances which in many respects come close to those of the print book. They can be held comfortably in the hands, positioned, tilted and angled to accommodate comfortable postures, whether for solo or shared reading settings.

In addition to hardware affordances, content possibilities abound on tablets which make them particularly appealing as reading devices for young children. Touch-screen tablets can present a variety of multimedia stories, combining audio, video, animations, text and graphics in any conceivable manner and configuration, replete with options for interactivity and story engagement. This integration of audiovisual materials with print text and interactivity enables the presentation of content that can simultaneously 'stimulate visual, auditory, tactile, and kinesthetic sensory systems and respond to a child's input with instant feedback' (Neumann and Neumann 2014: 232). It is unsurprising, then, that the appearance of tablets has seen a parallel upsurge of storytelling apps for children. Whether based on classic

children's literature (*Winnie the Pooh; Alice in Wonderland; Pippi Longstocking*) or created from scratch without a print predecessor (i.e. the award-winning *Fantastic
Flying Books of Mr. Morris Lessmore*), apps provide interactive, multimedia stories
that make use of the affordances of touch-screen technologies – most importantly,
interactivity and a combination of modalities (audiovisuals, text, graphics).

The audiovisual effects and technological features plentiful in these apps, however, run the risk of interfering with the most important consideration of all: the
quality of the story (the narrative). That is, as storytelling becomes digital, balancing
the attention-grabbing nature of dynamic audiovisuals (e.g. animations) with the
static modality of verbal text is essential for allowing a verbal narrative to unfold.
Smooth combinations of narrative and interactivity, however, are remarkably challenging to create, to such an extent that the compatibility of interactivity and narrative has been questioned (see for instance Ryan 2015, 2001; but see Jenkins 2004
for an attempt at reconciliation). Interactivity – explicit invitations to the reader/
listener to physically (haptically) engage with the content by, for example, clicking
on hot-spots – typically results in an interruption of the flow of the story. Thus,
instead of being entry points through which we can become immersed in the story,
such invitations interfere with our sense of transportation in the story (see Holland
2009; Mangen and van der Weel 2015) and marginalize the narrative. This can cause
digital stories to resemble games rather than stories proper, and provides a qualitatively different setting for verbal exchanges than listening to a story.

We get immersed in stories because we, the readers, know that we will not be
able to change the story with our actions in the real-world. In contrast, when playing a game (for instance, on a computer or an iPad), we enter the role of a character
in a 'story', concretely, and our actions and involvement are what drives this 'story'
forward. Albeit perhaps more intrinsically 'active', such a mode of engagement may
in fact negatively affect the dialogue surrounding the story, in the sense that language becomes more oriented towards the haptic interaction ('click there!') rather
than on the more potentially enriching story-related discourse. Further, finding
appropriate places to pause and engage in meaningful dialogue may prove challenging in e-books. In print stories, the reader is in total control over the temporal
unfolding of the narrative, and adult readers can easily find appropriate places to
stop and invite children to discuss and reflect upon the story. With dynamic multimedia narratives such as e-books, however, finding places to pause may prove
more unnatural, as it may entail artificially stopping an audiovisual narrative more
akin to a movie, or it may require deliberate manipulation of the presentation (e.g.
turning off the audio altogether). Thus, the affordances of electronic books, such
as interactivity and audiovisual features, provide a host of opportunities to engage
readers in ways not possible with print. At the same time, these features may contribute to a reading experience that is more game-like and less conducive to story
immersion and language-rich dialogue. Indeed, evidence suggests that, although
often highly engaging, e-books influence the language and interactions surrounding one of the most important home literacy practices, that of early shared storybook reading.

Digital influences on shared storybook reading

The young child's first foray into the world of books often begins on the lap of a loved one, where they feel safe and ready to explore (e.g. Wolf 2007). Nestled in a cosy spot, shared book reading becomes a time of bonding and language exposure. The voice of a familiar loved one reading, pausing, explaining words and events, even slightly editing the texts so that the story resonates more strongly with that child (e.g. Vander Woude *et al.* 2009), creates an ideal space for learning and participation in the reading experience. Through the dialogic reading that often unfolds as parents and children interact around text, children are encouraged to expand on the story content, infer, predict and connect the text to their own lives (e.g. Whitehurst *et al.* 1994). This process serves to enrich children's language and literacy skills (e.g. Bus 2001; Bus *et al.* 1995; Mol and Bus 2011; Mol *et al.* 2008; Lonigan and Whitehurst 1998; Scarborough and Dobrich 1994; 1997; Wasik and Bond 2001), while also shaping children's developing view of reading as an intimate time of focused attention where meaning arises through connection and contemplation. Indeed, early shared book reading is associated with not only superior language and literacy skills (e.g. Fletcher and Reese 2005; Hood *et al.* 2008; Mol *et al.* 2008) but also with increased enjoyment and interest in reading (Baker *et al.* 2001).

The introduction of e-books, with clickable characters and animations into the home literacy environment, however, may alter the practice of shared storybook reading before the interaction even begins. That is, the format of storybook apps, with 'read to me' options and various games, may sway parents into assuming that young children can and should use them on their own. Indeed, several studies suggest that parents frequently give children tablets and iPads and their associated apps and games to use independently when they are occupied with other tasks (Chiong and Shuler 2010; Kucirkova and Littleton 2016), and often to calm or distract the child (e.g. Radesky *et al.* 2016; see also Kucirkova and Radesky, Chapter 1, this volume, for relevant discussion). Thus, the device and its affordances may lead parents to remove themselves from the reading interaction, even as it is their very presence in shared storybook reading that marks it as a time of bonding and language growth (e.g. Korat and Segal-Drori 2016).

Even when parents are engaged with their children in shared reading, the presence of e-books can significantly influence the language and behaviour surrounding the interaction. For example, Parish-Morris *et al.* (2013) observed parent-child dyads (3-year-olds) as they read stories in print or on electronic consoles. Their observations revealed that parents in the print group made more content-related utterances and distancing prompts, asking children to relate the story to their own lives, whereas parents in the electronic group displayed significantly more behaviour-related utterances, such as asking the children to interact with specific elements of the screen ('Touch the puppy and it will play a song!', Parish-Morris *et al.* 2013: 211), or to turn the page. Children's language across conditions reflected these differences, with more expansions observed among children in the print group and more mechanical utterances evident among children reading electronic books. In both conditions, children were adept at identifying events and characters, but those who read print storybooks outperformed their peers on questions of content and recalling story event sequences. Results thus highlight the efficacy of shared print storybook reading, in supporting the type of rich language and literacy experience essential for comprehension and continued growth of literacy skills.

The advantage of print books over e-books for fostering language-rich interactions is evident across a number of studies that examine parents reading to their pre-school or kindergarten-aged children (e.g. Krcmar and Cingel 2014; Lauricella *et al.* 2014; Robb 2010; Segal-Drori *et al.* 2010). In print storybook conditions, parents are observed to engage in the most evaluations and expanding talk, including discussions around word meanings and connections to personal experience. They ask more questions and point out more aspects of print with their kindergarten age children than do parents reading digital storybooks (Korat and Segal-Drori 2016; Krcmar and Cingel 2014; Lauricella *et al.* 2014; Robb 2010; Segal-Drori *et al.* 2010). Conversely, although children tend to be significantly more engaged in the e-book conditions (Chiong *et al.* 2012; *Lauricella et al.* 2014), more distracted talk is observed in these conditions. That is, parents make significantly more utterances related to the mechanics of the digital device and engage in less content-related discussion (Chiong *et al.* 2012; Krcmar and Cingel 2014; Lauricella *et al.* 2014). These differences were sometimes (Chiong *et al.* 2012; Krcmar and Cingel 2014), but not always, to the detriment of their children's comprehension (Lauricella *et al.* 2014).

Thus, research suggests that digital books have a tangible influence on the parent–child interactions that occur during storybook reading. The traditional print book format is consistently seen to foster the kind of rich dialogic reading that helps scaffold children's language and comprehension skills, by clarifying content and making the story meaningful in a very personal way. Digital books, on the other hand, although often prompting increased levels of engagement, tend to also encourage discussions related to the mechanics of the digital device or the behaviour surrounding the book. Such a shift of parental focus when engaging with e-books may reflect that parents are also distracted by the various attractions of digital devices. It may reflect too the changing strategies parents must adopt to help their children cope with the increased cognitive demands of reading e-books.

Demands of digital books on the young child

Electronic books are rife with hotspots and activities, colours and sounds that vie for the attention of young children. Indeed, investigations reveal that three-quarters of the most popular electronic storybooks include hotspots, the majority of which are game-like, and only about one-fifth of which are relevant to the story (Guernsey *et al.* 2012). Results from a recent review and meta-analysis reveal that such interactive features are distracting and detrimental to comprehension and learning (Reich *et al.* 2016; Takacs *et al.* 2015). Within this context, engaging in storybook reading while navigating through a maze of moving images, sounds and games places a heavy burden on the child's executive function skills, such as the capacity to stay goal oriented, discern relevance and curtail distractions (e.g. Garon *et al.* 2008; Meltzer 2011), at a time when these are only developing. With their executive function skills lacking, children are left at the mercy of highly seductive bells and whistles (Radesky and Christakis 2016) to be easily pulled from one attractive, entertaining hotspot to another, following a potentially haphazard path through the e-book that often impedes comprehension (e.g. de Jong and Bus 2002; Labbo and Kuhn 2000; Trushell and Maitland 2005). For example, de Jong and Bus (2002) found that when given unrestricted access to games and hotspots in electronic storybooks, kindergarteners elected to spend nearly half their time playing games, navigated through the story randomly, and barely listened to the audio narrative. In addition, when reading an alphabet e-book, 3–4-year-olds spent 43.6 per cent of their time activating irrelevant hotspots. They activated letter hotspots only 11 per cent of the time and named letters, the purported goal of an alphabet book, less than 1 per cent of the time (Willoughby *et al.* 2015).

In order to wisely navigate through these interactive elements then, young children must possess the kind of executive skills that are beyond their developmental level (e.g. Garon *et al.* 2008). Reading digital books with an adult who can aid them in sorting through the digital debris may provide the help they need to stay goal directed and focused. Thus, the increased comments by parents on the technological features of e-books during shared reading of electronic books (e.g. Lauricella *et al.* 2014) may serve to direct children's attention away from distracting aspects of the technology and keep them on task. Indeed, Robb (2010) found that young children who read interactive storybooks with adults showed better story comprehension than when they read the interactive books by themselves. Further, among low socio-economic status (SES) children, the most robust gains in early literacy skills, such as word reading and concepts about print, were seen when adults assisted the children as they read electronic storybooks (Segal-Drori *et al.* 2010). Thus, parental guidance through digital elements is advantageous for young children reading e-books, as it may help them properly attend to the story and the feedback given. Although this is inarguably of great importance for helping children develop technological literacy (Neumann and Neumann 2014), it should happen in addition to, and not at the expense of, shared reading that focuses on the book, the story and the rich language of storybooks, the kind of reading best done, for now, in print.

Developing attitudes towards reading

Opting for digital texts during storybook interactions can thus influence the language and behaviour surrounding storybook reading, turning the focus from content and literacy skills to the properties of and abilities needed to navigate digital devices. In addition, as discussed earlier, electronic books in which text is overshadowed by hotspots and multimedia elements can come to resemble games more than they do stories. This, in turn, may foster within young children an attitude towards reading as a game-like experience, requiring only passive attention. Labbo and Kuhn

(2000) observed this passive state in a child interacting with an e-book replete with hotspots and animations. Lefever-Davis and Pearman (2005) also identified such a spectator stance among first graders interacting with electronic storybooks, noting that it was characteristic of those children who approached electronic books as a source of entertainment. Tellingly, in their comparison of parent–child storybook reading across media, Krcmar and Cingel (2014) found an interaction between children's experience with technology and comprehension such that, although technology experience did not differentiate children's comprehension in the print condition, in the iPad condition, children with greater familiarity with the technology performed more poorly on comprehension tasks. The authors suggested that these children associated the device with digital games and interactive apps. This led them to adopt an approach in which they invested less mental effort in reading on the iPad, to the detriment of their comprehension. These results simultaneously highlight the potent influence of media on the child's forming attitudes towards reading and the importance of providing children with reading experiences that nurture a view of reading as deserving of focused attention and thought.

E-books' influence on literacy skills

If digital technology cannot replace the voice of a loved one for children's earliest exposure to reading and storybooks, well-designed electronic books may hold the potential to support readers as they practice and develop their literacy skills. Indeed, several properties of digital text make it potentially advantageous for fostering literacy skills; the computer's neutral stance on mistakes, the malleability of digital texts, as well as the possibility of highlighting text as the story is read, breaking down words into their component sounds, providing definitions of keywords and embedding comprehension supports (e.g. Anderson-Inman and Horney 2007; Dalton and Proctor 2008). In addition, added multimedia, such as animations, sound and music that compliments story elements (e.g. scary music playing when the characters are frightened in the text) can create a synergy between story elements that enhances comprehension (e.g. Mayer 2005) while supporting the development of different reading skills and easing the executive function burden on the child (for relevant discussion, see Bus et al. 2015). Indeed, in their recent meta-analysis, Takacs et al. (2015) compared the effects of technology-enhanced narratives with print stories on children's language and literacy development. They found a small but significant additional benefit of multimedia elements such as music and animations for story comprehension and expressive vocabulary.

Research into the influence of electronic books on early literacy skills has further revealed that the benefits of such affordances are often tied to the abilities of the readers themselves (e.g. Lewin 2000; Littleton et al. 2006; Plak et al. 2016; Smeets and Bus 2012). That is, the way in which readers interact with digital storybooks, and either benefit or not from their affordances, has as much to do with their age and skill level as it does with the quality of the technology they are exposed to. In addition, certain profiles of readers may be particularly sensitive to the effects of technology. For example, research has revealed a population of learners for whom the multimodal presentation of material is particularly advantageous for learning. These are children who carry a specific allele that makes them susceptible to environmental influences and reduced attentional regulation (see Plak *et al.* 2016). In a noisy, crowded environment they tend to be the most ill-affected population. Plak *et al.* hypothesized that e-books providing multimedia comprehension supports would engage these children at multiple levels of sensory information (visual and auditory) and reduce the ability of environment distractions to influence their attention, allowing them to fully focus on the reading task. They assigned 565 5-year-olds to a digital reading support programme, an e-book reading condition or a control condition and measured the influence of each condition on literacy skills. Results indicated that the sample as a whole did not benefit from any of these interventions. Only the subsample of children with the allele showed a significant advantage in the e-book condition, making significant gains in their reading skills. Thus, without the appropriate support, these children lag behind in literacy skills, but when sufficiently engaged by e-books they are able to focus, learn and even outperform their peers (Plak *et al.* 2016).

Word reading skills

For children with different reading profiles, the benefits of e-book supports for such literacy skills as phonological awareness and word recognition may be similarly nuanced. In a series of experiments, Chera *et al.* (Chera and Wood 2003; Littleton *et al.* 2006; Wood 2005) examined the effects of electronic books that provided several options for text to speech support (including onset–rhyme, whole word and whole sentence feedback) on the phonological awareness of beginning readers. In the first experiment, 15 at-risk 3–4-year-olds read e-books crafted with speech feedback and various games that highlighted the phonological and orthographic properties of words. Results following the intervention indicated an advantage for the experimental group in phonological awareness skills when compared to a group who received phonological instruction using printed text. A delayed test, however, revealed that these differences were not sustained. Another study, with older, 5–6-year-old children did not reveal an advantage for children reading e-books when compared to reading print with an adult (Wood 2005). A more detailed analysis of a subsample of 18 boys, however, revealed an interaction between phonological awareness skills at pretest and reading strategies (Littleton *et al.* 2006). Boys with lower phonological skills were likely to request whole page and whole word speech feedback and chime in after the computer pronounced them, while boys with higher initial phonological skills were more likely to request feedback only for words they found difficult or not to access any computer supports at all. They were even observed to make significantly more mispronunciations than the boys with lower phonological skills as they attempted to use their developing phonological knowledge to decode unknown words. Improvements in phonological awareness were tied to ability level as well. Boys with low phonological awareness skills at the outset made greater gains in this area than those with higher initial phonological skills.

Lewin (2000) similarly found that the interaction patterns and literacy gains made by first graders using different versions of e-books were mediated by their reading ability at pretest. More specifically, low-ability readers benefitted most from in-text vocabulary exposure and pronunciations, regardless of whether the software included extended activities or not. The mid-ability students, however, made the most gains in word recognition skills when the e-book included extended activities focused on the phonological, semantic and syntactic properties of words. Thus, children were able to benefit from the e-book enhancements only after they had achieved a basic level of word knowledge. Indeed, when given unrestricted access to e-books, de Jong and Bus (2002) observed that 4–5-year-olds who began the study with some letter–sound knowledge improved their word recognition skills after exposure to electronic books, while those who began with a lower level seemingly ignored the text to such an extent that they weren't even aware that it changed colour as it was read. In addition, those with higher levels of emergent reading skills clicked more on hotspots that elicited reading while lower level readers clicked on hotspots with illustrations. These patterns of results illustrate how children's age and skill level influence both their reading strategies and the benefits they receive from e-books that emphasize word reading skills.

Vocabulary

The technological affordances of e-books may also hold potential benefits for improving children's vocabulary. Vocabulary knowledge is inherently incremental, developing with each exposure, and multidimensional, involving multiple aspects of a word's meaning, uses and associations (e.g. Beck et al. 2002; Kameenui et al. 1987; Nagy and Scott 2000; Stahl 2003). Thus, the multimodal presentation of word definitions and exposure to words in multiple contexts possible in e-books may provide a fitting path to enhancing vocabulary knowledge, particularly among those who struggle to read. Results from a recent meta-analysis attest to such an advantage for multimodal storybooks on expressive, although not receptive, vocabulary knowledge, particularly among disadvantaged and struggling readers (Takacs et al. 2015). The work of Korat et al. is similarly encouraging. In a series of studies, these researchers investigated the efficacy of electronic e-books that included automatic dictionary definitions of words including meanings and visualizations. For both typically developing children and those at risk of reading difficulties, findings indicated that children who read the electronic storybook with dictionary options consistently made gains in their vocabulary knowledge, outperforming those without access to the digital definitions (Korat 2010; Korat et al. 2014; Shamir et al. 2011; Shamir et al. 2012). Importantly, the presentation of the dictionary definitions occurred after the text was read, thus children did not have the added burden of having to decide whether or not to access the definition, nor the added distraction of a flashing hotspot with a definition, and were able to reap the benefits of word exposure without cognitive overload.

Results from several lines of research further highlight the influence of a child's initial level of word knowledge on the efficacy of different digital affordances for vocabulary learning. Research comparing children's learning from animated storybooks that included either multiple choice questions focusing on word meanings or hotspots including dictionary definitions, revealed an interaction between initial world knowledge and the effectiveness of these supports (Smeets and Bus 2012). More specifically, when children had some receptive knowledge of vocabulary items, both hotspot definitions and multiple choice questions were effective in supporting vocabulary growth. When the words were completely novel, however, gains in expressive knowledge were seen only when multiple choice questions were embedded in the text.

The initial level of word knowledge further mediated the effects of electronic books on kindergarteners' vocabulary learning in a study by Segers *et al.* (2004). They found that immigrant children with poor initial vocabularies benefited more from teacher-read presentations of books than from an electronic version with limited interactivity, whereas their non-immigrant peers benefitted from both. Verhallen *et al.* (2006), on the other hand, found that second language learners reaped significant benefits from multimedia stories. Findings indicated that the additional non-verbal information from music and animations congruent with the story supported their comprehension and vocabulary learning. Pre-kindergarteners in a Head Start program benefited too from the inclusion of e-books in the classroom when these complemented the books they read in print (Roskos *et al.* 2016). Having access to both print books and e-books allowed the children increased exposure to multiple instances of vocabulary words, and a broader array of book reading options. Results attested to the efficacy of this approach as children who began the study with a poor vocabulary were able to learn new words at a pace comparable to those who began the study with an average vocabulary. Thus, digital books may hold great promise for the enhancement of vocabulary learning, particularly if they are used in tandem with print stories, and provided the vocabulary affordances are well-matched to the child's skill level.

Concluding perspectives

Assessing the appropriateness of e-books for fostering children's reading and literacy skills requires taking into account a number of factors pertaining to the child, the parent, as well as to the software and hardware affordances of the e-book itself. For very young children, the print book, so inviting to parent–child interactions, has much to offer their language and literacy development as well as their notion of what reading is. Engaging with their parents in discussions that help them reflect upon stories and connect them to their own lives shapes the development of children's attitudes towards reading as an activity deserving of deep attention and thought. Digital books, while full of motivating and interesting sounds and pictures, often shift the parent–child conversation around the book to its mechanics and to the behaviour surrounding it. Although this is invaluable for helping the child navigate through the deluge of digital attractions that often grace storybook apps, it should not replace the language and meaningful conversation that surround print storybook reading. Further, early and frequent exposure to the many attractive animations and hotspots present in so many storybook apps may foster an attitude towards reading as a game-like and passive activity, to the detriment of immersion, comprehension and future reading. Thus, it is essential to ensure that the developing child, on the brink of discovering all that reading entails, receives as much exposure to print and shared reading as possible. The enormous language and literacy benefits of early shared print-reading if it is available cannot at present be fully matched by current e-book offerings.

This is not to dismiss the potential of digital books for literacy learning. To the contrary, the greatest potential of electronic books in supporting growth in literacy skills may come from their flexibility and malleability. That is, an overriding theme across much of the research reviewed is that digital affordances significantly enhance literacy skills, but that this influence is often dependent on the child's skill level and the technology itself. Hotspots or multimodal features that foster word reading in one child or support vocabulary learning in another, may have quite a different impact for yet another child. Thus, in going beyond the 'one size fits all' format of paper books, e-books offer *both* promises and perils to different types of readers. This, in turn, creates both promise and peril for parents and educators – an unparalleled opportunity to individualize learning experiences hand-in-hand with a dizzying array of decisions we all need to make as our children's digital partners.

Future directions

Moving forward, it is critical that caregivers and early years practitioners are key partners in the research cycle of generating questions and disseminating what is learned. The research reviewed in this chapter highlights the importance of parents and caregivers in positively scaffolding digital reading experiences. Research such as that of Kucirkova and Littleton (2016) also makes salient the questions these groups have and their potential difficulties in accessing research-based advice.

With respect to future research, digital storybook reading is a thriving area, with important contributions from pedagogy and literacy, as well as from psychology and experimental sciences. We look forward to increasingly interdisciplinary research on e-books and children's reading and literacy development, in which qualitative, (predominantly) socio-culturally oriented approaches are combined with experiment-based research, in systematic, multi-level designs (for an example of such an approach in reading research, see Mangen and van der Weel [2016] – two COST Actions dedicated to reading and literacy). The ongoing transition of storybook reading from print to screens provides an ideal occasion to bring scholars from the humanities and social sciences together with scientists doing experimental research, in the shared pursuit of optimal reading and literacy environments for children.

This article is the result of a collaboration made possible by the COST Action IS1404 E-READ: Evolution of Reading in the Age of Digitisation, supported by COST (European Cooperation in Science and Technology).

References

Anderson-Inman, L., and Horney, M. (2007) 'Supported etext: Assistive technology through text transformations', *Reading Research Quarterly*, 42: 153–160.

Baker, L., Mackler, K., Sonnenschein, S., and Serpell, R. (2001) 'Parents' interactions with their first-grade children during storybook reading and relations with subsequent home reading activity and reading achievement', *Journal of School Psychology*, 39: 415–438.

Beck, I. L., McKeown, M. G., and Kucan, L. (2002) *Bringing words to life: Robust vocabulary instruction. Solving problems in the teaching of literacy*, New York: Guilford Press.

Bus, A. G. (2001) 'Joint caregiver-child storybook reading: A route to literacy development', in S. Neuman and D. Dickinson (eds.) *Handbook of early literacy research*, New York: Guilford Press (pp. 179–191).

Bus, A. G., van Ijzendoorn, M. H., and Pellegrini, A. D. (1995) 'Joint book reading makes for success in learning to read: A meta-analysis on intergenerational transmission of literacy', *Review of Educational Research*, 65: 1–21.

Bus, A. G., Takacs, Z. K., and Kegel, C. A. (2015) 'Affordances and limitations of electronic storybooks for young children's emergent literacy', *Developmental Review*, 35: 79–97.

Chera, P., and Wood, C. (2003) 'Animated multimedia 'talking books' can promote phonological awareness in children beginning to read', *Learning and Instruction*, 13: 33–52

Chiong, C., and Shuler, C. (2010) *Learning: Is there an app for that? Investigations of young children's usage and learning with mobile devices and apps*, New York: The Joan Ganz Cooney Center at Sesame Workshop.

Chiong, C., Ree, J., Takeuchi, L., and Erickson, I. (2012) *Comparing parent-child co-reading on print, basic, and enhanced e-book platforms. A Cooney Center quick report*. Available online from www.joanganzcooneycenter.org/wp-content/uploads/2012/07/jgcc_e-books_quickreport.pdf [22 November 2016].

Couse, L. J., and Chen, D. W. (2010) 'A tablet computer for young children? Exploring its viability for early childhood education', *Journal of Research on Technology in Education*, 43: 75–96.

Dalton, B., and Proctor, C. P. (2008) 'The changing landscape of text and comprehension in the age of new literacies', in J. Coiro, M. Knobel, C. Lankshear, and D. J. Leu (eds.) *Handbook of research on new literacies*, New York: Routledge (pp. 297–324).

de Jong, M. T., and Bus, A. G. (2002) 'Quality of book-reading matters for emergent readers: An experiment with the same book in a regular or electronic format', *Journal of Educational Psychology*, 94: 145–155.

Evans, M. D. R., Kelley, J., Sikora, J., and Treiman, D. J. (2010) 'Family scholarly culture and educational success: Books and schooling in 27 nations', *Research in Social Stratification and Mobility*, 28: 171–197.

Fletcher, K. L., and Reese, E. (2005) 'Picture book reading with young children: A conceptual framework', *Developmental Review*, 25: 64–103.

Garon, N., Bryson, S. E., and Smith, I. M. (2008) 'Executive function in preschoolers: A review using an integrative framework', *Psychological Bulletin*, 134: 31–60.

Guernsey, L., Levine, M., Chiong, C., and Severns, M. (2012) *Pioneering literacy in the digital wild west: Empowering parents and educators*, Washington, DC: Campaign for Grade-Level Reading.

Holland N. N. (2009) *Literature and the brain*, Gainesville, FL: The PsyArt Foundation.

Hood, M., Conlon, E., and Andrews, G. (2008) 'Preschool home literacy practices and children's literacy development: A longitudinal analysis', *Journal of Educational Psychology*, 100: 252–271.

Jenkins, H. (2004) 'Game design as narrative architecture', in N. Wardrip-Fruin and P. Harrigan (eds.) *First person: New media as story, performance, and game*, Cambridge, MA: The MIT Press (pp. 118–130).

Kameenui, E. J., Dixon, D. W., and Carnine, D. (1987) 'Issues in the design of vocabulary instruction', in M. G. McKeown and M. E. Curtis (eds.) *The nature of vocabulary acquisition*, Hillsdale, NJ: Erlbaum (pp. 129–143).

Korat, O. (2010) 'Reading electronic books as a support for vocabulary, story comprehension and word reading in kindergarten and first grade', *Computers & Education*, 55: 24-31.

Korat, O., and Segal-Drori, O. (2016) 'E-book and printed book reading in different contexts as emergent literacy facilitator', *Early Education and Development*, 27: 532–550.

Korat, O., Levin, I., Atishkin, S., and Turgeman, M. (2014) 'E-book as facilitator of vocabulary acquisition: Support of adults, dynamic dictionary and static dictionary', *Reading and Writing*, 27: 613–629.

Krashen, S. (2013) 'Access to books and time to read versus the Common Core State Standards and tests', *English Journal*, 103: 21–29.

Krcmar, M., and Cingel, D. P. (2014) 'Parent–child joint reading in traditional and electronic formats', *Media Psychology*, 17: 262–281.

Kucirkova, N., and Littleton, K. (2016) *The digital reading habits of children: A national survey of parents' perceptions of and practices in relation to children's reading for pleasure with print and digital books*, Book Trust. Available online from: www.booktrust.org.uk/news-and- blogs/news/1371 [22 November 2016]

Labbo, L. D., and Kuhn, M. R. (2000) 'Weaving chains of affect and cognition: A young child's understanding of CD-ROM talking books', *Journal of Literacy Research*, 32: 187–210.

Lauricella, A. R., Barr, R., and Calvert, S. L. (2014) 'Parent–child interactions during traditional and computer storybook reading for children's comprehension: Implications for electronic storybook design', *International Journal of Child-Computer Interaction*, 2: 17–25.

Lefever-Davis, S., and Pearman, C. (2005) 'Early readers and electronic texts: CD-ROM storybook features that influence reading behaviors', *The Reading Teacher*, 58: 446–454.

Lewin, C. (2000) 'Exploring the effects of talking book software in UK primary classrooms', *Journal of Research in Reading*, 23: 149–157.

Littleton, K., Wood, C., and Chera, P. (2006) 'Interactions with talking books: Phonological awareness affects boys' use of talking books', *Journal of Computer Assisted Learning*, 22: 382–390.

Lonigan, C. J., and Whitehurst, G. J. (1998) 'Relative efficacy of parent and teacher involvement in a shared-reading intervention for preschool children from low-income backgrounds', *Early Childhood Research Quarterly*, 13: 263–290.

Mangen, A., and van der Weel, A. (2015) 'Why don't we read hypertext novels?' *Convergence: The International Journal of Research into New Media Technologies*. Available online first, doi:10.1177/1354856515586042

Mangen, A., and van der Weel, A. (2016) 'The evolution of reading in the age of digitisation: An integrative framework for reading research', *Literacy*, 50: 116–124.

Mayer, R. E. (2005) 'Cognitive theory of multimedia learning', in R. E. Mayer (Ed.), *The Cambridge handbook of multimedia learning*, New York: Cambridge University Press (pp. 31–48).

Meltzer, L. (Ed.). (2011). *Executive function in education: From theory to practice*, New York: Guilford Press.

Merchant, G. (2015) 'Keep taking the tablets: iPads, story apps and early literacy', *Australian Journal of Language & Literacy*, 38: 3–11.

Mol, S. E., and Bus, A. G. (2011) 'To read or not to read: A meta-analysis of print exposure from infancy to early adulthood', *Psychological Bulletin*, 137: 267–296.

Mol, S. E., Bus, A. G., de Jong, M. T., and Smeets, D. J. (2008) 'Added value of dialogic parent–child book readings: A meta-analysis', *Early Education and Development*, 19: 7–26.

Nagy, W. E., and Scott, J. A. (2000) 'Vocabulary processes', in M. L. Kamil, P. B, Mosenthal, P. D, Pearson, and R. Barr (eds.), *Handbook of reading research, Vol. 3*. Mahwah, NJ: Lawrence Erlbaum Associates, Inc. (pp. 269–284).

Neumann, M. M., and Neumann, D. L. (2014), 'Touch-screen tablets and emergent literacy', *Early Childhood Education Journal*, 42: 231–239.

Parish-Morris, J., Mahajan, N., Hirsh-Pasek, K., Golinkoff, R. M., and Collins, M. F. (2013) 'Once upon a time: Parent–child dialogue and storybook reading in the electronic era', *Mind, Brain, and Education*, 7: 200–211.

Plak, R. D., Merkelbach, I., Kegel, C. A., van Ijzendoorn, M. H., and Bus, A. G. (2016) 'Brief computer interventions enhance emergent academic skills in susceptible children: A gene-by-environment experiment', *Learning and Instruction*, 45: 1–8.

Radesky, J. S., and Christakis, D. A. (2016) 'Keeping children's attention: The problem with bells and whistles', *JAMA Pediatrics*, 170: 112–113.

Radesky, J. S., Peacock-Chambers, E., Zuckerman, B., and Silverstein, M. (2016) 'Use of mobile technology to calm upset children: Associations with social-emotional development', *JAMA Pediatrics*, 170: 397–399.

Reich, S. M., Yau, J. C., and Warschauer, M. (2016) 'Tablet-based ebooks for young children: What does the research say?', *Journal of Developmental & Behavioral Pediatrics*, 37: 585–591.

Robb, M. B. (2010) *New ways of reading: The impact of an interactive book on young children's story comprehension and parent-child dialogic reading behaviors* (Unpublished dissertation). University of California, Riverside.

Romeo, G., Edwards, S., McNamara, S., Walker, I., and Ziguras, C. (2003) 'Touching the screen: Issues related to the use of touch-screen technology in early childhood education', *British Journal of Educational Technology*, 34: 329–339.

Roskos, K. A., Sullivan, S., Simpson, D., and Zuzolo, N. (2016) 'E-books in the early literacy environment: Is there added value for vocabulary development?', *Journal of Research in Childhood Education*, 30: 226–236.

Ryan, M.-L. (2001) *Narrative as virtual reality: Immersion and interactivity in literature and electronic media*, Baltimore, MD: Johns Hopkins University Press.

Ryan, M.-L. (2015) *Narrative as virtual reality 2: Revisiting immersion and interactivity in literature and electronic media*, Baltimore, MD: Johns Hopkins University Press.

Scarborough, H. S., and Dobrich, W. (1994) 'On the efficacy of reading to preschoolers', *Developmental Review*, 14: 245–302.

Segal-Drori, O., Korat, O., Shamir, A., and Klein, P. S. (2010) 'Reading electronic and printed books with and without adult instruction: Effects on emergent reading', *Reading and Writing*, 23: 913–930.

Segers, E., Takke, L., and Verhoeven, L. (2004) 'Teacher-mediated versus computer-mediated storybook reading to children in native and multicultural kindergarten classrooms', *School Effectiveness and School Improvement*, 15: 215–226.

Sénéchal, M. (1997) 'The differential effect of storybook reading on preschoolers' acquisition of expressive and receptive vocabulary', *Journal of Child Language*, 24: 123–138.

Shamir, A., Korat, O., and Shlafer, I. (2011) 'The effect of activity with e-book on vocabulary and story comprehension: A comparison between kindergarteners at risk of learning disabilities and typically developing kindergarteners', *European Journal of Special Needs Education*, 26: 311-322.

Shamir, A., Korat, O., and Fellah, R. (2012) 'Promoting vocabulary, phonological awareness and concept about print among children at risk for learning disability: Can e-books help?', *Reading and Writing*, 25: 45–69.

Smeets, D. J., and Bus, A. G. (2012) 'Interactive electronic storybooks for kindergartners to promote vocabulary growth', *Journal of Experimental Child Psychology*, 112: 36–55.

Stahl, S. A. (2003) 'How words are learned incrementally over multiple exposures', *American Educator*, 27: 18–19.

Takacs, Z. K., Swart, E. K., and Bus, A. G. (2015) 'Benefits and pitfalls of multimedia and interactive features in technology-enhanced storybooks a meta-analysis', *Review of Educational Research*, 85: 698–739.

Trushell, J., and Maitland, A. (2005) 'Primary pupils' recall of interactive storybooks on CD-ROM inconsiderate interactive features and forgetting', *British Journal of Educational Technology*, 36: 57–66.

Vander Woude, J., van Kleeck, A., and Vander Veen, E. (2009) 'Book sharing and the development of Meaning', in P. Rhyner (ed.), *Emergent literacy and language development: Promoting learning in early childhood*, New York: Guilford Press (pp.36–77).

Verhallen, M. J., Bus, A. G., and de Jong, M. T. (2006) 'The promise of multimedia stories for kindergarten children at risk', *Journal of Educational Psychology*, 98: 410-419.

Wasik, B. A., and Bond, M. A. (2001) 'Beyond the pages of a book: Interactive book reading and language development in preschool classrooms', *Journal of Educational Psychology*, 93: 243–250.

Whitehurst, G. J., Arnold, D. S., Epstein, J. N., Angell, A. L., Smith, M., and Fischel, J. E. (1994) 'A picture book reading intervention in day-care and home for children from low income families', *Developmental Psychology*, 30: 679–689.

Willoughby, D., Evans, M. A., and Nowak, S. (2015) 'Do ABC eBooks boost engagement and learning in preschoolers? An experimental study comparing eBooks with paper ABC and storybook controls', *Computers & Education*, 82: 107–117.

Wolf, M. (2007) *Proust and the squid: The story and science of the reading brain*, Harper Collins.

Wood, C. (2005) 'Beginning readers' use of 'talking books' software can affect their reading strategies', *Journal of Research in Reading*, 28: 170–182.

3

TYPEWRITING ON ELECTRONIC DEVICES AND CHINESE CHILDREN'S LITERACY DEVELOPMENT

Duo Liu and Zhengye Xu

Introduction

Along with the rapid development and popularization of information and communications technology (ICT), the traditional form of writing, i.e. handwriting, that has been adopted for thousands of years in human history is being challenged by typewriting on physical or virtual keyboards. Currently, typewriting on computers, smart phones and tablets has become a major method applied in work and daily communication (e.g. Kiefer *et al.* 2015). This phenomenon is also occurring in school education and in the lives of children around the world (e.g. Couse and Chen 2010). Children in the United States have been required to learn how to typewrite since 2013, while handwriting has been dropped from the Common Core Curriculum Standards (Chemin 2014). As indicated by Holloway *et al.* (2013) in their report, in the last 5 to 6 years, the number of children under 9 years old using electronic devices and ICT has increased tremendously. The situation in China is quite similar (China Young Pioneers Undertaking Development Centre 2016). However, at the same time, many researchers and educators are highlighting the merits of handwriting, or cursive writing, namely writing in which the pen is not raised between characters, for children's overall cognitive development (e.g. Hopman 2014), and the effects of handwriting and typewriting on children's learning and development remain unclear. More systematic research, thus, is required in this area to help better understand the pros and cons of both handwriting and typewriting, so that the current instruction approaches could be modified accordingly and children could benefit from the development of techniques and be less influenced by their drawbacks.

Chinese characters, as a type of logograph, are constructed with strokes in a two-dimensional space, rather than with letters in a linear direction. Handwriting and typewriting do not substantially differ in alphabetic languages, such as English, as both pertain to spelling a word by combining letters. The major difference is how individual letters are written, either by typing or by handwriting. However, for Chinese, typewriting and handwriting are quite different in this sense. During handwriting, a character is written stroke by stroke. However, during typewriting, a Chinese character is recoded based on either its orthographic or phonological features to match it with the keys on the QWERTY keyboard. Considering the greater difference between typewriting and handwriting in Chinese, systematic investigations on the advantages and disadvantages of typewriting in Chinese people's processing of scripts in the writing system, and especially on Chinese children's literacy performance, should be conducted. However, studies on this topic are very limited. In this chapter, first a comparison between typewriting and handwriting is made with reference to the available research evidence and theory. Second, the nature of the Chinese writing system and the different types of typewriting input methods applied in Chinese societies are introduced and then critically considered in relation to Chinese children's literacy performance. Lastly, some future directions are offered and discussed concerning the modification of current Chinese input methods to improve Chinese children's literacy development.

Typewriting vs. handwriting: The current findings

There are several major differences between typewriting and handwriting in general (e.g. Kiefer *et al.* 2015; Mangen and Velay 2010). First, although both are related to the physical posture and movement of the body (e.g. the fingers, hands and arms), the motor programming related to typewriting is much easier than that of handwriting. During handwriting, fine sensory–motor skills are required to reproduce the shape of any language unit (e.g. alphabetic letters or Chinese characters) in a smooth manner. The shape or overall configuration of the words written on paper will largely be influenced by the coordination of different muscles, the posture of the body and the way the pen is held. During typewriting, however, no matter how hard a key is pressed, which finger is used, or the angle between the finger and key, the letter or Chinese character typed will be exactly the same. Therefore, compared to typewriting, handwriting is related to a closer connection between sensory–motor input and the produced output.

The relative simplicity of typewriting makes it easier to be grasped by children and other people whose sensory–motor skills are relatively weak. Even children as young as 3 years old are likely to know how to interact with digital devices by typing or touching (e.g. Couse and Chen 2010). Mainly because of the ease of its use, typewriting was thought to be a useful skill for helping young children or children with weak sensory–motor skills learn to write or even to improve their overall literacy performance (see Couse and Chen 2010; Shiling 1997; Zheng *et al.* 2013). For example, Shiling (1997) found that typewriting on computers could facilitate kindergarten children to learn about the functions and features of prints. A survey study conducted with 2,158 upper elementary students in the U.S. found positive roles of writing with laptop computers in improving achievement of English language arts (Zheng *et al.* 2013). This positive role was more significant in at-risk learners (i.e. Hispanic students and low-income learners, as indicated by the authors).

Nevertheless, as argued by Kiefer *et al.* (2015), handwriting still possesses some key features that suggest it cannot be simply replaced by typewriting. As mentioned above, typewriting and handwriting involve different body postures and movements, both quantitatively and qualitatively. The relatively complex coordination of the sensory–motor system of the body could provide some residual memories to facilitate the learning of new words in children (Kiefer *et al.* 2015). This perspective is supported by theories about embodied cognition, which indicate that cognitive processing, including learning, is closely related to the experience of the body and the context (e.g. Barsalou 2008; Ionescu and Vasc 2014; Stapleton 2013). The richer sensory–motor experience and the immediate and vivid feedback during handwriting provide essential information for children learning to read and write.

Additionally, the different tactile experiences between holding a pen and touching a piece of paper during writing and pressing keys during typing may also contribute to the fact that handwriting cannot simply be replaced by typewriting because these experiences may also provide unique sensory–motor interactions between the body and the brain. Moreover, during handwriting, the motion and product of the motion occur in the same space (both occur on the surface of a piece of paper), while during typewriting, they occur in two different places (typing happens on the keyboard, but the words appear on the screen) (Mangen and Velay 2010). Therefore, during typewriting, the typewriter's attention needs to be allocated to at least two different places, which may reduce the cognitive resources available to processing and learning the typed words. On the other hand, during handwriting, attention can be concentrated on a very limited area. At the same time, because handwriting requires more time and effort to produce an adequate stroke and then a comprehensible word, the hand writer will spend more time processing the specific language units, which could facilitate word acquisition. Mueller and Oppenheimer (2014) found in their study that students who took notes longhand during a course learned better than students who took notes on their computer by typing because taking notes by typing may result in a shallower processing of information.

There have been a number of training studies that show the effectiveness of handwriting training in improving children's learning of language units (e.g. Cunningham and Stanovich 1990; Kiefer *et al.* 2015; Longcamp *et al.* 2005). For example, Longcamp *et al.* (2005) found that children who learned letters by writing them by hand were better at recognizing them than children who learned these letters by typing them on a computer. In Kiefer *et al.*'s (2015) study, 23 German children (mean age = 5.5 years) were assigned to either a handwriting (12 children) or typewriting (11 children) condition to learn eight German letters. There were a total of 16 training sessions in this study, lasting over four weeks for four days per week. A series of literacy measures were administered, including letter-level recognition, naming, writing tasks and word-level reading. Typewriting did not show better training effects than handwriting in any of these tasks. In contrast, handwriting showed better training effects on word reading and writing, although the effects on word reading were only marginally significant.

Evidence from neurobiological studies supports the importance of handwriting for literacy development and even the development of the overall cognitive system (e.g. James 2010; James and Engelhardt 2012; Pangelinan *et al.* 2011). Visuomotor abilities have been found to be associated with cognitive abilities both at the neurobiological level and the behavioural level (Pangelinan *et al.* 2011). Neuroimaging studies have shown that during the visual recognition of letters, in addition to the visual areas, the motor regions of the brain were also activated (e.g. James and Gauthier 2006; Longcamp *et al.* 2003). During handwriting, but not typewriting, the activation patterns of the brain were similar (e.g. James and Atwood 2009). This consistency in brain activation during reading and handwriting may be a reason why the latter could enhance the former. In James and Engelhardt's (2012) study, preliterate 5-year-old English-speaking children were asked to write, type or trace letters and shapes while undergoing an fMRI scan. They found that after handwriting, letter perception recruited more brain regions that were associated with reading and writing than after typing or tracing, which indicated the importance of handwriting for reading acquisition in young children.

The Chinese writing system

To facilitate understanding of the principles of different types of Chinese input systems and their possible influences, some relevant features of the Chinese language and writing system are introduced below. The Chinese language is morphosyllabic (i.e. with few exceptions, one morpheme – the smallest meaningful unit in a language, e.g. the word *sunlight* is composed of two morphemes, namely *sun* and *light* – corresponds to one syllable and one Chinese character), while the Chinese writing system is logographic in nature (i.e. unlike most other alphabetic writing systems, a grapheme directly represents a word/morpheme rather than a phoneme). Thus, the scripts in this system are mainly designed to represent the meaning, rather than speech sound, in the corresponding oral language. The basic unit in the Chinese writing system is the character, which is composed of strokes with many different combinations in a two-dimensional space. There are eight basic strokes, namely spot (``), horizontal (—), vertical (|), left-falling (ノ), right-falling (乀), rising (⁄), hook (亅) and turning (乙); the different combinations of these strokes construct approximately 90,000 Chinese characters (Bai and Huo 2005).

Based on the building rules introduced in Shuowen Jiezi (Shen 2005), there are six basic principles for constructing Chinese characters. These include pictographs (the characters are graphical depictions of the objects that they represent; for example, 山 [mountain] is a stylized description of the shape of a mountain), ideographs (the characters denote some abstract meanings; for example, 上 [up] and 下 [down] just represent two different directions), logical aggregates (two or more pictographic components are combined to indicate the meaning; for example, in 休, the meaning of 'have a rest' is indicated by a person where亻is a component derived from the pictographic character 人 [person] leaning on a tree [木]), phonetic–semantic compound (a phonetic–semantic compound character is composed of a phonetic radical that can provide some cues on the pronunciation of the character and a semantic radical that can indicate the meaning of the character; for example, in 清 [clean], 氵 is a semantic radical that indicates that the meaning of the character is related to water; and 青 is a phonetic radical and can provide cues for pronouncing the whole character), transference (two characters that share the same radical and have similar pronunciation can indicate the same meaning; for example, both 老 /lao3/ and 考 /kao3/ indicate old) and borrowing (in ancient Chinese because there were limited Chinese characters, a character could be used to represent a morpheme that shares the same/similar pronunciation of the morpheme originally represented by this character; for example, 然 /ran2/ [correct] was used to represent the meaning of 燃 /ran2/ [burn]). There are seven basic constructing structures in Chinese characters, including single (e.g. 人, 口, 手), left-to-right (e.g. 林, 双, 清), left-to-middle-and-right (e.g. 树, 街, 晰), above-to-below (e.g. 炎, 盖, 笛), above-to-middle-and-below (e.g. 膏, 蓝, 暴), semi-surround (e.g. 区, 边, 庆) and full-surround (e.g. 国, 囚, 因).

Currently, two versions of Chinese characters are used in different Chinese societies. For example, in Taiwan, Hong Kong and Macau, Traditional Chinese characters are used, while in Mainland China and Singapore (in most contexts), Simplified Chinese characters are used. The Simplified Chinese characters are derived from the Traditional ones, with the purpose of reducing the overall complexity (namely, the number of strokes) and the total number of Chinese characters to reduce the difficulty of learning the characters. According to a comparison between the average stroke number of 1,128 Simplified characters and the corresponding Traditional characters (Gao and Kao 2002), the average stroke number of the Simplified characters was 6.69, while the average stroke number of the Traditional characters was 13.62 (an illustration of the difference in stroke number between Simplified and Traditional Chinese characters: 惊吓 [Simplified] vs. 驚嚇 [Traditional] for the meaning of 'scare').

Chinese characters are written stroke-by-stroke following a specific order and are not randomly placed together. There are approximately 12 basic stroke orders in writing Chinese characters, such as from left to right, from top to bottom and horizontal before vertical (Law *et al.* 1998; Qi 2007). Each individual stroke is also written following a specific orientation (such as from left to right and from top to bottom). The stroke order and orientation of each stroke for writing the Chinese character 手 are illustrated in Figure 3.1. Although there are some minor differences in the character stroke order rules applied in Simplified and Traditional Chinese, the basic rules are the same.

Following the correct stroke order in writing a Chinese character is an important skill for Chinese children to grasp during literacy instruction. Knowledge of

FIGURE 3.1 The stroke order and the orientation of each stroke for writing a Chinese character 手.

stroke order was found to explain the unique variance in Chinese word spelling in second grade Chinese children in Hong Kong, even after controlling for age, IQ, word spelling in first grade, phonological awareness and morphological awareness (Lo *et al*. 2015).

Chinese is a tonal language. There are five tones in Mandarin Chinese (including 1. high level, 2. rising, 3. falling rising, 4. falling and 5. neutral) and nine tones in Cantonese (including 1. high level, 2. middle rise, 3. middle level, 4. low rise, 5. low level, 6. bottom level and another three tones that are similar to Tones 1, 3 and 6). The same syllables with different tones represent different meanings and thus correspond to different Chinese characters. For example, 锅 /guo1/ (pan), 国 /guo2/ (country), 果 /guo3/ (fruit) and 过 /guo4/ (pass) have totally different meanings.

In Mainland China, a phonological coding system, called the Pinyin system, is used to represent speech sounds in Chinese oral language (i.e. Putonghua). The Pinyin system is composed of 25 lower case Roman alphabetic letters from a to z, except for v, which is replaced with ü. Unlike Chinese characters, which are opaque in terms of the mapping from orthography to phonology, the Pinyin system is very transparent. Each letter in the system corresponds to one sound only. Therefore, children can easily learn the pronunciation of unknown Chinese characters by relying on Pinyin. This Pinyin system is taught to young children in the first several months after they enter primary school, even before they are formally taught Chinese characters. In Chinese literacy textbooks, for the first several semesters, Pinyin is printed on the top or bottom of the corresponding Chinese characters to help children read and learn those characters.

In Taiwan, another similar phonological coding system called Zhuyin Fuhao (or Zhuyin) exists. The Zhuyin system consists of 37 symbols and four tone markers.

As with Pinyin, this system is also transparent, although the symbols used in this system are not alphabetic letters but unique diacritic markings. Since 2009, Taiwan has begun using Pinyin to replace Zhuyin as the official phonological coding system on a voluntary basis. Pinyin is also instructed and used in Singapore. In Hong Kong, when children learn Putonghua, Pinyin is also referred to in some situations. Hong Kong also has a Cantonese Pinyin system, which was first developed in the 1970s by modeling the principles of the Pinyin system and thus also uses alphabetic letters to represent speech sounds. However, this system is not formally taught in schools.

An introduction to the different types of Chinese input methods

To allow Chinese characters to be typed using QWERTY keyboards, some computer input methods were developed to recode Chinese characters and thus match them with the QWERTY keys. Most, if not all, currently used input methods recode Chinese characters based on either phonological (see Figure 3.2) or orthographic information (see Figure 3.3). A few input methods consider both.

In brief, when using phonology-based input methods to type, what the user inputs is the pronunciation of a Chinese character. The computer will list the corresponding Chinese characters from a stored font pool for the user to select. An advantage of these phonology-based input methods is that they are easy to learn (e.g. Zhu *et al.* 2009). Most of these input methods are designed based on Pinyin, Zhuyin or Cantonese Pinyin, which people are very familiar with. This is why this type of input method is used by a large number of Chinese people. However, a major disadvantage of this type of input method is the speed of typing. There are approximately 6,000 Chinese characters that are used in daily life but only approximately 1,500 syllables (Chao 1976). This means that there are many homophones in Chinese (i.e. morphemes that share the same syllables; for example, 风 [wind], 丰 [rich], 封 [seal], 峰 [summit] and 枫 [maple] are homophones, since they share the same syllable /feng1/ in Mandarin Chinese). When using the phonology-based input method to type a Chinese character, the computer may provide a number of alternatives for the user to select. For example, if one types /guo/ using a Pinyin input method, over 50 characters will be shown on the list (on several pages, depending on how many characters are shown on each page). Thus, selecting the right character is time consuming.

FIGURE 3.2 Example of input methods recode Chinese characters based on the phonological information.

FIGURE 3.3   Example of input methods recode Chinese characters based on the orthographic information.

```
xi'yi'ji
1.洗衣机  2.洗衣剂
```

FIGURE 3.4   The result of inputting /xi yi ji/ by the Pinyin method.

There are some solutions that make the use of phonology-based input methods more efficient. First, inputting the Pinyin of a word or a longer syllable cluster will reduce the alternatives in the list. For example, when /xi/ is entered, more than 300 characters may be presented. If /xi yi/ is entered, there are less than ten choices. If /xi yi ji/ is entered, only two choices appear (i.e. 洗衣机and 洗衣剂, see Figure 3.4), and the first one has a much higher frequency and thus will most likely be the desired word.

Therefore, to increase the efficiency of typing with phonology-based input methods, some would suggest typing long phrases or sentences, rather than characters or words. However, this may also increase the error rate of the input, the correction of which will require some extra time. Some input methods also develop certain functions, such as only entering the initial letter of a syllable but not the full Pinyin, to increase the input speed. For example, to input 洗衣机, /x y j/ can be typed instead of the full Pinyin of this word. However, this may also increase the items in the selection list because some words will very likely share the same initial letters. For example, entering /x y j/ may lead to over 50 choices (see Figure 3.5).

Another useful function of many of the latest input methods is that they can adjust the order of the character or word in the list based on the frequency of the items previously selected. For example, for the Pinyin /fu shu/ that correspond to附属 (affiliate), 复数 (plural), 复述 (repeat), 负数 (negative), 服输 (give-up), etc., if previously the word 负数was selected several times, it may appear among the first several alternatives, or even become the first one. Some input methods can even predict what words to type based on the words inputted immediately before the current input. These self-learning functions of the input methods can make it easier to select the desired character or word.

Orthography-based input methods work by decomposing Chinese characters into specific visual-orthographic components and establishing an artificial correspondence between each decomposed component and one key on the QWERTY keyboard. Roughly speaking, these types of input methods are faster than the

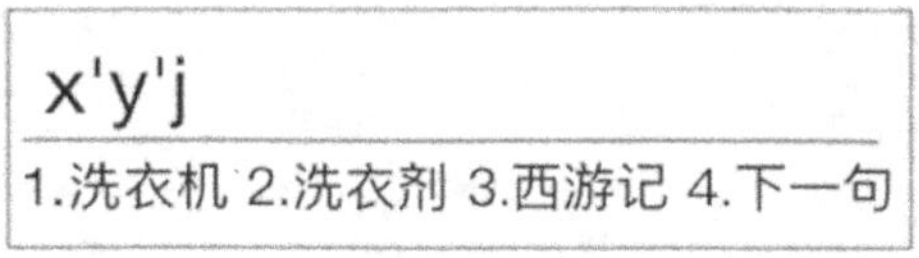

FIGURE 3.5 The result of inputting /x y j/ by the Pinyin method.

phonology-based ones because when typing with orthography-based input methods, the orthographic information can be directly mapped onto the keys, and there is no need to navigate the phonological path. Additionally, because these input methods directly recode the orthographic information of Chinese characters, the coincident code rate (i.e. the rate that different Chinese characters share the same key combinations) is much lower than in phonology-based input methods. This can also increase input speed.

An obvious disadvantage of the orthography-based input methods is the difficulty in mastering them. Different orthography-based input methods follow different rules in decomposing Chinese characters, which are somewhat artificial and thus need to be memorized. For example, in a popular input method, Wubi, the Chinese character 未 is deconstructed into 二 and 小, while the character 末 is deconstructed into 一 and 木; 午 is deconstructed into 丿 and 十, while 牛 is deconstructed into 二 and 丨. Different deconstructed components correspond with specific keys on the keyboards. Moreover, there are also certain simplified coding rules that need to be memorized to further improve inputting speed. For example, in Wubi, to type 工, 要, 在, 地 and some other frequently used characters, only one key plus the space needs to be typed and to type 式, 林, 大, 寺 and some other characters, only two keys need to be typed. Only when a typewriter is very familiar with these rules can he/she type efficiently with this input method. This is a main reason why the orthography-based input methods are not as popular as the phonology-based ones, although the overall inputting speed is higher when using the former (that is why professional typewriters still prefer to use orthography-based input methods, such as Wubi, to ensure a fast inputting speed).

In summary, the currently used Chinese input methods in different Chinese societies are based on the phonological and/or orthographic features of Chinese characters. Briefly speaking, the input methods that focus more on the phonological aspects are relatively easier to grasp. However, they are relatively less efficient. On the other hand, the ones based on the orthographic aspects of Chinese characters are relatively efficient. Nevertheless, they are not that easy to learn, because there are more rules to memorize. The features of these different types of Chinese input methods may also influence the users in processing Chinese characters. More importantly, the frequent use of these Chinese input methods may have some impact on children's literacy development. When these Chinese input methods were originally invented, the educational implications were not the main focus. In the next section, the educational impact of Chinese input methods in relation to children's literacy development is discussed.

The impact of Chinese input methods on children's literacy development

It is evident that the invention of these Chinese input methods is substantial because they provide a smooth connection between logographic Chinese scripts and alphabetic keyboards, thus keeping the Chinese language alive and active in the internet era. However, from the perspective of children's literacy acquisition, these input methods may lead to some negative influences that currently have not received enough attention from educators or relevant stakeholders.

For phonology-based input methods, first, because most methods of this type do not include the identification of tones, their use may influence the development of tone awareness (i.e. the awareness that the same syllable with different tones could represent different meanings). A number of studies have demonstrated the importance of tone awareness for Chinese children's literacy development (e.g. Ciocca and Lui 2003; Li *et al.* 2002; Shu *et al.* 2008; Zhang *et al.* 2013). For example, Siok and Fletcher (2001) found that tone awareness could be an effective index for predicting the reading success of primary students. The current design of phonology-based input methods may result in children not paying enough attention to, and thus lacking enough practice in, the processing and manipulation of tonal information.

Second, the focus on the phonological information when typing Chinese characters can influence the processing of the detailed visual-orthographic information of Chinese characters and thus may affect the development of orthographic knowledge and the learning of the details of Chinese characters. As shown in many studies, visual-orthographic processing skills, namely the awareness of the visual-orthographic structure of Chinese characters and the ability to manipulate this structural information, were among the important predictors of Chinese children's literacy performance (Chow *et al.* 2005; McBride-Chang *et al.* 2003; Siok and Fletcher 2001; Siok *et al.* 2008). When using phonology-based input methods, the main focus is on the phonological information of the characters, which thus may influence the fine processing of detailed orthographic information.

Some argue that using Pinyin input methods may increase the possibility of inputting homophonous characters (i.e. Chinese characters that share the same syllables) as typos and character amnesia. However, there are currently very few empirical studies that support these concerns. At the time of writing, only three peer-reviewed papers were found on this topic. Qian and Feng (2004) examined the influence of using both phonology-based and orthography-based Chinese input methods on the processing of phonological and orthographic information in 10-year-old Chinese children. A total of 120 children were selected as participants and were categorized into four groups based on the input methods they used, i.e. Pinyin (phonology-based) and CKC (orthography-based), and their proficiency level, i.e. low proficiency and high proficiency. There were 30 children in each of the four groups. Children were asked to perform both a homophone judgement task (to determine whether two Chinese characters were homophones) and a homograph judgement task (to determine whether two Chinese characters were identical). Children who used orthography-based input methods showed faster responses in the homograph judgement task, while children who used phonology-based input methods showed faster responses in the homophone judgement task. Furthermore, children who were proficient in either of the two input methods showed faster responses.

In Zhu *et al.*'s (2009) study, the influence of the Pinyin input method on the processing of phonological and orthographic information was investigated in 66 college students. These participants were categorized into two groups based on their own subjective judgement of their experience in using the Pinyin input method (i.e. low proficiency or high proficiency). The participants were asked to judge whether the pronunciation of a presented Chinese character included a given onset or rhyme in the phonological task and to judge whether there was a given component in the presented Chinese character. The high-proficiency group out-performed the low-proficiency group in both tasks. Considering the findings of these two studies presented here, it seems that phonology-based input methods could facilitate the processing of Chinese characters and the relevant phonological information. As stated by the authors of these research papers, an individual's experience or proficiency level with a certain Chinese input method determined the facilitation effect. However, in addition to the issues in sampling (i.e. we are uncertain whether the high-proficiency group and low-proficiency groups were selected properly and whether they were equal in other cognitive abilities or academic performance), the tasks adopted in these two studies differ from what children do when learning to read and write. Therefore, we should be very cautious about the optimistic conclusions derived from these studies.

In another recent study (Tan *et al.* 2013), the opposite conclusion was drawn. Tan *et al.* (2013) measured the non-verbal IQ, Chinese character reading ability, time spent every day on handwriting, typing using the Pinyin input method and e-communication of a total of 5,851 children in Mainland China and found that the use of the Pinyin input method was negatively correlated with Chinese character reading performance. Moreover, the prevalence rate of severe reading difficulty was found to be much higher in this sample than in data previously reported on Chinese reading, which was at least partially attributed to the decreased time in practicing handwriting and the increase in using Pinyin to type.

The orthography-based Chinese input method may also have some influence on the literacy development of children. Unlike the phonology-based input methods, orthography-based input methods mainly focus on orthographic information. This characteristic may lead to children who use this type of input method lacking enough exposure to the phonological information of Chinese characters because typing using orthography-based input methods does not require access to phonological information. As mentioned earlier, to use orthography-based input methods to type Chinese characters, children need to recode Chinese characters following specific artificial rules that may not be consistent with formal orthographic structures. Moreover, stroke order information, which has been proven to be important for Chinese children's literacy acquisition, is not emphasized. These factors may influence the learning of orthographic information and thus the process of learning to read and write.

Compared to the very limited number of studies on the influence of typewriting (i.e. the use of different types of input methods) on the development of Chinese children's literacy, a number of empirical studies have been performed to emphasize the importance of handwriting for literacy acquisition in Chinese (e.g. Guan *et al.* 2011; McBride-Chang *et al.* 2011; Tan *et al.* 2005; Wang *et al.* 2014). For example, Tan *et al.* (2005) found that both character copying and pseudo-character copying could significantly predict Chinese primary school children's word reading performance, even after controlling for other cognitive/linguistic skills, such as rapid automatic naming (RAN), non-verbal IQ and phonological awareness. McBride-Chang *et al.* (2011) also found that the performance of Chinese primary school children in copying scripts of foreign languages (including Hebrew, Korean and Vietnamese) accounted for a unique variance in Chinese word reading after controlling for non-verbal IQ, RAN, morphological awareness and orthographic awareness.

Therefore, considering both the general weaknesses of typewriting (compared to handwriting) in terms of facilitating children's literacy development (e.g. Chemin 2014; Kiefer *et al.* 2015; Mangen and Velay 2010) and the specific disadvantages resulting from the use of different types of Chinese input methods, substantial evidence has indicated the need to pay attention to the role of typewriting in Chinese children's education and cognitive development. Currently, the utilization of electronic devices (such as smart phones, tablets or laptops) is becoming increasingly popular in everyday life and in educational settings (Radesky *et al.* 2015). To the authors' knowledge, at the time of writing, many schools in Mainland China and Hong Kong are using electronic devices to implement elearning in multiple subjects. This relatively innovative teaching approach clearly has many strengths and advantages, such as active interaction and immediate feedback (e.g. Maynard and Cheyne 2005). However, considering the lack of empirical studies on the impact of these electronic devices and of the increased frequency of typewriting on children's literacy development, caution is needed during the development and implementation of this teaching approach.

Suggestions and future directions

Admittedly, in the foreseeable future, digitalization and cyberization are expected to be global trends, and it seems conservative to refuse new technological advances in this trend. Children inevitably need to learn and be exposed to electronic devices, and typewriting is a basic skill that children need to master. Therefore, the purpose of this chapter is not to prevent parents and educators from instructing children in typewriting. Rather, based on the information introduced in this chapter, we should design ways to optimize the role of typewriting and to balance handwriting and typewriting according to the characteristics of children in different developmental stages to maximize the positive influences of both.

From a technical perspective, we can propose the following strategies. First, some Chinese input methods could be designed for children, with the purpose of not only facilitating the efficient typing of Chinese, but also assisting them in learning to read and write. For example, when typing Chinese using orthography-based input methods, the Pinyin of the typed Chinese characters could be shown below the character in the typing window to facilitate the processing of phonological information. At the same time, Chinese character recoding rules that are more consistent with formal orthographic construction rules could be designed. When using phonology-based input methods, the selected Chinese characters or words could be enlarged momentarily to highlight their orthographic features. The alternatives presented after inputting Pinyin could be more formal to avoid confounding between formal and informal or casual expressions.

Moreover, most of the existing Chinese input methods have functions to estimate the possible characters based on the uncompleted or even incorrect inputs. As mentioned before, children could type 洗衣机 only by typing /x y j/ rather than the whole Pinyin of it (/xi yi ji/). The same situation could happen in the orthography-based method, namely children only need to input parts of the character, and the possible characters/words would appear automatically. Sometimes, the input methods could correct the input errors intelligently. For example, the Pinyin for 实验 (experiment) is /shi yan/. However, if you type /si yan/, the input method will automatically correct your input, and present the word 实验. This intelligent function may disturb children's learning of the completed phonological and/or orthographic information. Therefore, for children who are beginning to learn literacy, it may be good to shut down these functions.

Along with the development of the technology, besides that of the traditional physical keyboard and mouse, some new input devices and methods, such as touch screen, virtual keyboard and digital pen, have been developed. The popularization of these new techniques requires our attention as well. For example, the use of a touch screen and virtual keyboard will make typewriting different from the traditional typewriting using a physical keyboard. Some may think that handwriting input and a digital pen could be a good solution to save handwriting in this 'digital age'. However, although currently the digital pen technique has been developed well to mimic the real physical writing, the differences between them are still obvious. For example, the tactile impression of paper and screen is different. So is the friction between the nib and the paper/screen during writing. Although it is increasingly improving, the stroke lag issue during writing with a digital pen is still not perfectly resolved. Currently, the utilization of new techniques is far beyond the relevant research on the effect of them. We should always be careful in implementing these new techniques in an educational setting, and sufficient and rigorous research studies should be conducted beforehand, in order to ensure the effectiveness and avoid risks if there are any.

From the children's perspective, we should consider how to balance handwriting and typewriting. For preschoolers and children in early grades in primary school, since one main task in literacy development is to learn Chinese characters, the time for them to typewrite Chinese should be controlled at both school and home in order to ensure they have enough handwriting practice. We can select some proper Chinese input methods to teach children how to type Chinese characters after they have developed sufficient metalinguistic awareness and have learned enough Chinese characters, perhaps after third grade (Shu *et al.* 2003); typewriting may thus be less likely to present distractions in learning to read and write. Another suggestion is that even after children begin typewriting, sufficient handwriting practice should be ensured so that children can benefit from this activity. Even for adults who are experts in reading and writing, character amnesia would happen if they have rare practice in handwriting. It is worth noting that the home–school collaboration is critical for guaranteeing the effects of any of these suggestions. To some extent, the parents' role may be more important in practice because in most cases children are exposed to e-environments more frequently outside school (Davidson and Gottschalk 2011). At the same time, we have to admit that, because there is currently very limited research investigating the influence of typewriting on Chinese children's literacy and overall cognitive development and how to maximize the advantages and minimize the disadvantages of typewriting, more related research studies need to be conducted before we can take any action.

Conclusion

The features of the Chinese language and writing system determine the unavoidable differences between typewriting using the dominant QWERTY keyboard and handwriting in Chinese. Based on the discussions in this chapter, there are many advantages of handwriting for children's literacy development or even for the development of their general cognitive abilities; therefore, handwriting cannot be simply 'replaced' by typewriting. However, research studies in this area are still sparse in Chinese. We hope this chapter can motivate more researchers to investigate the different influence of typewriting and handwriting on the development of Chinese children's literacy, and thus provide research-based suggestions and evidence for guiding practice. On the other hand, we also hope the information provided in this chapter can alert the education policy-makers and frontline educators in promoting and implementing typewriting-related projects. It is possible that many elements of those projects can indeed benefit the learning experience of students. However, the impact of typewriting, as a kind of side effect, should also be given appropriate and sufficient attention.

References

Bai, Z., and Huo, Q. (2005) 'A study on the use of 8-directional features for online handwritten Chinese character recognition', *Document Analysis and Recognition - Conference Proceedings*, Eighth International Conference, Korea, pp.262–266.

Barsalou, L. W. (2008) 'Grounded cognition', *Annual Review of Psychology*, 59: 617–645.

Chao, Y. R. (1976) *Aspects of Chinese sociolinguistics: Essays*. Stanford, CA: Stanford University Press.

Chemin, A. (2014) *Handwriting vs typing: Is the pen still mightier than the keyboard?* Available online at http://gu.com/p/4445y/sbl [16 December 2014].

China Young Pioneers Undertaking Development Centre. (2016) *Dibaci zhongguo weichengnianren hulianwang yunyong zhuangkuang diaocha baogao.* Available online at http://news.xinhuanet.com/video/2016-01/06/c_128600939.htm [6 January 2016].

Chow, B. W., McBride-Chang, C., and Burgess, S. (2005) 'Phonological processing skills and early reading abilities in Hong Kong Chinese kindergarteners learning to read English as a second language', *Journal of Educational Psychology*, 97(1): 81–87.

Ciocca, V., and Lui, J. (2003) 'The development of the perception of Cantonese lexical tones', *Journal of Multilingual Communication Disorders*, 1(2): 141–147.

Couse, L. J., and Chen, D. W. (2010) 'A tablet computer for young children? Exploring its viability for early childhood education', *Journal of Research on Technology in Education*, 43: 75–96.

Cunningham, A. E., and Stanovich, K. E. (1990) 'Early spelling acquisition: Writing beats the computer', *Journal of Educational Psychology*, 82(1): 159–162.

Davidson, J., and Gottschalk, P. (2011) *Internet child abuse: Current research and policy*. London: Routledge.

Gao, D., and Kao, H. S. (2002) 'Psycho-geometric analysis of commonly used Chinese characters', *Cognitive Neuroscience Studies of the Chinese Language*, 195–206.

Guan, C. Q., Liu, Y., Chan, D. H. L., Ye, F., and Perfetti, C. A. (2011) 'Writing strengthens orthography and alphabetic-coding strengthens phonology in learning to read Chinese', *Journal of Educational Psychology*, 103(3): 509–522.

Holloway, D., Green, L., and Livingstone, S. (2013) *Zero to eight: Young children and their internet use*. Available online at http://eprints.lse.ac.uk/52630/ [17 September 2013].

Hopman, L. (2014) *Cursive over typeface: The importance of teaching handwriting instead of typing*. Mater: Leiden University.

Ionescu, T., and Vasc, D. (2014) 'Embodied cognition: Challenges for psychology and education', *Procedia-Social and Behavioral Sciences*, 128: 275–280.

James, K. H. (2010) 'Sensorimotor experience leads to changes in visual processing in the developing brain', *Developmental Science*, 13(2): 279–288.

James, K. H., and Gauthier, I. (2006) 'Letter processing automatically recruits a sensory–motor brain network', *Neuropsychologia*, 44(14): 2937–2949.

James, K. H., and Atwood, T. P. (2009) 'The role of sensorimotor learning in the perception of letter-like forms: Tracking the causes of neural specialization for letters', *Cognitive Neuropsychology*, 26(1): 91–110.

James, K. H., and Engelhardt, L. (2012) 'The effects of handwriting experience on functional brain development in pre-literate children', *Trends in Neuroscience and Education*, 1(1): 32–42.

Kiefer, M., Schuler, S., Mayer, C., Trumpp, N. M., Hille, K., and Sachse, S. (2015) 'Handwriting or typewriting? The influence of pen- or keyboard-based writing training on reading and writing performance in preschool children', *Advances in Cognitive Psychology*, 11(4): 136–146.

Law, N., Ki, W. W., Chung, A. L. S., Ko, P. Y., and Lam, H. C. (1998) 'Children's stroke sequence errors in writing Chinese characters', in C. K. Leong and K. Tamaoka (eds.) *Cognitive Processing of the Chinese and the Japanese Languages*. Netherlands: Kluwer, Academic Publishers (pp. 113–138).

Li, W., Anderson, R. C., Nagy, W., and Zhang, H. (2002) 'Facets of metalinguistic awareness that contribute to Chinese literacy', in W. Li, J. Gaffney and J. Packard (eds.) *Chinese children's reading acquisition*. Norwell, MA: Kluwer Academic Publishers (pp. 87–106).

Lo, L., Yeung, P., Ho, C. S., Chan, D. W., and Chung, K. (2015) 'The role of stroke knowledge in reading and spelling in Chinese', *Journal of Research in Reading*, 39(4): 367–388.

Longcamp, M., Anton, J., Roth, M., and Velay, J. (2003) 'Visual presentation of single letters activates a premotor area involved in writing', *Neuroimage*, 19(4): 1492–1500.

Longcamp, M., Zerbato-Poudou, M., and Velay, J. (2005) 'The influence of writing practice on letter recognition in preschool children: A comparison between handwriting and typing', *Acta Psychologica*, 119(1): 67–79.

McBride-Chang, C., Chung, K. K., and Tong, X. (2011) 'Copying skills in relation to word reading and writing in Chinese children with and without dyslexia', *Journal of Experimental Child Psychology*, 110: 422–433.

McBride-Chang, C., Shu, H., Zhou, A., Wat, C. P., and Wagner, R. K. (2003) 'Morphological awareness uniquely predicts young children's Chinese character recognition', *Journal of Educational Psychology*, 95: 743–751.

Mangen, A., and Velay, J. (2010) 'Digitizing literacy: Reflections on the haptics of writing', in M. H. Zadeh (Ed.), *Advances in haptics* (pp. 385–402).

Maynard, S., and Cheyne, E. (2005) 'Can electronic textbooks help children to learn?', *The Electronic Library*, 23: 103–115.

Mueller, P. A., and Oppenheimer, D. M. (2014) 'The pen is mightier than the keyboard: Advantages of longhand over laptop note taking', *Psychological Science*, 25(6): 1159–1168.

Pangelinan, M. M., Zhang, G., VanMeter, J. W., Clark, J. E., Hatfield, B. D., and Haufler, A. J. (2011) 'Beyond age and gender: Relationships between cortical and subcortical brain volume and cognitive-motor abilities in school-age children', *Neuroimage*, 54(4): 3093–3100.

Qi, H. (2007) *Xian Dai Han Yu [Modern Chinese]*. Beijing: The Commercial Press.

Qian, H. and Feng, C. (2004) 'The impact of Chinese input method on the processing of Chinese characters', *Psychological Science*, 6: 1368–1370.

Radesky, J. S., Schumacher, J., and Zuckerman, B. (2015) 'Mobile and interactive media use by young children: The good, the bad, and the unknown', *Pediatrics*, 135(1): 1–3.

Shen, X. (2005) *Shuo Wen Jie Zi (Xian Dai Ban) [The etymology of Chinese characters: The modern version]*. Beijing: Shehui Keixue.

Shiling, W. A. (1997) 'Young children using computers to make discoveries about written language', *Early Childhood Education Journal*, 24: 253–259.

Shu, H., Chen, X., Anderson, R. C., Wu, N., and Xuan, Y. (2003) 'Properties of school Chinese: Implications for learning to read', *Child Development*, 74: 27–47.

Shu, H., Peng, H., and McBride-Chang, C. (2008) 'Phonological awareness in young Chinese children', *Developmental Science*, 11(1): 171–181.

Siok, W. T., and Fletcher, P. (2001) 'The role of phonological awareness and visual-orthographic skills in Chinese reading acquisition', *Developmental Psychology*, 37(6): 886–899.

Siok, W. T., Niu, Z., Jin, Z., Perfetti, C. A., and Tan, L. H. (2008) 'A structural-functional basis for dyslexia in the cortex of Chinese readers', *Proceedings of the National Academy of Sciences of the United States of America*, 105(14): 5561–5566.

Stapleton, M. (2013) 'Steps to a "Properly embodied" cognitive science', *Cognitive Systems Research*, 22: 1–11.

Tan, L. H., Spinks, J. A., Eden, G. F., Perfetti, C. A., and Siok, W. T. (2005) 'Reading depends on writing, in Chinese', *Proceedings of the National Academy of Sciences of the United States of America*, 102: 8781–8785.

Tan, L. H., Xu, M., Chang, C. Q., and Siok, W. T. (2013) 'China's language input system in the digital age affects children's reading development', *Proceedings of the National Academy of Sciences of the United States of America*, 110(3): 1119–1123.

Wang, Y., McBride-Chang, C., and Chan, S. F. (2014) 'Correlates of Chinese kindergarteners' word reading and writing: The unique role of copying skills?', *Reading and Writing*, 27(7): 1281–1302.

Zhang, Y., Tardif, T., Shu, H., Li, H., Liu, H., McBride-Chang, C., Liang, W., and Zhang, Z. (2013) 'Phonological skills and vocabulary knowledge mediate socioeconomic status effects in predicting reading outcomes for Chinese children', *Developmental Psychology*, 49(4): 665–671.

Zheng, B., Warschauer, M., and Farkas, G. (2013) 'Digital writing and diversity: The effects of school laptop programs on literacy processes and outcomes', *Journal of Educational Computing Research*, 48(3): 267–299.

Zhu, Z., Liu, L., Ding, G., and Peng, D. (2009) 'The influence of pinyin typewriting experience on orthographic and phonological processing of Chinese characters', *Acta Psychologica Sinica*, 41(9): 785–792.

4

MAKING SENSE OF CUTTING-EDGE WEB-BASED LITERACY TECHNOLOGIES

Robert Savage, Aishwarya Nair, Miriam McBreen, and Eileen Wood

Technology in literacy

The advent of technology has redefined literacy instruction over the last two decades. In recent years, there has been a proliferation of digital literacy tools, including web-based platforms, classroom-integrated or independent programmes, applications on mobile devices, online discussion forums, e-books, interactive learning portfolios or tutors, sometimes exceeding paper approaches to literacy instruction in numbers and diversity. The growing importance of web-based platforms is evidenced, for example, by the fact that, in 2014, more e-books were accessed online than through CD-ROM format (Korat *et al.* 2014). It has been argued that schools must find ways of integrating these technologies into their curriculum or run the risk of perpetuating an outdated curriculum which offers little connection with children's present or future lives (Gee 2004; Pahl and Rowsell 2005). Despite the availability of these diverse instructional tools and the impetus to integrate these tools within the educational environment, reviews of research into literacy and technology suggest that relatively few empirical studies have explored web-based literacy tools in primary schools (i.e. Kindergarten to sixth grade [K-6]; Lankshear and Knobel 2003). Faced with the vast array of digital media, it can sometimes become difficult for parents and educators to distinguish between those digital literacy tools that are most likely to be beneficial for emerging readers from those of lesser quality. Efficacy of online software depends both on the quality of their content and the quality of their use, and more empirical investigations of both these aspects of technology use are needed.

Investigations into the merits of digital literacy point to several promising results. Indeed, a variety of findings suggest that children can obtain both social and cognitive benefits from using effective instructional software (e.g. Archer *et al.* 2014; Flynn and Richert 2015; McKenney and Voogt 2010; Savage *et al.* 2013). In the field of early literacy in particular, technology has important instructional potential for a number of reasons. These instructional affordances include opportunities for information to be presented in multiple modalities (e.g. visual, verbal, touch), immediate reactive feedback, scaffolding and modelling to help young learners develop independent learning strategies, increased engagement resulting from higher interactivity between the student and the software and increased motivation to persist because of the 'game-like aspect' of many programmes (Clark and Mayer 2008; Gee 2008; Huizenga *et al.* 2009; Karemaker *et al.* 2010). In addition to these general instructional supports, technology may also be able to provide useful additional instruction on key aspects of literacy, which are amenable to such teaching. Van Daal and Sandvik (2013), for example, in a systematic review of studies investigating technology's impact on literacy in early childhood (0–8 years), found that technology-assisted interventions had positive effects on concepts of print and phonological awareness (i.e. the ability to associate letters, or graphemes, with their given pronunciation, or phoneme), suggesting both of these can benefit from technology-assisted instruction. What most programmes lack, however, is a systematic evaluation of their internal and external validity.

As will be outlined in this chapter, the methods used to evaluate these programmes vary considerably, making it hard to draw firm conclusions about their efficacy. The following is an attempt to provide a review of the research evidence available to assess the quality of digital aids used in early reading acquisition. The research included ranges from descriptive evaluations, observational studies, quasi-experiments and multiple baseline designs to randomized control trials. The selection of studies involved a search of two major databases in education, (i.e. PsycInfo and ERIC), limiting results to peer-reviewed publications published since 2000. The search terms 'technology' OR 'web-based' AND 'reading' were used. Results were further restricted to studies working with emerging readers (i.e. K–6 elementary school students, aged between 5 and 11 years). These original searches identified 4,144 articles. From these, a subset of the most relevant 102 articles was selected. The scope of the search was then snowballed to include relevant citations from the references of the subset articles. Using this data, we can provide an overview of the different approaches that can be used to evaluate digital literacy tools along with a comparison of stand-alone and integrated approaches to digital reading programmes. Finally, a description of different types of digital reading tools, their implementation and the methods used to evaluate them is presented.

Approaches to evaluating digital literacy tools

Hall and Bierman (2015) note that different digital tools vary in how they are evaluated, ranging from parent and teacher reports of usefulness, feasibility and acceptability judgements, to more rigorous evaluations of outcomes. They note that only a few randomized-controlled trials (RCTs) of technology-assisted interventions which rely on multiple measures of child and parent outcomes exist, and that this number is lower still for interventions which compare technologically assisted intervention with those delivered face-to-face or in print (e.g. Antonini *et al.* 2014; Baggett *et al.* 2010; Sheeber *et al.* 2012). Comprehensive evaluations assess both the quality of content and of implementation. While the development of technological tools is fast-paced, elaboration of a standard evaluation scheme addressing both of these characteristics would be beneficial for current and future programme evaluation.

Content evaluation

In order to be able to provide a sound judgement of technological tools, it is important to evaluate how digital tools fare in terms of pedagogical strength of their content and instructional design. Such a framework appears necessary, given that formal evaluations are rarely conducted on software prior to release, making it hard for parents and teachers to select which ones are most likely to benefit their child or students (Wood *et al.* 2016). Notably, the programmes which bear in mind empirical evidence of key skills in literacy acquisition during development are most often those developed by experts for research or community use (e.g. Grant *et al.* 2012; Savage *et al.* 2013; Tamim *et al.* 2011). One such initiative, the Center for Study of Learning and Performance at Concordia University, proposes a way for software to be developed along best-practice guidelines for ensuring maximum alignment with children's literacy needs (Abrami *et al.* 2007). They argue that software should be developed on the basis of peer-reviewed empirical evidence, refined through research evidence, emphasize meaningful motivational and learning outcomes, be attractive and easy to use for the target population and address the specific needs of the latter. *ABRACADABRA* (http://abralite.concordia.ca) is an example of a tool developed along these guidelines, in the sense that it was developed based on systematic reviews of key skills in reading and spelling.

Wood *et al.* (2016) propose a framework for evaluating web-based literacy tools in terms of how they measure up to empirical findings in the field of literacy. They suggest that programmes can be evaluated in terms of how well they address a number of important reading skills, based on Grant *et al.*'s (2012) taxonomy. This taxonomy presents a developmental sequence of the skills associated with becoming a proficient reader. It includes nine key literacy skills (i.e. Concepts of Print, Alphabetic Knowledge, Phonological Awareness, the Grapheme–Phoneme Relationship, Phonics, Syntactic Awareness, Decoding, Fluency and Text Comprehension) and 45 sub-skills. Concretely, concepts of print involve recognizing how print works in regards to reading (e.g. reading from left to right): alphabetic knowledge involves naming letters and recognizing letter shapes and sounds; phonological awareness involves recognizing the sound structure of words; the grapheme–phoneme relationship involves recognizing the relationship between letters and sounds; phonics involves correlating sounds with letters or groups of letters; syntactic awareness involves manipulating or judging word order based on grammatical rules; decoding involves making meaning from words and sentences; fluency involves reading accurately, rapidly and with the correct expression; and text comprehension involves understanding the content of text. All of these skills have been found to be important to the development of early literacy and to improve with appropriate instruction (Grant *et al.* 2012; Wood *et al.* 2016). Consequently, any digital tool that integrates these skills adequately can reasonably be expected to be more effective. Within this framework, pedagogical strength of literacy programmes can be evaluated on the basis of appropriateness of content and of the developmental sequence of the skills taught. Beyond content and sequence, digital tools can also be evaluated in terms of quality of their instructional supports, in particular, feedback and scaffolding (i.e. teaching geared towards the learner's specific ability level and competencies). Scaffolding is important, given that matching tasks to skill level and ability has been found to ease learning (Palincsar 1998). Online platforms have the potential to be particularly useful in this respect, in that immediate and accurate feedback delivered through software can promote learning through the opportunity to immediately correct one's errors.

On the basis of the above taxonomy, Wood *et al.* (2016) compared three commonly used online programmes, *ABRACADABRA*, *Starfall* (www.starfall.com) and *Ooka Island* (www.ookaisland.com), and 17 popular offline literacy programmes. The software was designed to teach children in kindergarten and Grade 1. Across formats, it emerged that while some skills were being trained in a developmentally appropriate manner, others were incomplete or fully absent. In online games, the skills that were trained with highest quality were alphabetic knowledge, phonological awareness and the grapheme–phoneme relationship, all of which are important early skills in literacy acquisition, which may be indicative of the developmental period targeted by these games. The quality of instruction was assessed based on the amount of practice with each skill that was provided and how often the skill was trained in the programmes. Instructional scaffolding was assessed on the basis of whether the software included different difficulty levels, and whether the increase in levels was set manually by the learner or automatically through a performance diagnostic by the software. The authors found that both Starfall and Ooka Island trained eight of the nine key literacy skills, while *ABRACADRA* trained all nine and that, overall, the number of skills trained in kindergarten and Grade 1 online programmes was higher than for offline programmes. This suggests that online programmes may have the ability to be more comprehensive than their offline counterparts. Additionally, evaluation of quality of instruction showed that online platforms gave students more opportunities to practice each skill. However, the ability of programmes to appropriately determine the initial level of learner ability was limited in all contexts, suggesting that the scaffolding of many online literacy programmes may be an important area to develop.

Implementation: from quasi-experiments to randomized controlled trials (RCT)

Beyond assessing how well online literacy platforms are designed on the basis of empirical findings in the field of literacy instruction, an important step in establishing their usefulness is assessing how effective they are at improving literacy when compared to or integrated into regular, face-to-face reading instruction. Brooks *et al.* (2006), for example, compared the reading and spelling gains of 11- and 12-year-old students who received a literacy programme delivered through computers to those who received traditional, face-to-face instruction. The authors found no significant differences in spelling gains across groups, and reported a decrease in reading gains for the students using the computer programme. The programme involved the students recording their voice during reading of a text, and obtaining immediate feedback for any mistakes. However, no formal evaluation of the programme's content is mentioned by the authors, and students were pulled out of class to receive the intervention, both of which may be responsible for the lower gains observed and hence limit generalizability. Importantly, trials must include a valid control condition, which allows conclusions to be drawn concerning the benefits of using a given programme above and beyond traditional literacy instruction.

Multiple baseline designs, which use subjects' prior performance as the control measure, although imperfect tools for the generalization of findings, provide some measure of validity. Gibson *et al.* (2014), for example, examined the effects of the *Read Naturally Software Edition* (*RNSE*; www.readnaturally.com) on oral reading fluency (ORF) and comprehension for first graders at-risk for reading difficulties. *RNSE* incorporates empirically based findings of skills related to ORF, such as instruction based on multi-component strategies and generalizing (i.e. learners are exposed to multiple examples of correct answers they can then generalize to novel situations) (Lo *et al.* 2011; Silber and Martens 2010). During the intervention, students continued to receive their usual classroom instruction, and all students demonstrated gains on reading comprehension and ORF. Along similar lines, Cullen *et al.* (2014) examined the effects of *Headsprout Comprehension* (www.headsprout.com), a computer-assisted instruction reading programme grounded in evidence-based practices which incorporates explicit instruction, guided practice with continuous feedback and numerous opportunities for independent reading, on the reading comprehension of students with high-incidence disabilities (i.e. emotional disturbance, ADHD, learning disabilities). Programmes that incorporate these components have been found to be effective in terms of improving reading skills such as word recognition, vocabulary and comprehension (National Reading Panel 2000; Macaruso and Walker 2008). The authors reported significant reading comprehension improvement for all six participants sampled.

Randomized controlled trials (RCT), for their part, include a separate and equivalent control group, thereby further enhancing external validity while potentially offering generalizability of findings. A number of such studies has found beneficial effects of digital programmes. For example, Savage *et al.* (2009) found that first graders who took part in computer-assisted instruction had significantly more immediate and long-term gains in reading comprehension and decoding ability than those having taken part in regular balanced reading instruction.

Stand-alone versus integrated digital programmes

An important distinction to be made in the field of online literacy is between programmes that are used as a stand-alone programme and those that are integrated into ongoing teaching. The majority of the evidence comparing stand-alone and integrated programming in technology-based contexts suggests that, while computer-assisted instruction can be effective in and of itself, still greater benefits may derive from technology interventions that are coherently integrated with the ongoing literacy curriculum. An obvious reason for this may be that traditional 'pull out' intervention designs involve students missing class instruction time. Additionally, integrated programmes offer the opportunity to practice concepts learned in class in various settings. It may also be that integrated work provides a thematic synergy of benefits to students.

Cassady and Smith (2005), for example, compared the difference between a reading intervention delivered as a stand-alone technological instruction platform, and one delivered in alignment with the curriculum and used concurrently with the instructional plan. The authors examined the effects of the *Waterford Early Reading Program (WERP*; www.waterford.org) on first-grade students' reading attainment and found significantly greater gains for those students having received the integrated intervention than those having received it as a stand-alone. Interestingly, the students benefitting most from integrated instruction were those who had the lowest initial reading skills. Importantly the *WERP* was selected by teachers taking part in the study because they felt it met their students' instructional needs and mapped onto the curriculum they were teaching in school, which may in part explain its success. This finding provides evidence for the idea that, in order to be maximally effective, digital aids must be thoughtfully chosen in a way that is coherent with children's other early reading experiences.

Based on past research, it is apparent that the teacher's role in integrating digital programmes and activities into instruction with students is a critical factor in determining the effectiveness of these programmes with regard to student achievement. In a study designed to determine the most important factors influencing successful implementation, Mills and Ragan (1998: 8) concluded that 'integrated implementation must be teacher-driven. There is a perception that an integrated learning system runs itself … simply placing learners with computers does not ensure that they will grasp the underlying structure of important ideas and concepts'. They also found that teachers who were the most effective implementers of integrated digital instruction incorporated it in classroom instruction.

Even if a research-developed tool is thoughtfully developed with key literacy skills in mind, if teachers are poorly trained and supported in using the technology, it may not be effective. A meta-analysis conducted by Archer *et al.* (2014) found that when technology-based interventions were delivered with extended teacher training and support, the interventions can yield significant impacts as evidenced through large effect sizes. Alternatively, when interventions were delivered under sub-optimal conditions (e.g. those that were unspecified, or involved short training), effect sizes were close to zero.

Grant *et al.* (2012) also argue that once efficacy has been established (i.e. internal validity, delivered under optimal conditions), effectiveness needs to be established (i.e. external validity, when delivered under 'normal' conditions). Previous studies of *ABRACADRA* have shown it to have 'efficacy' when carried out by trained research assistants, for example, in terms of improved phonological awareness, grapheme-to-phoneme knowledge, phonological blending and reading comprehension (Abrami *et al.* 2014; Savage *et al.* 2009, 2013; Wolgemuth *et al.* 2013). Establishing whether the same gains are observed when instruction is delivered by regular classroom teachers is crucial to determine the potential of *ABRACADABRA*, and other literacy software to be included in general reading instruction. In an effort to investigate this, Grant *et al.* (2012) sought to observe whether the level of technological implementation of *ABRACADABRA* by elementary teachers affected its success. Here, the authors distinguish between different levels of technology integration, that is, entry, adoption and adaptation (Sandholtz *et al.* 1997). The biggest improvements in literacy scores following the *ABRACADABRA* interventions were found for teachers in later stages of integration (i.e. adaptation, wherein teachers linked technology to learning themes already present in the classroom). Strikingly, adaptation was 60% more effective than adoption (Grant *et al.* 2012).

A major reason for the lack of teacher involvement in some technologies is that teachers are sometimes (mis)informed that integrated digital programmes are designed to provide students with individualized instruction. This assumption tends to dissuade teachers from utilizing the software in ways that they believe are more educationally sound (Brush 1998). If teachers were provided with access to more open-ended software that provided them with greater flexibility in terms of coordinating web-based activities in the classroom, then perhaps teachers would use the software more appropriately. This software would allow teachers to take more ownership of the computer activities, provide a wider variety of activities to students and provide opportunities for interaction between and among students while they are working on the activities. In turn, the coordination between classroom and digital activities would have a positive effect on both student achievement and student attitudes. Having examined the state of affairs of evaluation methods for web-based reading tools, we now turn to different formats in practice and the methods most appropriate to their assessment.

Digital reading tools

Electronic books (e-books)

Shared book reading between parent and child sets the framework for the acquisition of emergent literacy skills during early childhood (Flouri and Buchanan 2004). However, innovative multimedia features in electronic books (e-books) such as animation, music and narration have transformed the traditional reading experience for the child who reads independently or with an adult (De Jong and Bus 2004; see also Barzillai *et al.* Chapter 3, this volume). The young child is able to control viewing the story through access to buttons that turn pages and activate dictionary features, picture animations and auxiliary games. Researchers have listed potential advantages to this format which include increased motivation and reading engagement, flexible opportunities to read the story multiple times independently, exposure to reading strategies and stories with more advanced vocabulary and ease of access for visual learners (Ciampa 2012; Korat and Shamir 2012). Independent reading is especially advantageous for children who lack adult availability and for teachers instructing different ability reading groups. The research shows that positive growth can occur when a child reads an e-book independently, under paired-peer reading conditions, and when a trained adult prompts discussion and engages the child's thinking (Korat *et al.* 2009). Ciampa (2012) additionally reported greater reading motivation for first graders given e-books (taken from the *Listening and Reading Comprehension* link on the Childtopia website, which targets children between infancy and 10 years of age; http://childtopia.com/) than for those continuing with regular classroom reading instruction. Interestingly, they found that students who typically exhibited off-task or learned helplessness behaviours during regular classroom reading instruction were on-task and motivated during online book reading. This study replicates findings from Ota and DuPaul (2002), who argue that online programmes have the potential to provide students with individualized, highly engaging instruction that may increase motivation. This is an important component to evaluate, given that getting students engaged in their reading is a crucial step in improving their literacy.

Despite the entertaining and motivating features in this format, researchers have questioned their viability to positively impact emergent literacy skill development rather than function as a distraction (De Jong and Bus 2004; Shamir 2009). Concerns focus on the disruption that occurs when the text is interrupted for games and features irrelevant to the story. As a result, the reader may take a more passive approach to understanding the story (Labbo and Kuhn 2000) and fail to use personal decoding skills or context clues when introduced to unfamiliar words (LeFever-Davis and Pearman 2005). As with other digital tools, it is important to distinguish between 'good' and 'bad' e-books. 'Good' or 'considerate' e-books tend to contain hotspots that are congruent with and integrated into the storyline, the beneficial effects of which have been found on comprehension and story-recall (Labbo and Kuhn 2000). Conversely, 'bad' e-books may have too much or irrelevant extra content, which can act as distractions and, ultimately, have negative effects on reading comprehension (Hendrickson 2014).

While evaluations of e-books differ on the methodology used, a wide number of these report beneficial effects. Hendrickson (2014), for example, examined the benefits of using e-books in a second grade classroom, in particular for students who did not benefit from traditional methods. Students in the experimental condition were exposed to the *Raz-Kids* e-books platform (www.raz-kids.com), a database of online books that offers books of increasing difficulty and of various types (e.g. serials, nursery rhymes, poetry and songs). The website offers users the option to hear word pronunciations, follow along during e-book reading, and play back recordings of themselves reading. Students who used the programme during computer time in school showed improvement in fluency, comprehension, expression and motivation when compared to students who did not use the programme. Here, however, lack of an equivalent control group limited the interpretability of results.

By combining content evaluation and an RCT design, Korat (2012) evaluated the benefits of reading e-books versus receiving regular literacy instruction in kindergartners and first graders. Across grades, those children who read the e-book made significantly more progress on measures of word meaning and reading than those in the control group, although kindergartners progressed more than first graders. This last finding may be due to the fact that first graders have more experience with word reading, so reach ceiling effects faster than the younger group. The e-book they used was developed specifically to target young readers with no or little reading experience, and was based on empirical findings (e.g. inclusion of a text tracking option which has been shown to support development of readers' orthographic knowledge) (Ehri and Sweet 1991).

E-portfolios

E-portfolio software programmes allow students to track their learning over time, and to monitor their effort and achievement in a given area, such as reading (Abrami *et al.* 2007). This can enable students to develop self-regulatory and metacognitive skills through a format that is appealing to them. Notably, they help students develop essential metacognitive skills, for example goal setting, strategy identification and reflection upon one's learning. In a randomized control trial, Meyer *et al.* (2010) examined the benefits on literacy skills of such a portfolio, *ePEARL* (www.concordia.ca/research/learning-performance/tools/learning-toolkit/epearl.html), which both contains student work in a multimedia format and supports self-regulated learning. The latter approach was developed on the basis of Zimmerman's (2000) model of self-regulation and teacher and student feedback. Students in grades four to six who regularly and appropriately used *ePEARL* during regular classroom instruction showed significantly more improvement in writing and certain metacognitive skills than those who continued to receive regular classroom instruction. Further findings show that how effective *ePEARL* is depends on further factors. Notably, *ePEARL* users in medium or high implementation classrooms showed greater learning gains on a standardized literacy measure and on self-regulated learning than in low implementation classrooms (Meyer *et al.* 2010). Again, this underlines the importance of digital tools being integrated into regular learning in thoughtful ways, as opposed to being used as a stand-alone instructional support.

Intelligent Tutoring Systems (ITS)

'An intelligent tutoring system would not just be capable of supporting learning. An intelligent tutoring system would behave as if it genuinely cared about the student's success' (Self 1998: 352). A new line of research is emerging based on the utilization of technological resources that use intelligent tutoring systems (ITS). This opens up new possibilities in education improvement, as well as providing an experimental field for testing teaching strategies. ITS are computer-assisted learning environments. They are highly adaptive, interactive and learner-paced learning environments. ITS are adaptive in that they adjust and respond to learners with tasks or steps to suit learners' individual characteristics, needs or pace of learning (Shute and Zapata-Rivera 2007). ITS have been developed to assist with the learning of reading (*READ 180*: Haslam *et al.* 2006; *iSTART*: McNamara *et al.* 2004) and writing (*R-WISE writing tutor*: Rowley *et al.* 1998). There are also ITS for specific skills, such as metacognitive skills (Aleven *et al.* 2006). The use of ITS as an educational tool has increased considerably in recent years in U.S. schools. *Cognitive Tutor* by Carnegie Learning, for example, was used in over 2,600 schools in the United States as of 2010 (What Works Clearinghouse 2010).

ITS may have important benefits in terms of providing individualized scaffolding and instruction. However, potential negative effects of ITS include the loss of opportunities for both teacher and peer learning and discussion. Learning activity does not occur in a vacuum. In classroom environments, a teacher assigns and evaluates the work. The relationship between the student and teacher has a dramatic impact on how students engage with the class and how they benefit from it. Further, other students in the same class are working on similar problems in the same locations, and parents and communities support students in doing their homework or pursuing after-school learning opportunities.

In terms of systematic approaches to evaluating ITS's content and implementation, Shute and Regian (1993) suggested seven steps: (1) Delineate goals of the tutor, (2) Define goals of the evaluation study, (3) Select the appropriate design to meet defined goals, (4) Instantiate the design with appropriate measures, number and type of subjects and control groups, (5) Make careful logistical preparations for conducting the study, (6) Pilot test tutor and other aspects of the study and (7) Plan primary data analysis concurrent with planning the study. These principles may also be employed as a framework for organizing, discussing and comparing ITS evaluation studies.

Using such evaluation schemes, intelligent tutoring systems have been proven effective, resulting in increased learning (Conati and VanLehn 2000). However, they are still not as effective as one-on-one human tutoring. An important factor in the success of human one-on-one tutoring is the tutor's ability to identify and respond to affective cues. Many researchers now agree that to restrict student modelling to simply interpreting answers is to overlook one of the human tutor's greatest allies, an appreciation of the student's nonverbal behaviour (e.g. Kort *et al.* 2001). Such is the nature of human communication, that tutors unconsciously process a continuous stream of rich nonverbal information that can suggest improved tutoring strategies. Competent human tutors adapt their tutoring according to the real-time, nonverbal behaviour of their students, as well as their answers to questions. Despite the advantages, few schools can afford to tutor all students who experience difficulties in learning to read.

Affective tutoring systems might just be the answer to this problem. These systems adapt to the affective state of students just as effective human tutors do (Sarrafzadeh *et al.* 2004). While technology has no face and no voice, the learner still reacts in a social way. Interestingly, recent results have shown that students can in fact learn more when an Artificial Intelligence in Education (AIED) system employs the type of polite language used by acquaintances (e.g. McLaren *et al.* 2011). There is building evidence that socially sensitive technologies have a more positive impact on learning than technologies that do not behave in social ways (Kumar *et al.* 2007). Politeness, rapport and feelings of accountability for one's collaborative agent–partner have all been shown to impact how much students learn from interactions with virtual agents (McLaren *et al.* 2011). In the future of AIED technologies, system social behaviours will be dependent on understanding the interaction context (Walker and Ogan 2016).

Mobile learning (M-learning)

Mobile technologies offer a variety of opportunities for application in the field of education including: use of mobile technology during classes; enabling teachers and students to share files; allowing students to ask anonymous questions, answer polls and give teachers feedback; delivering quizzes; disseminating information, collecting data during field trips and supporting students' inquiries; supporting collaborative learning; use as an instructional tool and a replacement to laptops; use as a tool for learning on the move, etc. (e.g. Ratto *et al.* 2003; Segall *et al.* 2005; Shen *et al.* 2009). Mobile technology enables the delivery of a range of multimedia material such as video, audio, graphics and integrated media. However, although mobile technologies have power to improve education, some researchers argue that it is not yet possible to make clear recommendations for educators, as the current research and practical recommendations are still in an embryonic stage (e.g. Liaw *et al.* 2010).

That being said, we have powerful demonstrations of the potentials of this type of technology following years of dedicated research. There exist systems that can provide support at every step of a student's thinking process (VanLehn *et al.* 2005), systems that can talk with students in natural language (Nye *et al.* 2014), systems that model complex teacher and tutor pedagogical strategies (Khachatryan *et al.* 2014) and systems that recognize and respond to differences in student emotion (Arroyo *et al.* 2014). Again, how mobile technology will be used in education depends largely on teachers' understanding of affordances of this technology. Klopfer and Squire (2008) describe five potential educational affordances of Personal Digital Assistants (PDA): (1) portability, can be taken to different locations; (2) social interactivity, can be used to collaborate with other people; (3) context sensitivity, can be used to gather real or simulated data; (4) connectivity, enables connection to data collection devices, other handhelds and to a network; and (5) individuality, can provide scaffolding to the learners.

Future directions

The future of web-based learning lies in creating systems that fully enable the development of successful students from diverse backgrounds and initial abilities. Such approaches are likely to attempt to support learner's socio-emotional needs as well as their cognitive ones, in an integrated intelligent system. The development of such systems needs to follow empirically based content elaboration, such as that proposed by Grant *et al.* (2012), and use best practice evaluation of implementation, such as an RCT design. Clearly documenting what is being taught, ensuring that skills are taught in a developmentally appropriate sequence are foundations necessary for design. Evaluation of impact needs to be comprehensive and well-controlled to ensure generalizability.

Conclusion

The digital tools reviewed in the present chapter are promising in a number of respects. From traditional digital approaches to reading such as web-based games, e-books and electronic portfolios to more recent innovations such as intelligent tutoring systems and mobile learning programmes, a number of research endeavours report the benefits of integrating technology into reading instruction. Notably, such programmes may be more cost effective than traditional paper or face-to-face delivery systems of reading instruction. Additionally, digital tools, when evaluated using rigorous methods such as randomized controlled trials, allow for a deeper understanding of how emerging readers learn, and what the most effective teaching tools are. For example, use of digital tools in reading instruction offers the opportunity to examine the importance of scaffolding, individualized instruction, multimodal learning and offloading of visual and verbal learning.

Despite the initial enthusiasm about systems that can use reinforcement learning to improve themselves (e.g. Beck *et al.* 2000), few programmes incorporate this capacity. While generally positive, the findings reviewed herein underline an important point: digital tools must be carefully examined, both in terms of content and of implementation, before their quality can be adequately determined. Moreover, it appears that digital tools are most effective when integrated into the wider curriculum and implemented by teachers who are well trained to do so. This suggests that technology should not be viewed as a stand-alone instructional tool, but rather as an additional tool in teaching emerging readers. More work needs to be done in order to deploy these solutions into approaches used at scale with emergent learners.

References

Abrami, P. C., Savage, R., Wade, C.A., Hipps, G., and Lopez, M., (2007) 'Using technology to assist children learning to read and write' in T. Willoughby and E. Wood (eds) *Children's learning in a digital world*, Oxford, UK: Blackwell Publishing Ltd. (pp. 129–171).

Abrami, P. C., Wade, C. A., Lysenko, L., Marsh, J., and Gioko, A. (2014) 'Using educational technology to develop early literacy skills in Sub-Saharan Africa', *Education and Information Technologies*, (online first): 945–964.

Aleven, V., Mclaren, B., Roll, I., & Koedinger, K. (2006). Toward meta-cognitive tutoring: A model of help seeking with a Cognitive Tutor. *International Journal of Artificial Intelligence in Education, 16(2)*, 101–128.

Antonini, T. N., Raj, S. P., Oberjohn, K. S., Cassedy, A., Makoroff, K. L., Fouladi, M., and Wade, S.L. (2014) 'A pilot randomized trial of an online parenting skills program for pediatric traumatic brain injury: Improvements in parenting and child behavior', *Behavior Therapy*, 45(4): 455–468.

Archer, K., Savage, R., Sanghera-Sidhu, S., Wood, E., Gottardo, A., and Chen, V. (2014) 'Examining the effectiveness of technology use in classrooms: A tertiary meta-analysis', *Computers & Education*, 78: 140–149.

Arroyo, I., Woolf, B. P., Burelson, W., Muldner, K., Rai, D., and Tai, M. (2014) 'A multimedia adaptive tutoring system for mathematics that addresses cognition, metacognition and affect', *International Journal of Artificial Intelligence in Education*, 24(4): 387–426.

Baggett, K. M., Davis, B., Feil, E. G., Sheeber, L.L., Landry, S. H., Carta, J. J., and Leve, C. (2010) 'Technologies for expanding the reach of evidence-based interventions: Preliminary results for promoting social-emotional development in early childhood', *Special Education*, 29(4): 226–238.

Beck, J., Woolf, B. P., and Beal, C. R. (2000) 'ADVISOR: A machine learning architecture for intelligent tutor construction', *AAAI/IAAI*, 2000: 522–557.

Brooks, G., Miles, J. N. V., Torgerson, C. J., and Torgerson, D. J. (2006) 'Is an intervention using computer software effective in literacy learning? A randomised controlled trial', *Educational Studies*, 32(2): 133–143.

Brush, T. A. (1998) 'Embedding cooperative learning into the design of integrated learning systems: Rationale and guidelines', *Educational Technology Research and Development*, 46(3): 5–18.

Carnegie Learning, Inc. (2016) 'Carnegie Learning® co-founder John Anderson earns highest honor from Association For Psychological Science - Carnegie Learning', Available online from www.carnegielearning.com (12 May 2016).

Cassady, J. C., and Smith, L. L. (2005) 'The impact of a structured integrated learning system on first-grade students' reading gains', *Reading & Writing Quarterly*, 21(4): 361–376.

Ciampa, K. (2012) 'Improving grade one students' reading motivation with online electronic storybooks', *Journal of Educational Multimedia and Hypermedia*, 21(1): 5-28.

Clark, R. C., and Mayer, R. E. (2008) 'Learning by viewing versus learning by doing: Evidence-based guidelines for principled learning environments', *Performance Improvement*, 47(9): 5–13.

Conati, C., and VanLehn, K. (2000, June) 'Further results from the evaluation of an intelligent computer tutor to coach self-explanation', in *International Conference on Intelligent Tutoring Systems*, Berlin Heidelberg: Springer (pp. 304–313).

Cullen, J. M., Alber-Morgan, S. R., Schnell, S. T., and Wheaton, J. E. (2014). Improving reading skills of students with disabilities using Headsprout Comprehension. *Remedial and Special Education*, 35(6), 356–365.

Daal, V., and Sandvik, J. M. (2013) '*The effects of multimedia on early literacy development of children at risk: A meta-analysis*' in A. Shamir and O. Korat (eds.) *Technology as a support for literacy achievements for children at risk, Literacy studies*. Dordrecht, Netherlands: Springer (pp. 73–119).

De Jong, M. T., and Bus, A. G. (2004) 'The efficacy of electronic books in fostering kindergarten children's emergent story understanding', *Reading Research Quarterly*, 39(4): 378–393.

Ehri, L. C., and Sweet, J. (1991) Fingerpoint-reading of memorized text: What enables beginners to process the print?', *Reading Research Quarterly*, 26: 442–462.

Flouri, E., and Buchanan, A. (2004) 'Early father's and mother's involvement and child's later educational outcomes', *British Journal of Educational Psychology*, 74(2): 141–153.

Flynn, R. M., and Richert, R. A. (2015) 'Parents support preschoolers' use of a novel interactive device', *Infant and Child Development*, 24(6): 624–642.

Gee, J. P. (2004) *Situated language and learning: A critique of traditional schooling*, New York: Psychology Press.

Gee, J. P. (2008) 'Getting over the slump: Innovation strategies to promote children's learning', in *New York: The Joan Ganz Cooney Center at Sesame Workshop* (Vol. 15).

Gibson Jr, L., Cartledge, G., Keyes, S. E., and Yawn, C. D. (2014) 'The effects of a supplementary computerized fluency intervention on the generalization of the oral reading fluency and comprehension of first-grade students', *Education and Treatment of Children*, 37(1): 25–51.

Grant, A., Wood, E., Gottardo, A., Evans, M. A., Phillips, L., and Savage, R. (2012) 'Assessing the content and quality of commercially available reading software programs: Do they have the fundamental structures to promote the development of early reading skills in children?', *NHSA Dialog*, 15(4): 319–342.

Hall, C. M., and Bierman, K. L. (2015) 'Technology-assisted interventions for parents of young children: Emerging practices, current research, and future directions', *Early Childhood Research Quarterly*, 33: 21–32.

Haslam, M. B., White, R. N., and Klinge, A. (2006) '*Improving student literacy: READ 180 in the Austin Independent School District 2004–05*', Washington, DC: Policy Studies Associates.

Hendrickson, B. (2014) 'The effectiveness of electronic books in the primary classroom', *The Eagle Feather Undergraduate Research Journal*.

Huizenga, J., Admiraal, W., Akkerman, S., and Dam, G. T. (2009) 'Mobile game-based learning in secondary education: engagement, motivation and learning in a mobile city game', *Journal of Computer Assisted Learning*, 25(4): 332–344.

Karemaker, A. M., Pitchford, N. J., and O'Malley, C. (2010) 'Does whole-word multimedia software support literacy acquisition?', *Reading and Writing*, 23(1)|: 31–51.

Khachatryan, G. A., Romashov, A. V., Khachatryan, A. R., Gaudino, S. J., Khachatryan, J. M., Guarian, K. R., and Yufa, N. V. (2014) 'Reasoning Mind Genie 2: An intelligent tutoring system as a vehicle for international transfer of instructional methods in mathematics', *International Journal of Artificial Intelligence in Education*, 24(3): 333–382.

Klopfer, E., and Squire, K. (2008) 'Environmental detectives – the development of an augmented reality platform for environmental simulations', *Educational Technology Research and Development*, 56(2): 203–228.

Korat, O. (2012) 'Mediating book reading, parental beliefs and child's emergent literacy' in O. Korat and D. Aram (eds.) *Literacy and language: Relationship bilingualism and difficulties*, Magnes: The Hebrew University Jerusalem.

Korat, O., and Shamir, A. (2012) 'Direct and indirect teaching: Using e-books for supporting vocabulary, word reading, and story comprehension for young children', *Journal of Educational Computing Research*, 46(2): 135–152.

Korat, O., Segal-Drori, O., and Klein, P. (2009) 'Electronic and printed books with and without adult support as sustaining emergent literacy', *Journal of Educational Computing Research*, 41(4): 453–475.

Korat, O., Shamir, A., and Segal-Drori, O. (2014) 'E-books as a support for young children's language and literacy: the case of Hebrew-speaking children', *Early Child Development and Care*, 184(7): 998–1016.

Kort, B., Reilly, R., and Picard, R. W. (2001, August) 'An affective model of interplay between emotions and learning: Reengineering educational pedagogy-building a learning companion', in *ICALT*, 1: 43–47.

Kumar, R., Rosé, C. P., Wang, Y. C., Joshi, M., and Robinson, A. (2007) 'Tutorial dialogue as adaptive collaborative learning support', *Frontiers in Artificial Intelligence and Applications*, 158: 383–390.

Labbo, L. D., and Kuhn, M. R. (2000) 'Weaving chains of affect and cognition: A young child's understanding of CD-ROM talking books', *Journal of Literacy Research*, 32(2): 187–210.

Lankshear, C., and Knobel, M. (2003) 'New technologies in early childhood literacy research: A review of research', *Journal of Early Childhood Literacy*, 3(1): 59–82.

Lefever-Davis, S., and Pearman, C. (2005) 'Early readers and electronic texts: CD-ROM storybook features that influence reading behaviors', *The Reading Teacher*, 58(5): 446–454.

Liaw, S. S., Hatala, M., and Huang, H. M. (2010) 'Investigating acceptance toward mobile learning to assist individual knowledge management: Based on activity theory approach', *Computers & Education*, 54(2): 446–454.

Lo, Y. Y., Cooke, N. L., and Starling, A. L. P. (2011) 'Using a repeated reading program to improve generalization of oral reading fluency', *Education and Treatment of Children*, 34(1): 115–140.

Macaruso, P., and Walker, A. (2008) 'The efficacy of computer-assisted instruction for advancing literacy skills in kindergarten children', *Reading Psychology*, 29(3): 266–287.

McKenney, S., and Voogt, J. (2010) 'Technology and young children: How 4–7 year olds perceive their own use of computers', *Computers in Human Behavior*, 26(4): 656–664.

McLaren, B. M., DeLeeuw, K. E., and Mayer, R. E. (2011) 'Polite web-based intelligent tutors: Can they improve learning in classrooms?', *Computers & Education*, 56(3): 574–584.

McNamara, D. S., Levinstein, I. B., and Boonthum, C. (2004) 'iSTART: Interactive strategy training for active reading and thinking', *Behavior Research Methods, Instruments, & Computers*, 36(2): 222–233.

Meyer, E., Abrami, P. C., Wade, C. A., Aslan, O., and Deault, L. (2010) 'Improving literacy and metacognition with electronic portfolios: Teaching and learning with ePEARL', *Computers & Education*, 55(1): 84–91.

Mills, S. C., and Ragan, T. R. (1998) 'An implementation model for integrated learning systems', Presented at Selected Research and Development Presentations at the National Convention of the Association for Educational Communications and Technology (AECT) Sponsored by the Research and Theory Division 1998.

National Reading Panel (US), National Institute of Child Health and Human Development (US), 2000. *Teaching children to read: An evidence-based assessment of the scientific research literature on reading and its implications for reading instruction*, Washington, DC: National Institute of Child Health and Human Development, National Institutes of Health.

Nye, B. D., Graesser, A. C., and Hu, X. (2014) 'AutoTutor and family: A review of 17 years of natural language tutoring', *International Journal of Artificial Intelligence in Education*, 24(4): 427–469.

Ota, K. R., and DuPaul, G. J. (2002) 'Task engagement and mathematics performance in children with attention-deficit hyperactivity disorder: Effects of supplemental computer instruction', *School Psychology Quarterly*, 17(3): 242–257.

Pahl, K., and Rowsell, J. (2005) 'Understanding literacy education: Using new literacy studies in the elementary classroom', London: Sage.

Palincsar, A. S. (1998) 'Keeping the metaphor of scaffolding fresh – A response to C. Addison Stone's "The metaphor of scaffolding its utility for the field of learning disabilities"', *Journal of Learning Disabilities*, 31(4): 370–373.

Ratto, M., Shapiro, R. B., Truong, T. M., and Griswold, W. G. (2003) 'The Active Class project: Experiments in encouraging classroom participation', in *Designing for change in networked learning environments*, Netherlands: Springer (pp. 477–486).

Rowley, K., Carlson, P., and Miller, T. (1998) 'A cognitive technology to teach composition skills: Four studies with the R-WISE writing tutor', *Journal of Educational Computing Research*, 18(3): 259-296.

Sandholtz, J. H., Ringstaff, C., and Dwyer, D. C. (1997) *Teaching with technology: Creating student-centered classrooms*, New York: Teachers College Press.

Sarrafzadeh, A., Fan, C., Dadgostar, F., Alexander, S., and Messom, C. (2004) 'Frown gives game away: Affect sensitive systems for elementary mathematics', in *2004 IEEE International Conference on Systems, Man and Cybernetics* IEEE Vol. 11 (pp. 13–18).

Savage, R. S., Abrami, P., Hipps, G., and Deault, L. (2009) 'A randomized controlled trial study of the ABRACADABRA reading intervention program in grade 1', *Journal of Educational Psychology*, 101(3): 590–604.

Savage, R., Abrami, P. C., Piquette, N., Wood, E., Deleveaux, G., Sanghera-Sidhu, S., and Burgos, G. (2013) 'A (Pan-Canadian) cluster randomized control effectiveness trial of the ABRACADABRA web-based literacy program', *Journal of Educational Psychology*, 105(2): 310–328.

Segall, N., Doolen, T. L., and Porter, J. D. (2005) 'A usability comparison of PDA-based quizzes and paper-and-pencil quizzes', *Computers & Education*, 45(4): 417–432.

Self, J. (1998) 'The defining characteristics of intelligent tutoring systems research: ITSs care, precisely', *International Journal of Artificial Intelligence in Education (IJAIED)*, 10: 350–364.

Shamir, A. (2009) 'Processes and outcomes of joint activity with e-books for promoting kindergarteners' emergent literacy', *Educational Media International*, 46(1): 81–96.

Sheeber, L. B., Seeley, J. R., Feil, E. G., Davis, B., Sorensen, E., Kosty, D. B., and Lewinsohn, P. M. (2012) 'Development and pilot evaluation of an Internet-facilitated cognitive-behavioral intervention for maternal depression', *Journal of Consulting and Clinical Psychology*, 80(5): 739–749.

Shen, R., Wang, M., Gao, W., Novak, D., and Tang, L. (2009) 'Mobile learning in a large blended computer science classroom: System function, pedagogies, and their impact on learning', *IEEE Transactions on Education*, 52(4): 538–546.

Shute, V. J., and Regian, J. W. (1993) 'Principles for evaluating intelligent tutoring systems', *Journal of Interactive Learning Research*, 4(2): 245–271.

Shute, V. J., and Zapata-Rivera, D. (2007) 'Adaptive technologies', *ETS Research Report Series*, 2007(1): 1–34.

Silber, J. M., and Martens, B. K. (2010) 'Programming for the generalization of oral reading fluency: Repeated readings of entire text versus multiple exemplars', *Journal of Behavioral Education*, 19(1): 30–46.

Tamim, R. M., Bernard, R. M., Borokhovski, E., Abrami, P. C., and Schmid, R. F. (2011) 'What forty years of research says about the impact of technology on learning a second-order meta-analysis and validation study', *Review of Educational Research*, 81(1): 4–28.

VanLehn, K., Lynch, C., Schulze, K., Shapiro, J. A., Shelby, R., Taylor, L., Treacy, D., Weinstein, A., and Wintersgill, M. (2005) 'The Andes Physics Tutoring System: Lessons learned', *International Journal of Artificial Intelligence in Education*, 15(3): 147–204.

Walker, E., and Ogan, A. (2016) 'We're in this together: Intentional design of social relationships with AIED systems', *International Journal of Artificial Intelligence in Education*, 26(2): 713–729.

What Works Clearinghouse. (2010, August). *WWC intervention report high school math: Carnegie Learning curricula and cognitive tutor software*. Retrieved from Department of Education, Institute of Education Sciences, website: http://ies.ed.gov/ncee/wWc/pdf/intervention_reports/wwc_cogtutor_083110.pdf.

Wolgemuth, J. R., Savage, R., Helmer, J., Harper, H., Lea, T., Abrami, P. C., Kirby, A., Chalkiti, K., Morris, P., Carapetis, J., and Louden, W. (2013) 'ABRACADABRA aids Indigenous and non-Indigenous early literacy in Australia: Evidence from a multisite randomized controlled trial', *Computers & Education*, 67: 250–264.

Wood, E., Gottardo, A., Savage, R. S., and Evans, M-A. (2016) 'Software to promote young children's growth in literacy: A comparison of online and offline formats', *Early Childhood Education Journal*, (online first): 1–11.

Zimmerman, B. J., Boekarts, M., Pintrich, P. R., and Zeidner, M. (2000) 'A social cognitive perspective' in M. Boekarts and P. R. Pintrich (eds.) *Handbook of self-regulation*, New York: Academic Press (pp. 13–39).

PART II

New technology

Supporting all learners or divisive tools

5

DIGITAL ASSISTIVE TECHNOLOGIES AND EDUCATIONAL NEED

Peter Zentel

Systematical and historical framing

> In the beginning there were bullhorns. That's what hearing impaired people used as tools to try to hear. In the 1870s, Alexander Graham Bell, whose wife was deaf, tried to develop a device for her to hear and ended up inventing the telephone.
>
> *(Robitaille 2010: 10)*

The improvement of concrete living conditions of people with disabilities is highly connected to technological progress. The rapid development of Information Communications Technology (ICT) has induced numerous developments, especially during the last few decades (Miesenberger 2015). New possibilities of participation in different areas have emerged due to the development of innovative Assistive Technologies (AT). A systematical use of technology to compensate disadvantages that occur due to disabilities, however, started much earlier and did not only start with the computer age. In fact, two World Wars created many new disabled people and had an impact on public awareness of disability. Internationally, this led to numerous efforts to develop special technological aids. The technologies that have been used were oriented towards the needs of people with disabilities. Prosthetic and orthopaedic aids were supposed to compensate the consequences of impaired bodily functions (Story *et al.* 1998). Parallel to these developments, since the 1950s another movement, which aims to obtain accessibility, has evolved. The term 'accessibility' initially only referred to the architectural area. In the 1980s, it was further developed into the concept of 'Universal Design', which claims to be relevant for all products and living environments. Universal Design aims to design/ create an environment (and products) that can be used by as many people as possible, whichever age and abilities they might have (Story *et al.* 1998). At the core of the Universal Design Concept are a set of principles. It should be taken into account that these products and environments are usable by all people, to the greatest extent possible, without the need for adaptation or specialized design. Examples of principles are: *Equitable Use,* which means that design should be useful and marketable for people with diverse abilities; *Flexibility in Use*, to accommodate a wide range of individual preferences and abilities; *Simple and Intuitive Use,* to make sure that the user will understand, regardless of the experience, knowledge, language skills or current concentration level (Story *et al.* 1998).

Capovilla and Gebhardt (2016) describe the difference between AT and Universal Design as follows: Universal Design aspires after a society that is open to all people, regardless of their subjective presuppositions. AT, on the other hand, tries to change the subjective presuppositions of people in a way that enables them to participate autonomously and confidently in a society that is not necessarily accessible. Since the ideal 'Universal Design' will practically not be completely achieved, AT will still be necessary in the future.

Following this, the authors define AT as technical aids that are developed for personal usage, which strengthen the physical, sensory or cognitive abilities of people with disabilities in a way that they gain more independence in different environments, and furthermore, the peculiarities that are specific for their disabilities fade into the background. In this sense, AT comprises hard- and software that supports people with disabilities to manage their life as independently and safely as possible – more independent and safer as would be possible without technology. In this sense, Becta defines AT as 'software and technology which helps people with disabilities to overcome the additional barriers they face in communication and learning' (Becta 2003: 3). In the US, many publications reference the Individuals with Disabilities Act of 2004. In it, AT is defined as 'any item, piece of equipment or product system, whether acquired commercially off the shelf, modified or customized, that is used to increase, maintain, or improve the functional capabilities of a child with a disability' (IDEA 2004: 6). Following the international ISO Standard on Assistive products for persons with disability (ISO 9999: 2016), AT are devices, endowments or software which are designed specifically for people with disabilities or general products that help people 'to protect, support, train, measure or substitute for body functions/ structures and activities; or to prevent impairments, activity limitations or participation restrictions' (ISO 2016: n.p.). These products can be low-tech products, as well as sophisticated ICT, software, cyber-physical and stem-cell applications (European Parliament 2015). Historically, AT has taken various forms and is most widely associated with applications that help individuals who are blind, visually impaired, deaf, hard of hearing or physically impaired. Applications of technology which serve as cognitive prostheses are considerably less accepted and understood (Edyburn 2004).

Blackhurst and Edyburn (2000) consider AT as a part of Special Education Technology, which they divide into six different types:

- Instructional Technology comprises those technologies that explicitly support learning, like computer-assisted learning, Distance Education, multimedia learning programmes, network-based learning, to name but a few examples.

- Assistive Technology is a technical, supportive device, which is used to obtain or improve the functional possibilities of persons with disabilities.
- Medical Technology in the context of Special Education Technology includes those devices that obtain the health and vitality of people with disabilities.
- Technology Productivity Tools are computer software, specific hardware and connected systems that enable people with disabilities to participate in working life.
- Information Technology makes it possible to access information and resources from very different domains of knowledge. In this context, the Internet and the World Wide Web are the most known source of information. In this regard, Blackhurst and Edyburn stress the particular importance of the information system by the Educational Resources Information Center (ERIC). People with disabilities profit from this technology rather indirectly, since it supports professional activities.
- Technology of Teaching involves teaching and learning methods that work with well-defined objectives, precise instructional procedures based on tasks that students are required to learn, small units of instruction that are carefully sequenced, high degree of teacher activity, high levels of student involvement, liberal use of reinforcement, and careful monitoring and evaluation of student performance (Blackhurst and Edyburn 2000: 33). As stated by the authors, these techniques can be implemented without technology. It is, however, possible to complementarily use software that is applicably programmed and based on such teaching and learning techniques.

By naming the different subtypes of Special Education Technology, the great broadness of application as well as the essential importance of technology for people with disabilities becomes clear. However, today the term 'Assistive Technology' is often used as a new umbrella term. This makes sense since technology for people with disabilities differs from 'normal technology' due to its supportive function. Educational software, for example, only becomes Special Education Technology when it takes the specifics of the target groups into account and operates supportively in this regard. One issue to mention is that Special Education Technology ceases to be special when it becomes ubiquitous. For example, spectacles are not seen as special education/disability technology but they are: they take the specifics of the target groups into account and operate supportively in this regard.

The term 'Assistive Technology' is also of interest, as it discloses the essential factor 'assistance'. 'Assistance', or synonymously 'aid', also always implies the dependence that results for the person who makes use of the assistance or aid. This dependence is accepted in order to expand one's own possibilities. This becomes especially clear in the context of Medical Technology. Without it, in some cases survival is not possible. In these cases, there is no alternative to the dependence that comes along with technology.

With reference to Melchior, Blackhurst and Edyburn (2000) systemize AT with regard to the special needs of people with disabilities. They identify areas in which people with disabilities might have problems that can be mitigated or compensated by technology. Areas that were identified by the authors are, for example life-sustainment, communication, mobility, control of the environment and learning (Blackhurst and Edyburn 2000).

A definition provided by LoPresti *et al.* (2008) describes AT with respect to how the available personal competences are complemented or expanded. They distinguish between AT to augment an individual's strength so that his or her abilities counterbalance the effects of any disabilities, and AT that provides an alternate mode of performing a task so that any effects from an individual's disabilities are compensated. It is important that the usage of AT has to be selected for and adjusted to each individual. The points mentioned here can serve as a grid that helps to identify the individual needs systematically (Blackhurst and Edyburn 2000). If media are deployed in this way, they can considerably extend the possibilities of people with disabilities. People of all ability levels can work within their own style preferences and readiness levels (Jeffs *et al.* 2003).

Personal vs. technical assistance

As mentioned above, in connection to technical assistance, questions arise that concern the dependence that comes with it and the interplay with personal assistance. In this context, Norman (1998) issued an interesting and striking juxtaposition of human and machine from the human's and machine's perspective (see Table 5.1).

The juxtapositions show the ambivalence that is embedded in the evaluation of human and technical assistance. Individual considerations are necessary to decide which kind of aid is suitable for a specific person and for a specific task. An appropriate usage of technical assistance can lead to a more effective use of personal assistance. This might possibly leave more time for conversations which would be missed out on otherwise due to the support.

The impact of AT for learners with a variety of educational needs and impairments

The application of AT for people with physical and motor impairments

People with motor disabilities have physical impairments which limit movement and fine motor controls. Problems can occur in lifting, walking or typing. In addition to that, physical disabilities might be accompanied by impairments of speech. The deficiencies in this context range from a blurred language that is hard to understand to the absence of speech and the possibility to make oneself understood through facial expressions and gestures.

In the last 30 years, the development of computer-based technologies has led to many new possibilities of support. The possibility to compensate the most different impairments via microelectronics and numerous techniques to perceive stimuli was pivotal. Besides controlling via special keyboards, joysticks or touchpads, smallest intentional movements, such as an eyelid movement, can be used to control complex processes. By this time, the gaze movement via Eye-Tracking has proven to be an influential tool of controlling.

If only one impulse can be received and a selection cannot be made through at least two stimuli, the so-called 'scanning-procedure' is used instead. In this variant, the different options switch automatically. Once the desired option appears, the impulse is triggered. Depending on the cognitive abilities, it is possible to work with different levels, which makes it possible to control elaborated applications as well. Code systems can be used and refined for this purpose, which partly can only be understood by the user himself.

For people with motor disabilities, technology-based communication aids are of great importance. Augmentative and Alternative Communication (AAC) devices range from switches that can record words or sentences and play them back to complex speech generating devices with dynamic surfaces and multiple levels. An example for a simple AAC device is a picture board. This device uses pictures or symbols of items or activities that are relevant for a person's daily life. It can be customized with regard to a person's age, education, occupation and interests. Devices with a text-based display face outward so that two people are able to exchange information while facing each other. Speech-generating devices can translate texts or pictures into speech. Some devices are using a set of vocabulary of prerecorded words while others synthesize speech as soon as words are typed. These devices have an unlimited vocabulary (NIDCD 2011).

If there is no movement ability and the eye movement cannot be deliberately deployed either, so-called Brain–Computer–Interfaces (BCI) are within the bounds of possibility. However, these systems are still in the research phase and are not yet applied in everyday practice. BCI are based on the discovery that the imagination of moving a hand or foot already leads to the activation of certain areas of the brain. During a training process, the BCI, which includes technology as well as the human, learns what kinds of changes in brain activity are linked to which imaginations. This information can then be transformed into a control signal for various applications. In the application of the previously described scanning technology, selection is made when the user imagines the movement of the left or right hand (Pantke 2010).

TABLE 5.1 Comparison of the human and machine

From the machine's perspective		From the human's perspective	
Humans are	Machines are	Humans are	Machines are
Imprecise	Precise	Creative	Uncreative
Unorganized	Organized	Flexible	Rigid
Illogical	Logical	Attentive to changes	Unreceptive to change
Emotional	Unemotional	Imaginative	Unimaginative

Adapted from Norman (1998).

Due to the fact that via computer-based interfaces each stimulus can be linked to countless applications, various scenarios are possible in which people with motor impairments can interact with their environment. With this kind of control, it is possible to operate computers and computer programmes, devices with synthetic speech output or even a wheelchair. Combined with Smart Home Concepts, many new possibilities of independent conduct of life appear beyond that. Smart AT can improve daily life at home, leisure, work and school.

The deployment of the computer for people with visual impairments and the blind

People with visual impairments are individuals who are blind, have low vision or colour blindness. People who are blind need text equivalents for the images used on the Web page, because neither they nor the assistive screen reader technology can obtain information from an image. People with colour blindness or those with low vision need good contrasting colours to be used in design or an alternate attribute of information being presented.

Only some decades ago, there was not much technology to assist people with visual impairments apart from a small supply of braille books. The development of technical aids has changed this situation fundamentally. Today people with visual impairments use computers and almost daily, whether for working, shopping online or listening to music (Robitaille 2010). With the aid of technologies, people with visual disabilities can now study largely independently at normal universities (Mulloy *et al.* 2014; Petz and Miesenberger 2012). Via the use of additional output devices and software, computers and cohesive technologies are made usable for the target group.

An essential component of this expansion is a screen reader, a programme that outputs computer-based content with automatically synthesized speech. It is possible to receive texts, however not pictures and graphics. The screen reading technology has established itself as a stable and matured standard (Miesenberger 2015). This was made possible due to the development of basic concepts of interaction towards windows, icons, menus and cursors that are arranged on a virtual desktop which can be selected by a pointing tool through different operations, for example point and click, drag and drop, etc. (Miesenberger 2015).

Additionally, a Braille line can be used for data output. Braille is a tactile writing system. In this system, letters are represented through combinations of palpable dots. A Braille line is typically attachable to a computer and allows a blind person to read computer-based content. Each Braille character consists of six or eight movable pins in a rectangular array. The pins can rise and fall depending on the electrical signals they receive. This simulates the effect of the raised dots of Braille impressed on paper (Miesenberger 2015).

Since much multimedia content also contains graphic representations, there is intensive research for solutions on how to make these tangible for blind or visually impaired people as well. Graphic tactile displays can for example dynamically output graphics (Taras 2011).

The use of magnification software is an important tool for people with visual impairments. With such a tool, the screen of a computer can be magnified (texts, scanned texts, photos, computer games, webcam pictures, etc.). Different to classic accessibility tools of operating systems that are already offered as a standard feature, commercial magnifying software offers more specific aids, for example distinctly higher magnifying factors, antialiasing, colour inversion and a read out function (Capovilla and Gebhardt 2016).

Furthermore, independent navigation is a big challenge for individuals with visual impairments. Reduced visual capacity challenges persons to solve spatial problems everyday in different ways. It's essential to know how to receive, perceive, interpret and process information that is needed to explore an unknown environment. To find a way inside and outside, several factors including the complexity of the environment need to be taken into account. In this context, the most common aid is the white cane. It has been extremely successful because of its simplicity and its price. But it has some limitations. A white cane can only scan the immediate surroundings. More distant obstacles can't be anticipated. In the last years devices have been developed that try to augment or complement the white cane to overcome these restrictions. New white canes, equipped with sensors and feedback systems are able to measure the distance to objects and alert the user of these by vibration bursts varying in frequency depending on the measured distance. As a complement to white canes, electronic GPS travel aids are available to help with finding the way. The white cane explores immediate surroundings whereas the GPS travel-aid notifies longer distances. Most of the time, these systems are giving an acoustic feedback.

Looking at cutting-edge technologies for blind people, so-called bionic eyes seem to be a new and promising approach. Similar to cochlear implants, which stimulate auditory nerve fibres, visual prostheses aim to provide patients with visual information by stimulating neurons in the retina, in the optic nerve or in the brain's visual areas. There are different bionic eye models which take aim at different target areas in the visual pathway. Future developments will try to improve the spatial resolution, increase the field of view that can be perceived and increase the number of electrodes to provide an even better view of the world.

AT for people with hearing impairments

Hearing impairment refers to hearing losses of varying degrees, ranging from hard-of-hearing to total deafness. People with hearing thresholds of less than 25dB in both ears have a hearing loss. It can be distinguished as mild, moderate, severe or profound and may affect one or both ears. 'Deaf' people mostly have profound hearing loss (>90dB), which implies very little or no hearing. Usually they use sign language for communication (Shemesh 2010).

The emergence of new technologies implies ambivalent consequences for hard-of-hearing and deaf people: 'Traditional uses of technology have provided tremendous support to individuals with hearing loss. Advances in computer use, however, have also provided challenges to persons with hearing loss because computers are inherently an auditory–visual medium' (Jeffs *et al.* 2003: 137). On the one hand, the target group can gain text-based information with computers or similar devices. On the other, the very nature of multimedia including auditive information obstructs the way to knowledge. Alternative information such as subtitles for pictures is often neglected because of the fast changing and usually private sources of the Internet.

Systematically, three kinds of AT can be distinguished: Mobility assistive listening devices; Augmentative and alternative communication; and Alerting devices. These are considered in turn.

- 'Assistive listening devices' (ALDs) help to amplify the sounds, independent of background noises. ALDs can be used combined with a hearing aid or cochlear implant. Whereas some ALDs are designed for large facilities such as classrooms, theatres, places of worship and airports, other types are constructed for personal use in small settings.
- 'Augmentative and alternative communication' (AAC) devices help people with communication disorders to express themselves. These devices can range from a simple picture board to a computer programme that synthesizes speech from text (see previous commentary). For many years, people with hearing loss have used text telephone or telecommunications devices to communicate by phone. With today's new electronic communication devices, these devices are no longer needed. People can place phone calls through using almost any device with a keypad, including a laptop, personal digital assistant and cell phone. Text messaging has also become a popular method of communication.
- 'Alerting devices' (ADs) give a visual or haptic sign when an acoustic event occurs. Visual alert signalers can monitor a variety of household devices and other sounds, such as doorbells and telephones (NIDCD 2011).

Most information on the internet becomes accessible without additional help. Two problems are often named in this context: On the one hand, the above-mentioned problems occur when information is represented auditorily. On the other, it is difficult for the target group to comprehend the content because of its linguistic complexity (Hellbusch 2005). In this context, the high frequent usage of social media to build up communities is of interest. There are numerous net-based communities used to discuss available aids and frequent problems. It is an enormous advantage especially for people lacking other persons with similar disabilities and challenges in their direct environment.

For people with hearing disabilities the Cochlear Implant (CI) induced a fundamental change. A CI is an electronic device which is able to replace a non-functioning inner ear. In contrast to hearing aids which amplify sounds, a CI can compensate damaged parts of the inner ear, providing signals directly to the brain. Today, CIs are used for many people, representing the only means to improve their hearing. Since the beginning, these devices have been discussed critically. One concern was that CIs reinforce pathological views of deafness rather than views of deaf life as independent, promising and emotionally fulfilling. Another criticism relates to the child's autonomy and is connected with the concern that an implant may impair a child's self-esteem, body image and the quality of the child's and family's acceptance of the hearing loss (Leonhardt 2009).

AT for people with speech and language disorders

Speech disorders affect the way a person creates sounds to form words. Speech disorders include having a lisp (causing someone to have difficulty pronouncing sibilant letters), stuttering (which induces difficulties with the flow of speech) and cluttering (which is difficult for listeners to understand due to the rapid speaking rate, erratic rhythm or poor syntax or grammar) (Robitaille 2010). 'While stuttering is a speech disorder, cluttering is a language disorder. A stutterer knows what he wants to say but can't say it; a clutterer can say what she is thinking, but her thinking becomes disorganized during speech.' (Robitaille 2010)

Other speech disorders are apraxia, a motor speech disorder caused by damage to the parts of the brain related to speaking, and dysarthria, a motor speech disorder in which the muscles of the mouth, face or respiratory system may become weak or have difficulty moving (Gargiulo 2006).

In the context of people with speech and language disorders AT is used in different ways. An important issue is the training with the help of specific computer programmes to develop speech and language skills. There are numerous software tools which can be used. Advantages of this way of learning are the neutral feedback, the possibility to repeat as often as necessary and the options to control spoken text or phrases auditorily and visually. The technical feedback is not dependent on an individual person and represents an exact record of the speech.

Fluency devices simulate the so-called 'chorale effect'. With this device, worn like a hearing aid, words are digitally replayed in the ear with a slight delay and frequency modification. 'As a result, the brain perceives them as speaking in unison with another person, which causes the chorale effect. Fluency devices can help control speech fluency, slow down speech rate, and increase confidence.' (Robitaille 2010: 146).

Additionally, people with speech and language impairments use augmentative or alternative communication (AAC). As mentioned above, AAC is the use of symbols, aids, strategies and techniques to enhance the communication process. This includes sign language and various communication boards, both manual and electronic, that are used by individuals with impaired oral motor skills.

The most basic AAC devices used for students with speech and language impairments are non-electronic communication boards. The boards usually are limited to a number of choices (two to four). The choices can be represented by real items, pictures of items and symbols for items (including print). The objective of the communication board is to have the student make a choice, typically of food or activity. Electronic AAC devices range from very simple devices with few buttons (such as the Cheap Talk) to very elaborate systems that use a keyboard and synthesized speech (such as the DynaVox and Liberator) (Turnbull *et al.* 2007).

AT for people with mild learning disabilities

The group of people with a mild learning disability makes up a great part of all people with disabilities. A learning disability is a disorder in one or more of the basic cognitive abilities. This can lead to reduced ability to think, speak, read, write, spell, calculate or communicate. In the context of this target group, AT usually refers to regular hard- and software, which is adjusted to the special needs and living conditions. If supportive media is deployed in a perfectly fitting way, the personal benefits are tremendous: the possibility of writing an almost errorless, neat looking text, for example, has only come along with computer-based writing programmes (Quenneville 2001). Considering the fact that by now texts can be written through speech recognition, the obstacle of errorless writing highly decreases, at least for this target group. The same applies to reading competences. By now, a read out function is part of the basic equipment of many devices, so that more difficult, longer words, which can lead to problems for weak readers, can be deduced too. With these expanded competences, people with a mild learning disability can fulfill the demands of everyday life more easily.

As described, difficulties that improve participation of the target group appear mainly in cultural techniques, and the usage of compensating programmes has to play a big role in school already. Especially since these are not specific media, there is a greater danger that the topic will not get sufficient attention or it is not followed up systematically. Allen (2015) therefore stresses that the imparting of media competence has to be systematical and guided by principles. In his opinion, AT cannot replace basal competences, they can only be expanded. They should be part of the pedagogic process and be used to establish basic competences. Furthermore, AT for children with mild learning disabilities is more than just an educational tool; it is a fundamental work tool that is comparable to pencil and paper for non-disabled children. A third point is that students with a mild learning disability use AT to manage regular tasks in class and to be able to learn together with their classmates. And finally, evaluation that is based as an ongoing process is necessary for the foundation of a long-term successful use.

Raskind and Higgens (1998) assume that competency acquisition that is led by principles increases the independence of people with a mild learning disability. The authors state that without media, the dependence on other people (parents, siblings, friends, professionals) increases, which makes the crossover to adulthood more difficult. Due to the dependence, people with a mild learning disability might experience less self-efficacy, which in some circumstances leads to them having difficulties in building a feeling of self-worth. AT, moreover, provides a way for children with learning disabilities to achieve specific tasks on their own. Besides reading, calculating and writing, navigation and a structured approach also belong to these tasks. With the help of free apps, it can be considerably easier to manage the challenge of complex connections of local public transport. Especially changes in the timetable often lead to excessive demand for people who are dependent on fixed and reliable executions and cannot find alternatives without further ado. Many tasks of everyday life and the job, but also the mastering of a whole daily routine, are bound to consequent consideration of sequence and structure. As it will be shown in connection to moderate to severe learning disabilities, media can be meaningfully deployed to give structure.

Another important area is the usage of social media. If the previously mentioned aids are deployed appropriately, people with mild learning disabilities can play a part in social media as equal members: 'Technology facilitates the students' ability to make personal connections with others and provides opportunities to focus on writing skills within a context that they value, without fear of being stigmatized.' (Hasselbring and Glaser 2000: 108). In this connection, it is important to emphasize that people need to be educated and trained on how to use social media responsibly.

Technical assistance for people with moderate to severe learning disabilities

A cognitive disability represents a substantial limitation in mental tasks (such as planning, information processing and understanding of social cues) that reduces a person's ability to perform desired activities ... Assistive technology can reduce the affect of these disabilities and provide improved quality of life (Lopresti *et al.* 2008: 29).

The target group of people with an intellectual disability is very heterogeneous. In consequence, the use of media highly differs as well. Whereas people with a moderate learning disability can use conventional media similarly to people with a mild learning disability, people with severe cognitive disabilities often need specific media or at least specific apps that are adjusted to their special needs. Due to frequent comorbidities like physical impairments, visual impairments and hearing impairments, specific sets of AT may be appropriate, depending on the individual impairment. Part of these aids are, for example, walking aids, hearing aids, glasses or communication aids within the meaning of AAC.

The accurately aligned choice of media is an important prerequisite for meaningful usage. Beyond that, however, the usage needs to be integrated into a holistic framework which is interconnected with the personal and material resources. This challenging process is described by Svensk (2001) in the *Design for Cognitive Assistance*. Svensk suggests a two-level selection process. On the one hand, this selection process describes criteria for technical aids, similar to the ones of Universal Design (Affordance, Visibility, Mapping, Feedback, Error reducing), and on the other, it phrases socio-economic conditions that are essential for a productive deployment of technical media: Safety: If a person who needs support does not feel as if he or she can depend on a person or on a technology, the person will use a lot of energy to build an alternative safety net instead of being active and socialize; Context: A person who needs support needs to have an overview about the aids and resources surrounding him or her and needs to know the relationships between them; Memory: People who are incapable of recalling people, objects or impressions that are not present at the moment need suitable aids to make connections to previous experiences; Accuracy/Clarity: The precise or clear knowledge of an activity is an important requirement for being able to perform this exact activity independently (Svensk 2001).

If these aspects are considered, an environment emerges that supports an individual as much as possible. Irritating or inhibiting factors are compensated or blanked out through the specific use of technology. Support of people with intellectual disabilities via AT is a holistic complex process which has to be accompanied by professional supporters. While not all impairments can be compensated by technology, an additional personal support is still necessary. In the best case, resources and independence of the person who needs support are expanded through specific, systematical networking with the material and personal environment (Fischer 2003).

Inclusion through AT?

The last section demonstrated the high potential of AT to facilitate the lives of people with special education needs. In many cases technology compensates impairments; hence it can be assumed that technology causes inclusion. This assumption corresponds with the modern belief that new technologies hold the key to human progress and was the motivation of many grant programmes all over the world in the last two decades. However, the question of whether AT can enable inclusion can't be answered easily. We need to look at different aspects of technology and society to obtain a clear and differentiated view.

'Normal' technology for people with disabilities

In the beginning, AT consisted mainly of isolated aids, which were built especially for people with disabilities (e.g. prosthetics, braille writers). In the last two decades, more and more conventional products have been built flexible enough to extend their use in manifold ways, so that people with disabilities can use them. One reason for this change process has been driven by legislation: in many countries accessibility has been included in the law. Hence, some operation systems have built-in AT, for example, basic screen reader or magnifier. Another reason is the growing evidence that these special settings are fruitful for many people and enhance the attractiveness of the products. In the first years of IT, only a few experts were working with computers using cryptic programming languages like Basic or Pascal. An important waymark was the development of the graphical user interface (GUI). These developments have led to a growing range of users and an expanding market. The more different types of people started using computers, the more important the usability of hard- and software became (Zentel *et al.* 2008). Hence, technologies expected to be used as mass media by many people consider the natural diversity and thereby open up access for special target groups.

It therefore appears that scenarios of the use of computer-based technologies have revolutionized in only a few years. In 1991 Weiser had already predicted that computer-based technology would change fundamentally in the twenty-first century. He thought about computers as ubiquitous and pervasive devices, which may support people within all circumstances (Weiser 1991). With the appearance of the smartphone and tablet-pc, this vision has become true.

In many cases specific hardware, which is closely related with a negative stigma, is no longer needed. State-of-the-art devices support plenty of functions able to compensate the disabilities of people. Due to multiple input and output options (e.g. keyboard, speech, touchscreen) manifold needs can be met. Technical resources are becoming more and more user-centred. Content can be displayed in manifold ways – adequate to the needs of the users. This is a fundamental step towards normalization and inclusion. Keeping this in mind, the main challenge is not only to develop more specific tools but to observe and, if possible, to influence the development of 'normal' technologies.

An ecological approach as a framework of AT

The concepts of AT that were presented show that the development of such technologies has to arise from an environment analysis. Such an ecological approach both enlivens and enlightens the process of matching man and technology (Tobias 2005). The theory of distributed cognition (Salomon 1993) provides an effective conceptual framework for such an understanding. In distributed cognition theory, cognition involves mental processes and representations in the mind as well as artefacts located in the environment. Anatomy and cognitive abilities are not a destiny; both are improvable through a well-chosen environment which compensates shortcomings and enhances competencies (Carmien et al. 2004). As Postman emphasized, this framework in not dependent on ICT: The invention of eyeglasses in the twelfth century not only made it possible to improve defective vision, but suggested the idea that human beings need not accept as final either the endowments of nature nor the ravages of time. Eyeglasses refuted the belief that anatomy is destiny by putting forward the idea that our minds as well as our bodies are improvable (Postman 1985: 14)! According to this understanding, *competence* and *disability* are not independent, unalterable factors, but depend on how much a person is included into his or her multi-layered human–environment–system (Hildeschmidt and Sander 2002). As shown above, media or technical aids can play an important role in such an environment.

AT – a tool for an inclusive society?

The integration of AT in the larger context of a socio-ecological framework makes us aware that media can be an important element of an inclusive environment such as an inclusive classroom, but it doesn't lead necessarily to inclusion – in certain circumstances it creates the exact opposite! Inclusion can be seen as a synonym for the acceptance of diversity. In other words, diversity can be considered as a determinant factor of an inclusive society. All people are accepted and have equal rights as members of an open society although they differ in gender, sex, race or even because of their disability. Inclusive societies are open and willing to reconstitute if their members are changing.

AT are raising hopes that disability as one variable of deviance can be compensated. In this sense people can live, learn and work inclusively because they are using AT, which helps to adapt on a presumed norm. But that's not inclusion! AT are neither causes nor cures for inclusion, and their use shouldn't be an imperative.

The digital gap as a danger for inclusive processes

The progressing digitalization of developed countries' social systems urges people to use technologies in order to participate in social environments – with high expectations towards competences and equipment. The so-called digital gap is still alive and produces difference – difference between people who are able to use ICT and those who are not. The more information is represented only digitally, the more people without the ability to use ICT are excluded. If information on the next train connection is no longer given by a person sitting behind a counter that is able to adapt to special communication needs, only people who are able to read a schedule or are familiar with the use of smartphones will get the right train. As stated above, it seems to be obvious that ICT cannot be seen as a pure technological artefact, but as a socio-digital innovation that needs to be embedded in social environments. The needs of people with disabilities, impairments or disadvantages can only be addressed by a blended approach of technological and social innovation. Hence, the development and use of new technologies should be part of the new paradigm of community orientation. The design of new public spheres should imply the use of personal and technical assistance as complementary resources in order to meet the needs of all people. Especially for people with physical or sensory disabilities, custom-fit individual arrangements in arbitrary formats can be created spontaneously from generic information: e.g. tactile or acoustic for blind people, visual for deaf. Furthermore, individual ways of communication can be transformed in accessible and intelligible formats through technology.

The automatic, computer-based transformation of complex content in easy formats such as easy language signs or pictures which could provide access to people with intellectual disabilities is still a big challenge. At least today, the didactical task of making content easier can't be solved through artificial intelligence.

Future directions

The development of specific AT based on state-of-the art technologies will open numerous new possibilities. These new emergent tools will bring the vision closer that the lame can walk, the blind can see and the deaf can hear. It remains to be seen whether the introduction of these systems will be accepted by people with disabilities. To meet the real needs of people with disabilities and to reduce rejection, the target group should be involved in the process of development. If that is the case, new possibilities will arise.

Standard hard- and software has to continue progressing on the path towards accessibility. People shouldn't be forced to adapt to complicated systems – technologies should provide access regardless of impairments and adapt to specific preferences. Technical devices and ubiquitous services should be further developed systematically and to enable new forms of usage.

A big challenge seems to be the involvement of people with intellectual disabilities. Although technologies have produced new possibilities to compensate cognitive difficulties, the digitalization induced many new hurdles and effected a digital gap, separating people that are overstrained due to the new technology-based complexities.

Discussion

AT has the potential to influence the lives of people with disabilities. Carefully designed environments including technologies can change a concrete situation in a fundamental way and lead to a decrease in a disability: 'For some students technology may be the only way to ensure they can make their thoughts and needs known. For them access to appropriate ICT-based solutions provides perhaps the only chance of participating in society and realizing their full potential.' (Becta 2003: 1). On the one hand, considerable advantages for people with disabilities are obvious. On the other, a growing responsibility comes along with the increasing importance of technology in society (Heumann 1998). Technology which is not accessible prevents the possibility of participating (Gallegos 2013; Miesenberger 2012). This should be avoided!

The UN Convention on the Rights of Persons with Disabilities (www.un.org) underlines the importance of accessibility and assigns a key role to ICT in the further development of an inclusive society. According to Articles 4, 9 and 24, AT should be provided to all people with disabilities to enable participation in all aspects of society and education, and to realize inclusion (Fisseler 2012; Welke 2012). Media competencies as a result of media education must be seen as an indispensable means to granting human and civil rights (Bosse 2012).

AT are effective media to support the lives and learning processes of people with disabilities. We are still far beyond tapping the full potential of technologies. But the further development of technologies will provide more accessibility to all people.

Future ICT will be an integrated part of cars, telephones, wristwatches, wheelchairs, and even clothing and jewellery. According to their individual competencies and strength, a tailor-made solution will be provided to '… put everyone in control and allow them to interact and manipulate their environment, regardless of ability, through the method of their choice' (Robitaille 2010: 181).

References

Allen, E. (2015) *Assistive technology for students with multiple disabilities*. Education Masters. Paper 299. Available online from: http://fisherpub.sjfc.edu/cgi/viewcontent.cgi?article= 1300&context=education_ETD_masters [29 December 2016].

Becta (British Educational Communications and Technology Agency) (2003) *What the research says about ICT supporting special education needs and inclusion*. Available online from http://webarchive.nationalarchives.gov.uk/20130401151715/http://www.education. gov.uk/publications/eOrderingDownload/15014MIG2799.pdf [03 November 2016].

Blackhurst, A. E., and Edyburn, D. L. (2000) 'A brief history of special education technology', *Special Education Technology Practice*, 2: 21–35.

Bosse, I. (2012) *Medienbildung im Zeitalter der Inklusion*, LfM Dokumentation, Bd. 45.

Capovilla, D., and Gebhardt, M. (2016) 'Assistive Technologien für Menschen mit Sehschädigungen im inklusiven Unterricht', *Zeitschrift für Heilpädagogik*, 1: 4–15

Carmien, S., Dawe, M., Fischer, G., Gorman, A., Kintsc, A., and Sullivan J. S. (2004) *Socio-technical environments supporting people with cognitive disabilities using public transportation*. Available online from http://l3d.cs.colorado.edu/clever/projects/maps/papers/TOCHI-submitted-2-26-04.pdf [03 November 2016].

Edyburn, D. L. (2004). 'Rethinking assistive technology', *Special Education Technology Practice*, 5: 16–23.

European Parliament (2015). Assistive technologies to support people with disabilities. Available online from http://www.europarl.europa.eu/EPRS/EPRS-Briefing-559513-Assistive-technologies-support-people-with-disabilities-FINAL.pdf [13 September 2017].

Fischer, G. (2003) 'Distributed cognition: A conceptual framework for design-for-all', in C. Stephanidis (ed.) *Proceedings of HCI International* 2003, Crete Greece, June 2003, Mahwah, NJ: Lawrence Erlbaum Associates (pp. 78–82).

Fisseler, B. (2012) 'Assistive und Unterstützende Technologien in Förderschule und inklusivem Unterricht', in I. Bosse (ed.) *Medienbildung im Zeitalter der Inklusion*, LfM Dokumentation, Vol. 45, Düsseldorf, Germany: LfM (pp. 87–91.

Gallegos, L. (2013) 'The ICT opportunity for a disability-inclusive development framework: Why now?', in Unesco (Hrsg.). T*he ICT opportunity for a disability-inclusive development framework*. Available online from: www.itu.int/en/action/accessibility/Documents/The%20ICT%20Opportunity%20for%20a%20Disability_Inclusive%20Development%20Framework.pdf [03 November 2016].

Gargiulo, R. M. (2006) *Special education in contemporary society: An introduction to exceptionality*, Belmont, CA: Thomson Wadsworth.

Hasselbring, T. S., and Glaser, C. H. W. (2000) 'Use of computer technology to help students with special needs', *Children and Computer Technology*, 10: 102–122.

Hellbusch, J. E. (2005) *Barrierefreies Webdesign. Praxishandbuch für Webgestaltung und grafische Programmoberflächen*, Heidelberg, Germany: d.punkt.

Heumann, J. (1998) *Keynote address to Microsoft employees and experts on disabilities and technology*, Redmond, Washington, February 19.

Hildeschmidt, A., and Sander, A. (2002) 'Der ökosystemische Ansatz als Grundlage für Einzelintegration', in H. Eberwein, and S. Knauer (eds.) *Integrationspädagogik*, Weinheim und Basel: Beltz (pp. 304–312).

IDEA (2004) *Individuals with Disabilities Education Act*. Available online from www.parent centerhub.org/wp-content/uploads/repo_items/PL108-446.pdf [08 December 2016].

ISO (2016) ISO 9999:2016 - Assistive products for persons with disability – Classification and terminology. Available online from www.iso.org/iso/catalogue_detail.htm?csnumber= 60547 [29 December 2016].

Jeffs, T., Morrison, W. F., Messenheimer, T., Rizza, M. G., and Banister, S. (2003) 'A retrospective analysis of technical advancements in special education', *Computers in Schools*, 20: 129–152.

Leonhardt, A. (2009) 'Cochlea-Implantate für gehörlose Kinder gehörloser Eltern?', in A. Ernst, R. D. Battner, and I. Todt (eds.) *Cochlear implant heute*, Berlin, Germany: Springer (pp. 63–71).

LoPresti, E., Bodine, C., and Lewis, C. (2008) 'Assistive technology for cognition: Understand the needs of persons with disabilities', *IEEE Engineering in Medicine and Biology Magazine*, 29–39.

Miesenberger, K. (2012) *Sieben Fragen zur inklusiven Medienbildung.* Available online from http://lfmpublikationen.lfm-nrw.de/catalog/downloadproducts/L137_Medienbildung_Inklusion.pdf [03 November 2016].

Miesenberger, K. (2015) 'Advanced and emerging solutions: ICT and AT in education of low vision and blind students', in G. Kouroupetroglou (ed.) *Proceedings of ICEAPVI*, Athens, Greece: (pp. 17–26).

Mulloy, A., Gevarter, C., Hopkins, M., Sutherland, K., and Ramdoss, S. (2014) 'Assistive technology for students with visual impairments and blindness', in G. E. Lancioni, and N. Singh (eds.) *Assistive technologies for people with diverse abilities*, New York: Springer (pp. 113–156).

NIDCD (2011) *NIDCD Fact sheet: Assistive devices for people with hearing, voice, speech, or language disorders NIH publication, No. 11-7672.* Available online from www.nidcd.nih. gov/sites/default/files/Documents/health/hearing/NIDCD-Assistive-Devices-FS.pdf [03 November 2016].

Norman, D. A. (1998) *Things that make us smart: Defending human attributes in the age of the machine*, New York, US: Perseus Books.

Pantke, K.-H. (2010) *Mensch und Maschine. Wie Brain-Computer-Interfaces und andere Innovationen gelähmten Menschen kommunizieren helfen*, Frankfurt am Main: Mabuse Verlag.

Petz, A., and Miesenberger, K. (2012) 'Dealing with changes in supporting students with disabilities in higher education', in K. Miesenberger, A. Karshmer, P. Penaz, and W. Zagler (eds.) *Computers helping people with special needs series LNCS, Vol. 7382*, Berlin, Germany: Springer (pp. 1–25).

Postman, N. (1985) *Amusing ourselves to death—Public discourse in the age of show business*, New York: Penguin Books.

Quenneville J. (2001) 'Tech tools for students with learning disabilities: Infusion into inclusive classrooms', *Preventing School Failure*, 45: 167–170.

Raskind, M. H., and Higgins, E. L. (1998) 'Assistive technology for postsecondary students with learning disabilities: An overview', *Journal of Learning Disabilities*, 31: 27–40.

Robitaille, S. (2010) *The illustrated guide to assistive technology and devices: Tools and gadgets for living independently*, New York: Demos Medical Publishing.

Salomon, G. (1993) *Distributed cognitions: Psychological and educational considerations*, Cambridge, UK: Cambridge University Press.

Shemesh R. (2010) 'Hearing impairment: Definitions, assessment and management', in J. H. Stone, and M. Blouin (eds.) *International encyclopedia of rehabilitation.* Available online from http://cirrie.buffalo.edu/encyclopedia/en/article/272/ [03 November 2016]

Story, M. F., Mueller, J. L. and MACE, R. L. (1998) *The universal design file: Designing for people of all ages and abilities,* Raleigh, NC: Center for Universal Design.

Svensk, A. (2001) *Design for cognitive assistance, Licentiate Thesis CERTEC, LTH number 1:2001.* Available online from www.english.certec.lth.se/doc/designforcognitive/designforcognitive.pdf [03 November 2016].

Taras C. (2011) *Presentation and interaction techniques for the efficient use of graphical user interfaces by blind and visually impaired.* Available online from http://dx.doi.org/10.18419/opus-2704 [03 November 2016].

Tobias, J. (2005) 'Network-based accessibility services for people with disabilities', in A. Pruski, and H. Knops (eds.) *Assistive technology: From virtuality to reality, Proceedings of the AAATE 2005,* Amsterdam, Netherlands: IOS Press. (pp. 69–72).

Turnbull, A., Turnbull, R., and Wehmeyer, M. L. (2007) *Exceptional lives: Special education in today's schools,* Upper Saddle River, NJ: Pearson.

Weiser, M. (1991) 'The Computer for the twenty-first-century', *Scientific American,* 3: 94–100.

Welke, A. (2012) *UN-Behindertenrechtskonvention. Mit rechtlichen Erläuterungen,* Freiburg im Breisgau, Germany: Lambertus.

Zentel, P., Lingnau, A., and Cress, U. (2008) 'Perspectives of ICT in special education: Potential and possibilities of Web 2.0 and social software', *Journal of Assistive Technologies,* 2: 22–33.

6

THE CONSTRUCTION OF DIFFERENCE

The impact of neurodiverse communities within the cyber and physical worlds

Charlotte Brownlow and Donna-Marie Thompson

Autism: Identity as a shifting categorical concept

Autism as a topic of research has attracted much attention since its initial introduction to the fields of psychiatry and psychology in the 1940s. While debate continues around whom should be recognised for 'discovering' autism and the appropriate terminology (see for example Silberman 2015), the adoption of autism as a diagnostic descriptor within psychiatric and psychological discourse has been widespread. However, as well as being a focus of research, autism is also a cultural identity, one that is often considered a contested area with respect to terminology. We acknowledge the constructive and contested nature of labels, and throughout this chapter we have followed the lead of Silberman (2015) and use 'autism' when discussing a categorical condition and 'autistic' when referring to an individual in order to reflect the adoption of autism by some as a cultural identity rather than a diagnostic disability attached to a person by others. Further, we seek to explore divergent understandings through considerations of identity construction within different technological spaces and the potential impacts of these.

One of the most recent impacts on, and challenges to, understandings of autism has been the introduction of the *Diagnostic and Statistical Manual of Mental Disorders*, Fifth Edition (DSM-5). Changes to the DSM-5 saw a major shift in the diagnostic conceptualisation of autism, with a new overarching diagnosis of autism spectrum disorder (ASD) that encompassed previous diagnostic categories such as Asperger's syndrome, childhood disintegrative disorder, autistic disorder and pervasive developmental disorder not otherwise specified (Spillers *et al.* 2014). This shift in diagnostic thinking has also been evident in a change from the conceptualisation of autism as comprised of a 'triad of impairments' to a 'dyad of impairments' (American Psychiatric Association 2013).

While clinicians may claim that such changes will enable a more accurate diagnosis, the impacts on individual identity making should not be underestimated. Spillers *et al.* (2014), for example, argue that the replacement of some diagnoses with the broader term of ASD may require some individuals to revisit their identity. For some this may lead to instability of identity, with a concern being that previous understandings of the 'self' built around being 'autistic' or an 'Aspie' potentially require re-negotiation due to an abrupt absence of validation by clinicians (Spillers *et al.* 2014). This would also suggest that, for some, identity construction was, in part, the responsibility of professionals rather than self-determined. Following their work in online discussion forums, Spillers *et al.* argued that the perceived impacts of changes to the DSM by adults with a diagnosis were a primary concern because labels such as 'Asperger's' and 'Autism' have much wider reaching implications for individuals rather than functioning purely as a diagnosis. For the individuals contributing to Spiller *et al.*'s work, such labels were seminal to self-identity as well as to the broader culture. For these participants, assurances by the clinicians that they would retain a diagnosis under the DSM-5 did not assuage their concerns as to the impacts on their positive identity making. Indeed, Giles (2014: 192) noted in his analysis of online autism-related forum threads relating to the DSM-5 diagnostic changes that some autistic individuals believed the 'highest authority' on matters pertaining to autism lay with the autistic community itself.

Such findings suggest the influence of technology, and particularly the age of the Internet, in opening up a means of communication to the autistic community leading, in part, to the development of a self-advocacy movement, advocacy that had previously been largely parent led (Giles 2014; Silverman 2012). Research has argued that the Internet provides a more 'comfortable communication medium' for autistic people in that it relies less on the non-verbal aspects of communication (Benford and Standen 2015: 44). As such it would appear that the Internet has provided a forum that equalises the autistic and neurotypical (NT, non-autistic) communities in sharing opinions and experiences, while allowing connections and relationships to develop.

Despite the changes witnessed with the various iterations of the DSM, the core essence of the clinical focus remains on the *deficits* associated with the diagnosis. This focus is largely reflected in the therapeutic interventions drawn upon by professionals when working with people on the spectrum. For example, Applied Behavioural Analysis (ABA) has been cited as the most successful empirically validated intervention for autism (Serna *et al.* 2015). Such an approach requires intensive early treatment with the prime purpose being to change behaviours deemed to be socially undesirable (Sturmey 2012). An example of this might be stimming behaviours used by some autistic people as a means to reduce sensory overload in order to better engage with their environment. Within particular social contexts such as a school classroom, however, these behaviours might be considered distracting by some non-autistic people. Safran *et al.* (2003) noted that students undertaking behavioural therapy must be specifically taught to be able to discriminate between socially acceptable and socially unacceptable behaviours, learning appropriate alternatives to unacceptable behaviour. Here the clear implication is that people with autism must change in order to accommodate the non-autistic majority. The presupposition of therapeutic interventions is therefore that the individual with autism is required to change rather than engage in a more accommodating interactional environment. Such therapeutic presuppositions further contribute to the dominant construction of the autistic individual within therapeutic discourse as having a *deficit* rather than displaying a *difference*.

The discourse of neurodiversity

Within dominant ways of thinking that are largely influenced by the medical model, the positioning of individuals on the autism spectrum is one of 'impaired', 'lacking' and requiring of interventions in order to 'fix' such deviations from the 'norm'. The medical model continues to dominate the larger cultural view of autistic individuals as being 'impaired'. This definition suggests a diminished 'quality or strength of physical or psychological functioning' that requires intervention to address any deviation from cultural norms (Colman 2015: 366). In the context of autism, this would include contextual social interactions and behaviours or interests deemed unusual. In more recent years, there has been a movement that seeks to challenge such impairment discourse, instead viewing autism through a lens of *neurodiversity*. Neurodiversity reflects both terminology and an advocacy movement, and is credited to self-advocate and activist Judy Singer (Ortega 2009). A core premise of the neurodiversity movement is one of the removal of stigma operationalised in the discourse of impairment, and instead embraces the differences that characterise the diversity found on and within autistic people. Ortega argues that through adopting a position of neurodiversity, an individual is able to challenge stereotypes of being either severely mentally impaired or in the possession of savant skills. This presents alternative possibilities in terms of the presentation of knowledge about autism, and the resultant opportunities for the framing of positive self-identities.

Neurodiversity advocates propose that autism and related conditions are a reflection of natural variations in neurological make-up, and consequently autistic individuals display unique neurological differences to non-autistic people (Sarrett 2016). The appeal to the discourse of neurology is therefore central to this position in the management of *differences* rather than *deficits*, and the position calls for a re-interpretation of autism as a difference that needs to be both accepted and embraced within society rather than an impairment that requires intervention and cure. The understanding underpinning neurodiversity is therefore one that is echoing of the wider disability rights movement, challenging the medical model's focus on impairment and cure, and instead focusing attention on autism as being both a difference and as central to self-identity (Kapp *et al.* 2013).

Ortega (2009) argues that psychiatric labels remain central in identity constructions, and the diagnosis provides a powerful framework for the individual, their family and others through which to understand autism. Within this, neurodiversity offers the possibility for alternative understandings, ones that can enable positive self-identities to be constructed. However, Ortega warns that the core assumption of the neurodiversity movement as being one in which individuals are 'wired differently' requires caution, as to do so may imply that any challenges are attributable to biological essences. In doing so, there is a risk that the focus of support provision as being a societal obligation could shift to that of individual responsibility. Whilst on one hand neurodiversity discourse may enable a positive identity and the connection of like-minded others, the appeal to neurology may serve to act in reductionist ways where individuals are merely a reflection of their own neurology. Furthermore, Orsini (2012) argues that we also need to recognise the divergent positions adopted concerning neurodiversity. For example, Orsini notes that not all autistic individuals choose to frame their identity around neurodiversity, and do not wish to be considered part of this wider movement. Orsini argues that these individuals may instead choose to construct their identity around elements that do not necessarily reflect their diagnosis. Similarly, Orsini notes that some parents of children with autism may equally not want to embrace the discourse of neurodiversity due to fears that it may trivialise their child's needs through the appeal to a spectrum of neurological possibilities.

Arguably, the appeal to neurology is strong; however, importantly Ortega (2009) points out that despite several positions being presented in the research literature, there remains no general agreement concerning the aetiology of autism. Despite this, self-advocates appear to largely agree on the aetiology of autism as one reflecting neurological difference. Such a position is intuitively appealing due to the possibilities it affords to individuals in the construction of positive autistic identities. What remains in question is whether the location of interactions has any impact on the crafting of positive identities. As previously discussed, scholars such as Robertson and Ne'eman (2008) note an expansion in advocacy movements both online via social media and in face-to-face contexts, indicating a potential synthesis across the two environments. In this chapter, we present examples from research conducted in both face-to-face and online forums in order to explore the relative influence of technological spaces and the impact and pertinence of these in face-to-face contexts.

Adopting an abilities framework

Refocusing our thinking through a lens of neurodiversity and individual difference lends itself to the adoption of an abilities perspective when considering autism, one where the presumption is of competence rather than impairment. Such a framework challenges the assumptions that serve to restrict individual expression of difference and the associated disabling societal practices, while emphasising the need to accommodate some of the challenges that might be faced by individuals as a minority population situated within a dominant non-autistic culture. Importantly, adopting this view creates space for positive identity construction and the positioning of adults with differing abilities as contributing citizens within society. One of the ways in which this may be achieved is through employment and engaging in Higher Education. Concerningly, national statistics indicate a lower rate of employment for ASD demographics, and expressed difficulties in the navigation of the Higher Education environment. For example, according to the Australian Bureau of Statistics (2014), in 2012 the workforce participation rate for autistic individuals was 42 per cent compared to people with a disability (53 per cent) and people without a disability (83 per cent). These figures indicate that there may be a high number of disadvantageous factors for autistic people in the workforce, including (1) employers' overestimation or lack of understanding of the accommodations required to support autistic employees, (2) stigma and negative stereotypes of autistic traits and (3) the reluctance of autistic individuals to disclose being on the spectrum for fear of the previous two points (see for example Neely and Hunter 2014). Similarly, the same statistics reported that 86 per cent of respondents had difficulties at school, with 81 per cent not completing a post-school qualification.

Somewhat in contrast to these statistics, Sheedy (2016) reflects on the benefits of having a diverse workforce, which he notes was evident as far back as World War 2, during which time the unique skills of people with colour blindness proved beneficial in making sense of aerial photographs without the distractions commonly encountered by people who had full colour vision. Sheedy argues that the diversification of the workforce has increasingly become a focus of interest following the seminal work of organisations such as the Danish company Specialisterne, which was among the first to recruit autistic individuals based on individual, and often highly specialised, skill sets. Sheedy also cites the international software company Systemanalyse und Programmentwicklung (SAP) and their commitment to engaging a minimum of 1 per cent of their target workforce from among autistic individuals by 2020. Other technology-based companies, such as Microsoft and Hewlett-Packard, are reported to be launching similar programmes (Florentine 2015).

Sheedy (2016), however, argues that in order to increase the proportion of autistic employees, employers must adopt more sophisticated recruitment strategies that enable the skills of prospective employees to shine rather than falling short at the first hurdle, the interview. Frequently, traditional interview techniques require an individual to manage complex social interactions and emphasis is placed not only on the ability of the individual to carry out role responsibilities, but also to 'fit in' with the workplace culture. Often such complex social interactions are a challenge for an autistic interviewee, and the mastery of such abilities frequently bears little resemblance to the actual requirements of the job. Given that many occupations increasingly depend upon technologies such as email and video-conferencing for communication, and in educational contexts via online learning management systems, the mediating influence of these could potentially buffer against some of the challenges in managing the inherent social obligations associated with work and educational spaces. Additionally, the ever-expanding growth in interactive apps for smartphones and tablets may offer targeted support to assist individual employees or students (Chandler 2016). Such tools expand potential employment and learning opportunities, not just for autistic individuals, but also for all those challenged by social interactions and offer much scope for future research.

In recognising the acknowledged preference that many autistic individuals have for utilising technology as a communication tool, researchers have turned to increasingly novel approaches to engage autistic learners and employees. For example, Beaumont *et al.* (2015) have trialled a computer-based social skills programme initially designed for children with high-functioning autism spectrum conditions, the Secret Agent Society, in mainstream classrooms in Australia with resulting improvements in social-emotional functioning at school and home with implications for improved peer relationships and learning. Other emerging developments involving technology include utilising video-conferencing rather than face-to-face interactions to reduce extraneous environmental stimulation in learning environments and virtual simulation systems that allow people with social difficulties to have conversations with a simulated person and receive immediate feedback on non-verbal behaviours (Fung *et al.* 2015; Mokashi *et al.* 2013). Such findings support the need to maximise structured opportunities for students with autism to excel, thereby increasing opportunities for individual mastery to build stronger self-identity and to provide a more positive lens for both themselves and their peers to view autistic students' abilities (Bottema-Beutel and Smith 2013; Wolfberg *et al.* 2008). In agreeing with Frauenberger (2015), we would caution that while designing such interactive technologies, it is of utmost importance that a collaborative and participatory approach be adopted and maintained in designing such tools in order to ensure that the focus remains on the well-being and self-determination of autistic individuals rather than simply addressing perceived diagnostic deficits.

Exploring the construction of identities

We can therefore see that the discussions surrounding understandings of autism and the consequent possibilities for identity making amongst such a population are complex. The different voices of professionals, advocates and parents each stake claims as 'expert' voices, with each drawing on knowledge from distinctly subjective and highly personal perspectives. In order to explore this further, and in line with our argument for the necessity of recognising the participatory 'voice' of the autistic community, this chapter will now draw on data contributed by adults on the autism spectrum in two different contexts: online discussion forums and face-to-face discussion groups. While the two sources are divergent in their methodological approach, both prioritise the core objectives of encouraging autistic individuals to represent themselves and support them in crafting self-determined self-identities. Both research approaches received ethics approval from university Human Research Ethics committees prior to data collection.

The data collected from four online discussion forums took place in an asynchronous environment, where discussions between participants were 'natural' in that there was no involvement from the researchers in its production. The identity of the participants in this sample could not reliably be established due to the anonymity that the online environment affords, although all identified themselves as autistic individuals, as a parent of an autistic child or as a professional who worked with autistic people. In contrast, the data collected in the face-to-face discussion groups involved a researcher facilitating the discussions and these took place synchronously. These face-to face focus groups were specific in their participant pool in that all participants were autistic university students who had attended a programme, *A-Skills*, designed by the second author to support autistic higher education students in navigating their university journeys. The participants in this discussion therefore had developed relationships with each other throughout the 8-week duration of the A-Skills programme. Excerpts will be presented from these unique arenas in order to illustrate the complexities in the construction of identity and difference in both online and face-to-face contexts. We have presented these through our identification of two key themes drawn from these research studies: (1) *Redefining 'disorder' as 'difference'* and (2) *Neurodiverse communities*. All names used to identify the participants are pseudonyms.

Redefining 'disorder' as 'difference'

One of the core themes shared by both contributors to the online and face-to-face discussion forums was that of identifying the qualities perceived as making autistic people different to non-autistic people. This theme echoes some of the more recent research that indicates a general shift towards the construction of autism as a difference rather than a deficit (see for example Lorenz and Heinitz 2014). In our work the adoption of the discourse of neurodiversity in both the face-to-face and the online discussion groups was evident, and its central tenets reflected in (1) the way that autism was positioned and (2) the use of language when referring to non-autistic people as being 'neurotypical' (NT). For example, Robert was a contributor to the face-to-face groups and noted:

> People who come here and realise that we're, um…well, understand that we're different; we're not disabled; alright? That, um, though that's cool right?

A resistance to positioning autism as a disability was also reflected in some of the discussions in the online groups. For example, Archie said:

> I won't use the term 'disability' to describe AS… I do not feel disabled or impaired. I am not broken and I do not need to be fixed or cured. If I were to become NT, I would not be 'me' anymore, and a lot of my good qualities would disappear.

The repositioning therefore of autism in the language as a difference rather than as a deficit was a core issue that was reflected in discussions both in online and face-to-face arenas. Robert, for example, went on to clearly state this position, but in doing so he did not seek to trivialise some of the challenges that may be faced in being an autistic individual. He elaborated on his perspective of autism as follows:

> A group for people whose brains are wired differently; alright?...I mean... yeah, unless your brain is wired differently, you know, what... and no matter how it's wired differently, you don't get how seemingly simple things are really, really hard and conversely, some stuff that's really, really hard for ordinary people is pretty damn easy for us...I'd hate to be a normal person.

It can be seen from Robert's quotes that a discourse of neurodiversity is one that can be drawn on in complex ways that serve to highlight positive differences, while not negating the challenges of existing within a culture dominated by social norms determined by the NT majority.

Some of the discussions in the online forums also mirrored Robert's neurological view of autism. There were contributions to the discussion lists that defined autistic people as being a group significantly different from non-autistic people. This difference was constructed as real, and weight was again given to this position by referencing neurology. This is most strongly reflected in the choice of terminology for non-autistic people as being NT. Such presuppositions about neurological differences are evident throughout the discussions and are used to construct both individuals with autism and NTs. Abigail described her experience in terms of physiological functioning:

> The hunger is intense, and this is where the AS brain makeup can cause a lot of worry to the Aspie.

Similarly, Archie reported perceiving brain-based diversity:

> I know they are all individuals, and that we shouldn't blame every NT for the action of every other NT ... but there is a common thread that ties them together, and it is at the core of their being. It is more than cultural; it is how they are hardwired from the factory.

As can be seen, both quotes serve to highlight the perception of existing differences between the two groups of autistic and NT members, and while the quotes are from two different contributors, both appeal to neurology as the basis for justification of the constructed differences. The quotes also exemplify that such a reliance on neurological explanations is applied to both groups, with the common presupposition being the neurological origins of the exclusiveness, and thus separateness, of each group.

In addition to the adoption of an empowering position, discussions in the online forums further explored the nature of difference between 'autistics' and 'non-autistics'. Such discussions frequently highlighted the positive characteristics associated with an autistic identity and positioned these against the negative features attributed to a non-autistic identity. In doing so, the dominant view of 'normal' (i.e. non-autistic) characteristics are no longer prioritised and valued by contributors. For example, some contributors to the online discussions, while acknowledging some of the challenges faced by people with autism with respect to communication, rejected the idea that autistic communication is in some way inferior or lacking. This is reflected in contributions to the discussion lists that examine the communicative interactions of neurologically typical individuals, and position such exchanges as 'illogical'. For example, Archie wrote that:

> Humans, even NTs, possess the linguistic ability to express concepts, ideas and emotions verbally with clarity, but the NT brain seems incapable of actually doing so. They rely heavily on the animalistic means of body language. It's primitive and unnecessary, I think. Further, NTs can't seem to express thoughts completely. They use an irritating form of verbal shorthand, where significant gaps are left to be filled by the listener. It's absurd!

This quote questions some common assumptions surrounding the traits of autism and specifically the diagnostic criteria of impairments in communication and social interaction. Here the much-researched 'impairments' in social interaction commonly associated with autistic people are positioned as being a consequence of the illogical behaviour of NTs.

Academic literature discussing autism frequently refers to a spectrum of autism, and has done this for many years prior to the introduction of the DSM-5 (see for example Wing 1981). The conceptualisation of a spectrum, ranging from abilities to impairments, is a pervasive one and is reflected in contributions to the discussion groups. For example, the online groups' postings draw upon the differences proposed between the various abstract categories or points on the spectrum, such as the differences between autism, Asperger's syndrome and high functioning autism. However, at the same time participants use a series of terms inter-changeably, notably AS, HFA (high functioning autism), autism and Asperger's Syndrome. This was also something that was reflected in professional discourse, for example, in a quote by Tom, a professional:

> That brings me to Andrew, the high functioning autistic (he wasn't high functioning enough to be Asperger [sic], but was higher functioning than the severe autistics).

Distinctions are also made regarding the 'severity' of autism by conceptualising autism as being on a continuum of severity with some individuals more seriously 'affected' than others. For example, one parent, Tracy, comments:

> Our son, Andrew, is 4 and a half years old. He was diagnosed 2 months ago by his pediatrician with mild autism.

Once differences between positions on the spectrum are identified, different values are inferred for the various points. For example, in addition to the classification differences between autism and high functioning autism, there is a view expressed which suggests that high functioning autism is 'better', the child has 'moved along' the spectrum and hence become more 'normal', through exposure and interaction with 'normal' children. For example, another parent contributor to the online discussions, Natalie, commented that:

> [Y]es my son does benefit from the exposure from normal children. That is why he is now high functioning.

What is interesting about these discussions reflecting the theme *redefining 'disorder' as 'difference'* is the ability to adopt two quite contrasting positions of autism almost simultaneously. For example, focus is placed on a discourse that enables a uniquely 'autistic identity' where reference is made to neurology to strengthen claims to such a difference and the distinct nature of this from NTs. At the same time a discourse of a spectrum of difference is also invoked, positioning everyone on a spectrum, with the implication of NTs being at one end and the 'severely autistic' at the other. Kapp *et al.* (2013: 59) suggested that these apparent divergent views reflect a 'deficit-as-difference conception of autism' with nuanced neurological differences reflecting equally valid positions amongst diverse humanity.

It remains clear throughout the discussions had by both the online and the face-to-face groups that labelling was a key issue and that self-identification with a specific label was a central feature in many of the interactions. Within the autism community online there is a powerful discourse privilege through which an individual is able to embrace autism, and therefore their differences, and reject the less-valued non-autistic traits, perhaps due to a sense of control through the anonymity provided by online communication and without the associated angst of the confusing non-verbals when interacting with an NT audience (Benford 2015). Additionally, online forums comprised of autistic individuals are reported to develop a sense of shared community, providing a safe environment in which to disclose and within which to self-define an autistic culture derived from shared experiences (Brownlow and O'Dell 2006; Davidson and Henderson 2010). In such a discourse, change, as an achievable goal, is positioned as neither desirable nor necessary.

The rejection of the 'normalisation' goal as a focus of psychosocial or psychopharmacological therapeutic interventions is given weight by the construction presented of autism as a neurological difference rather than as a neurological deficit. By constructing autism as a difference, the need for a 'fix' is removed. In line with this alternative construction of difference, the goals to make people with autism more 'normal' through therapy are countered by a rejection of the desire to change and become less autistic. For example, Ronald explained:

> There is no pill to make you more social and I am not sure that I would take one if there were ...

… This medicine is mostly for behavior control. The Applied Behavior Analysis is mostly for behavior control. I don't want to pretend to be normal. I want to be me.

The perceived importance of resisting change while maintaining a positive autistic identity is further reflected in the second theme, *neurodiverse communities*.

Neurodiverse communities

Drawing on a discourse of neurodiversity enables the crafting of a positive identity by drawing on an abilities framework within which an individual's skills, rather than impairments, are highlighted. Often, however, in order to capitalise on such frameworks the ecological context needs to be one that is supportive, with a shift in thinking required by the wider society. Such shifts in thinking have implications at the individual, family and societal levels. This is particularly evident, in terms of identity making and broader negotiations of a label, within the contexts of education and employment. Previous commentators have explored the extent to which specific environments such as online discussion groups can facilitate not just a mechanism for social support, but also the possibilities for the crafting of activist positive identities (Brownlow and O'Dell, 2006; Chamak, 2008; Davidson, 2008).

The importance of having a supportive and enabling environment was something highlighted by several contributors. For example, in reflecting on the face-to-face group specifically for autistic higher education students, one contributor, Rose, discussed the importance of gaining broader acceptance for autism:

I haven't really been in an environment where I could just be ASD, just be me but also people knowing that I have [autism] and accepting it. So I think this is the first environment I've been in where people know and they accept it and it doesn't matter, and I feel like being accepted so much for all my weirdness.

Such acceptance reduced the need to 'pass' as NT or to minimise autistic traits in favour of more societally acceptable NT traits. For example, Margie said:

I think I never realised how much when I was at uni, I really tried to be normal until I came here and didn't feel like I had to be normal anymore, like, um, you guys just did a really great job of making it feel like a really safe space where we could actually say honestly what we thought and it wasn't like you were going to baby us or pamper us, like you were going to challenge us and question us, but you understood that it was hard and so you … like, I generally got a vibe that you really wanted to learn from us which is nice.

For Margie, a central importance of the A-Skills group was one of finding a 'safe place' in which to be herself and to feel respected for her strengths. This was a position echoed by Robert:

> I'll take acceptance over support any day.

For Rose, one of the benefits of being with other autistic people was one of experiential understanding and knowledge, and, in recognising this, Rose advocated for the establishment and maintenance of specific autism groups within university settings. For example, she explained:

> If I was in a room and I was the only person with ASD, I would not feel comfortable talking about my hypersensitive hearing and how painful it is and how it effects my studies and I would not feel comfortable about having to sit in the same seat as often as possible, like I would feel silly if I was the only person with ASD who was in the room … If I was the only one who had to fiddle with things … I wouldn't feel part of the group.

This stated desire for groups tailored specifically to the autistic community reflects the position that the challenges faced by autistic people are distinct, but that despite these difficulties, membership to this group was something that was considered desirable, and particularly within the confines of a safe and accepting environment, whether online or face-to-face. Here we will focus on the challenges faced by autistic people in negotiating life situations as a minority within a largely NT majority. An example of this would be managing career opportunities and the negotiation of a place in the workforce when faced with a socially demanding environment.

The management of integration into communities through tasks such as employment is something that was focused on by the discussion groups. Within the online group autistic adults posted advice for parents of autistic children regarding future educational and work environments. For example, Edward suggested:

> If you have an AC [ASD] child, you better make sure to help him or her to learn what he or she wants to learn. Getting them interested in 'meta-subjects', such as Sociology, Digital Physics, Accelerated Learning and general Computer Science could help. However, sometimes the AC children just need to know that they can get what they want, for instance, by learning to programme, and they will learn to do so willingly.

Parents are therefore encouraged by autistic adults to adopt an 'autism as difference' construction of individuals by enabling their autistic children to follow their interests. The often narrow range of interests typically identified as a problem in professional literature is thereby reconstructed as a positive asset in providing focus for individuals. Such a positive emphasis on autistic traits can lead to disbelief that people with such positive talents and abilities might be omitted from work opportunities. For example, Edward said:

> When I first heard of HFA and AS unemployment I almost didn't believe that. I thought, why would people with such unusual talents and abilities have to suffer such a fate?

Such difficulties in autistic people achieving gainful employment are attributed by contributors to workplaces being largely populated by NT's and, as a consequence, the workplace becoming an extension of the larger social domain. For example, Edward rationalised:

> With the 'New Economy' now sweeping us, the NTs had made a comeback with the 'New Age' employment tactics, including making a work place extremely sociable. This gives [autistics] an extremely troubling headache.

It could be suggested, therefore, that it is not a lack of ability that restricts employment opportunities for many autistic people, but rather the domination by NTs of the workplace and the resulting social demands. This echoes debates common to the social model of disability in which an individual is considered disabled by their 'impairment' of autism principally because of the socially demanding nature of a workplace created by NTs. Alternatively, traits typically associated with autism, such as the ability to identify detail, could be considered as valuable within a workplace and channelled accordingly into meaningful employment and lifestyle opportunities for autistic people. Areas of interest could be capitalised upon as exemplified by technological companies such as SAP, and difficulties accommodated simply and meaningfully through the introduction of computer-based tools, such as tablets and iPhones or through utilising apps in order to facilitate communication, to improve individual skills and to increase accessibility of learning (Chandler 2016; Florentine 2015; Mokashi *et al.* 2013). With adequate support people with autism may be able to apply their unique skills effectively and make significant contributions within the classroom and the workforce.

Renegotiating understandings of normative difference

Negotiating the label of autism is complex, one an individual may negotiate several times throughout their life span. Important constructions of autism are presented through clinical interventions, however, these serve largely to construct autism as a deficit rather than a difference. A renegotiation of this construction focusing on the individual differences within and between autistic people allows for an alternative understanding of autism, one grounded within a positive abilities framework. In this construction, the potential value of diversity through the inclusion of autistic people in education and employment domains is highlighted, thus allowing a position of neurodiversity to be maintained. By introducing inclusive, universal design strategies within the classroom or workplace initiatives to expand acceptance of neurodiverse persons, greater awareness of difference by the NT majority may offer increasingly safe and supportive environments to autistic individuals beyond online communities or dedicated autistic face-to-face programmes. The development of viable computer-delivered programmes and apps could provide affordable, accessible and sustainable approaches to achieving these aims (Couzens *et al.* 2015; Remy and Seaman 2014).

The constructive nature of powerful deficit discourses, such as that by professionals and clinicians, can be a challenge in the crafting of positive identities; and supportive face-to-face and online environments, both within and beyond the classroom and employment environs, may enable the facilitation of these through a privileging of a discourse of neurodiversity. For example, early research by Folstein (1999) proposed that a lack of socially acceptable communication abilities can lead to many autistic adults being under-employed relative to their measured intelligence, a premise reflected in several postings to the discussion lists contributing to the current research, and reflections in the face-to-face groups. These points are echoed by Barnard *et al.* (2001), who comments that autistic people often have little choice in where they live, the work they do and who, if anyone, cares for them. Barnard *et al.* further cite that only 19 per cent of adults in their study had access to any sort of advocacy to support them in expressing their views during decision-making around choice of care, housing and activities.

A call for research and future challenges

In adopting an abilities framework, we would argue that the skills of people with autism need to be brought to the fore and future research directions need to reflect the priorities of autistic people. A powerful avenue towards achieving this is through the deliberate and meaningful inclusion of autistic individuals within research programmes through a participatory and collaborative framework (Wright *et al.* 2014). To do so would enable a comparative 'insiders' examination of the implications and influence that the label of autism has on the construction of self-identity. It should be acknowledged that such a research methodology does not come without significant challenges. Indeed, Wright *et al.* identify the added time-intensive burden required to collaborate meaningfully between stakeholders. In considering neurodiversity as a fluid range of people with neurological strengths and challenges within and beyond autism, there is also disagreement as to the scope of eligibility criteria (Kapp *et al.* 2013). Additionally, in acknowledging the inherent social communication challenges of autism and the complex power differentials between the autistic minority and the NT majority, a level of communication scaffolding and advocacy is also required (Frauenberger 2015). Nevertheless, by including the wider views of people with autism in professional dialogues, a less negative and stigmatised construction of autism can be presented. This alternative construction of autism may lead to a more enabling vision of practice, as highlighted by Todd

(2005) wherein following the bestowment of the autism label upon an individual, the focus is shifted from professionals prescribing interventions as modalities of change and, instead, onto the individual as the self-determining co-constructor of personal support directions. Indeed, Frauenberger (2015) argues that a move from the medical deficit model in designing interactive technologies for autistic individuals towards one based on empowerment and well-being demands the direct involvement of autistic people in developing needs-based solutions. To do so requires the unequivocal participation of autistic stakeholders in order to meet user needs.

Issues of empowerment raise important questions concerning the impact of online cyber-social movements in the non-virtual world. In early online work, Seymour and Lupton (2004) question the impact of the Internet on disability politics, due to the anonymity that the online environment offers, and with it the opportunity to 'pass as non-disabled'. Seymour and Lupton propose that talking with people perceived as like-minded within cyber communities may serve to 'ghettoise' disability discussions rather than bringing them forth as a challenge to wider society. Such discussions may provide comfort and support for an individual, but they do not challenge the fundamental issues that arise in the physical world. The authors question whether the privacy awarded to such discussions risks isolating issues raised and serves, instead, to fragment the political voices of people with disabilities. Thus important issues are confined within the 'special world' of disability rather than discussed, and addressed, by society at large.

While the ghettoisation of the online voices of people with autism is a concern, this research has highlighted a strong alternative discourse surrounding autism that is drawn upon by autistic people to construct an alternative positive identity, and that this is something reflected in both online and face-to-face discussions. We would therefore argue that the boundaries between the online and face-to-face world are becoming blurred, with a carry-over effect of neurodiverse language evident across two quite distinct contexts. Contributors within both forums crafted, and identified with, a strong autistic identity, one that was frequently favourably positioned against an NT identity. In so doing, these contributors were not seeking to 'pass as non-autistic' or to appear NT; indeed, quite the opposite goal was espoused, with some contributors voicing a rejection of the dominant NT ways in favour of autistic understandings. While many of these discussions did occur between 'like-minded individuals', the collective positive acceptance of an alternative autistic identity was something shared in both on- and off-line communities. The possibilities for an individual, through the construction of a more enabling concept of autism, may provide the leverage for influencing wider society, with impacts experienced at both the educational and employment levels. The opportunities, therefore, for the formation of communities that enable discourse between like-minded autistic individuals should be prioritised and offered in a variety of formats in order to increase access and meet the needs of the autistic community at large. The development of these more positive concepts can only be further enhanced through the continued development and implementation of technology to enhance communication between autistic and NT communities, and to increase awareness and acceptance of neurodiversity in the classroom and employment environments. To ensure that such technologies are designed to provide meaningful solutions in the lives of autistic people, it is essential that stakeholders participate in the research, development and implementation stages (Frauenberger 2015). Promisingly, there is emerging research evidence pointing to discourses of neurodiversity becoming mainstreamed within professional contexts, particularly in the UK, where the use of terms such as NT are becoming more common (Runswick-Cole 2014). Such seepage of terminology, previously contained within autistic communities, suggests increasing acceptance of neurodiversity as a framework for understanding autism amongst the wider community, and may hold promise for extending similar understandings to other developmental disabilities, such as attention or learning disorders.

Conclusion

In conclusion, the impact of a discourse of neurodiversity in our research was evident in both online and face-to-face communities, highlighting the difficulties of disentangling online and face-to-face spaces. We would argue that the online world, and in particular social media, has become so pervasive in everyday interactions with the advent of technology that it is now very much part of everyday life. What does however remain key are the opportunities afforded by a particular environment for the crafting of positive identities. The operation of a supportive, accommodating, enabling environment, be it online or face-to-face, can therefore be considered crucial in key contexts such as education or the workplace in order to positively construct the abilities of difference.

Future directions

- Increased opportunities to engage autistic individuals in participatory research, thereby engaging the autistic voice and perspective as a meaningful driver of research directions.
- The continued development of technological applications and programmes tailored to support autistic people within NT environments and wider universally designed programmes to enhance understanding and acceptance of neurodiverse persons within the larger community. Importantly, focus should be maintained on evaluative research of such technologies to determine efficacy.
- An exploration of the tension between experiential and professional knowledge and the need to engage with the experiential voice, one that is all too often marginalised. This would require a broader understanding of the abilities of individuals reflected in research, among professional discourses, and within the broader community.

- A further empirical exploration of the importance of 'safe spaces', both on- and off-line, that are committed to fostering a narrative of neurodiversity with a focus on an abilities framework of autism.
- A recognition of the potential value and societal benefits involved in adopting a perspective of neurodiversity within the domains of education and employment, and how this can be achieved.

References

American Psychiatric Association (2013) *Diagnostic and statistical manual of mental disorders (5th ed.)*, Washington, DC: American Psychiatric Association.

Australian Bureau of Statistics (2014) *Autism in Australia 2012*, Canberra.

Barnard, J., Harvey, V., Potter, D., and Prior, A. (2001) *Ignored or ineligible? The reality for adults with autism spectrum disorders*, London, UK: The National Autistic Society.

Beaumont, R., Rotolone, C., and Sofronoff, K. (2015) 'The Secret Agent Society social skills program for children with high-functioning autism spectrum disorders: A comparison of two school variants', *Psychology in the Schools*, 52: 390–402.

Benford, P., and Standen, P. J. (2015) 'The internet: A comfortable communication medium for people with Asperger syndrome (AS) and high functioning autism (HFA)?', *Journal of Assistive Technologies*, 3: 44–54.

Bottema-Beutel, K., and Smith, N. (2013) 'The interactional construction of identity: An adolescent with autism in interaction with peers', *Linguistics and Education*, 24: 197–214.

Brownlow, C., and O'Dell, L. (2006) 'Constructing an autistic identity: AS voices online', *Mental Retardation*, 44: 315–321.

Chamak, B. (2008) 'Autism and social movements: French parents' associations and international autistic individuals' organisations', *Sociology of Health & Illness*, 30: 76–96.

Chandler, D. L. (2016) 'Opening new worlds for those with autism: Technology is creating great new possibilities for those on every part of the spectrum', *IEEE Pulse*, 7: 43–46.

Colman, A. (2015) *A dictionary of psychology: Oxford quick reference*, Oxford, UK: Oxford University.

Couzens, D., Poed, S., Kotaoka, M., Brandon, A., Hartley, J., and Keen, D. (2015) 'Support for students with hidden disabilities in universities: A case study', *International Journal of Disability, Development, and Education*, 62: 24–41.

Davidson, J. (2008) 'Autistic culture online: Virtual communication and cultural expression on the spectrum', *Social & Cultural Geography*, 9: 791–806.

Davidson, J., and Henderson, V. L. (2010) 'Coming out on the spectrum: Autism, identity and disclosure', *Social & Cultural Geography*, 11: 155–170.

Florentine, S. (2015) *How SAP is hiring autistic adults for tech jobs*, Available online from http://www.cio.com.au/article/590493/how-sap-hiring-autistic-adults-tech-jobs/ [10 May 2017].

Folstein, S. E. (1999) 'Autism', *International Review of Psychiatry*, 11: 269–277.

Frauenberger, C. (2015) 'Rethinking autism and technology', *Interactions*, 22: 57–59.

Fung, M., Jin, Y., Zhao, R., and Hoque, M. E. (2015) *ROC speak: Semi-automated personalized feedback on nonverbal behavior from recorded videos*, in Proceedings of the 17th International Conference on Ubiquitous Computing (Ubicomp) (pp. 1167–1178). Osaka, Japan.

Giles, D. (2014) 'DSM-V is taking away our identity: The reaction of the online community to the proposed changes in the diagnosis of Asperger's disorder', *Health*, 18: 179–195.

Kapp, S. K., Gillespie-Lynch, K., Sherman, L. E., and Hutman, T. (2013) 'Deficit, difference or both? Autism and neurodiversity', *Developmental Psychology*, 49: 59–71.

Lorenz, T. and Heinitz, K. (2014) 'Aspergers – Different, not less: Occupational strengths and job interests of individuals with Asperger's syndrome', *PLoS ONE*, 9: e100358.

Mokashi, S., Yarosh, S., and Abowd, G. D. (2013) *Exploration of videochat for children with autism*, In Proceedings of the 12th International Conference on Interaction Design and Children, New York, USA (pp. 320–323).

Neely, B. H., and Hunter, S. T. (2014) 'In a discussion on invisible disabilities, let us not lose sight of employees on the Autism Spectrum', *Industrial and Organisational Psychology*, 7: 274–277.

Orsini, M. (2012) 'Autism, neurodiversity and the welfare state: The challenges of accommodating neurological difference', *Canadian Journal of Political Science*, 45: 805–827.

Ortega, F. (2009) 'The cerebral subject and the challenge of neurodiversity', *BioSocieties*, 4: 425–445.

Remy, C., and Seaman, P. (2014) 'Evolving from disability to diversity: How to better serve high-functioning autistic students', *Reference & User Services Quarterly*, 54: 24–28.

Robertson, S. M., and Ne'eman, A. D. (2008) 'Autistic acceptance, the college campus, and technology: Growth of neurodiversity in society and academia', *Disability Studies Quarterly*, 28: online.

Runswick-Cole, K. (2014) "Us' and 'Them': The limits and possibilities of a 'politics of neurodiversity' in neoliberal times', *Disability & Society*, 29: 1117–1129.

Safran, S. P., Safran, J. S., and Ellis, K. (2003) 'Intervention ABCs for children with Asperger's syndrome', *Topics in Language Disorders*, 23: 154–165.

Sarrett, J. C. (2016) 'Biocertification and neurodiversity: The role and implications of self-diagnosis in autistic communities', *Neuroethics*, 9: 23–36.

Serna, R. W., Lobo, H. E., Fleming, R. K., Curtin, C., Foran, M. M., and Hamad, C. D. (2015) 'Innovations in behavioural intervention preparation for paraprofessionals working with children with Autism Spectrum Disorder', *Journal of Special Education*, 30: 1–12.

Seymour, W., and Lupton. D. (2004) 'Holding the line online: Exploring wired relationships for people with disabilities', *Disability & Society*, 19: 291–305.

Sheedy, C. (2016) *Autism as an asset in the workplace, Human Resources Media*, Available online from <http://www.hrmonline.com.au/section/featured/autism-in-the-workplace/?utm_source=HRM&utm_medium=e%2Dnews&utm_campaign=HRM+announcement> [4 May 2016].

Silberman, S. (2015) *Neurotribes: The legacy of autism and how to think smarter about people who think differently*, New York, NY: Penguin Random House.

Silverman, C. (2012) *Understanding autism parents, doctors, and the history of a disorder*, Princeton, NJ: Princeton University.

Spillers, J. L. H., Sensui, L. M., and Linton, K. F. (2014) 'Concerns about identity and services among people with autism and Asperger's regarding DSM-5 changes', *Journal of Social Work in Disability & Rehabilitation*, 13: 247–260.

Sturmey, P. (2012) 'Treatment of psychopathology in people with intellectual and other disabilities', *Canadian Journal of Psychiatry*, 57: 593–600.

Todd, L. (2005) 'Enabling practice for professionals: The need for practical post-structuralist theory', in D. Goodley and R. Lawthom (eds.), *Disability and psychology* Basingstoke, England: Palgrave MacMillan (pp. 141–154).

Wing, L. (1981) 'Asperger's syndrome: A clinical account', *Psychological Medicine*, 11: 115–129.

Wolfberg, P. J., McCracken, H., and Tuchel, T. (2008) 'Fostering peer play and friendships: Creating a culture of inclusion', in P. Wolfberg and K. D. Buron (eds.) *Learners on the autism spectrum: Preparing highly qualified educators*, Shawnee Missions, KS: Autism Asperger Publishing (pp. 182–207).

Wright, C. A., Wright, S. D., Diener, M. L., and Eaton, J. (2014) 'Autism spectrum disorder and the applied collaborative approach: A review of community based participatory research and participatory action research', *Journal of Autism*, 1: online.

7

TEACHING ABOUT ABILITY EXPECTATION AND ITS GOVERNANCE

The issue of STEM

Gregor Wolbring

Background

In 1853, the *New York Times* argued that power comes with the ability to obtain knowledge, and that the exclusivity of knowledge is often used to oppress the ones who lack the knowledge (Wolbring and Yumakulov 2015). Access to the right to education as a means of challenging oppression is the theme of many international documents, such as Article 26 of the UN Universal Declaration on Human Rights (UN General Assembly 1948) and Article 24 of the UN Convention on the Rights of Persons with Disabilities (United Nations 2007). Education encompasses many different aspects that address oppression and social justice issues. The United Nations Educational, Scientific and Cultural Organization (UNESCO) focuses on Education for All (EFA), Education for Sustainable Development (ESD), Education for Human Rights (EHR), Inclusive Educations (IE) and Adult Education (AE) (Burke and Wolbring 2010). Education for sustainable development remains a main aspect of the global sustainability agenda (Jucker 2011; UNESCO Conference on Education for Sustainable Development 2009), as is education for sustainable consumption (Mackay and Wolbring 2013). Citizenship education is another area that has been debated for some time (Keating *et al.* 2009; Wolbring 2012a), including a focus on active citizenship (Hoskins *et al.* 2008; Hoskins and Crick 2010).

Science, technology, engineering and mathematics (STEM) is a significant focus of education (Kuenzi 2008). STEM advancements impact on how we teach, with different impacts on different social groups (Fabry and Higgs 1997; Volman and van Eck 2001). Indeed, this book covers various scientific and technological products used to teach within educational settings. Advancements in STEM knowledge also impact on the nature of what we teach, bringing with it social consequences (for example, later in this chapter the linkage between the appearance of the first satellite, Sputnik, changes in the ability expectations of pupils and students, and the appearance of the term 'learning disability' in the USA is highlighted (Wolbring and Yumakulov 2015)).

Indeed, education can be seen as fulfilling society's changing ability expectations of others and oneself. As for the ability expectations one may have of oneself, some might cherish the ability to be competitive in sport or to be able to buy the newest phone or newest trend in clothing, others won't. Some might cherish the ability to build friendships, others won't. Some might cherish the ability to obtain a lot of money, others won't. Ability expectations people have of themselves appear endless, change often and are within a hierarchy of which ability expectations are relatively more important to themselves than others. As for the expectations others have of them, if one wants to have a job, then one has to have learned the abilities required for the given job. Consequently, the abilities one has to learn change constantly (Wolbring and Yumakulov 2015). These individual ability expectations reflect cultural and historical developments. For example, having the ability to read was not seen as essential a few hundred years ago whereas being able to use a computer is a more recent ability expectation. Ability expectations are not permanent. Learning to drive a car was not essential 150 years ago, and is likely to become a non-essential ability once more if the autonomous car comes to pass. Ability expectations are a constant societal reality impacting every aspect of life including, and profoundly impacting on, how we educate and what we teach.

The field of Ability Studies is about investigating the impact of ability expectations. The purpose of this chapter is to expose the reader to the Ability Studies field, by discussing how we teach, what we teach and whom we teach, with a special emphasis on the interrelationship between STEM and ability expectations. In this chapter, a case is made for the need to teach about the social reality and social dynamic of ability expectations, and the need to manage (govern) ability expectations people have of each other and themselves. It argues for the utility of the lens of ability expectation as a means for discussing 'the social' constructions and consequences of numerous topics, such as advancements in STEM. In developing this argument, the chapter outlines the concepts of ability expectation and ableism and the academic field of Ability Studies, and the latter's linkage and difference to Disability Studies. It examines various aspects and areas of education through an Ability Studies lens and focuses on the impact of the ability expectations associated with STEM on education. It concludes with proposing an 11-step reflexive exercise, which includes examples of various scientific and technology advancements and their linkages to ability expectations. The purpose of the proposed exercise is to facilitate the reader and others in obtaining an initial idea about the pervasiveness of ability expectations, their own role in the ability expectation reality and the need to govern ability expectations.

Ability Studies

The field of Ability Studies emerged in 2008 with the focus on investigating how ability expectation hierarchies and preferences come to pass and the impact of such hierarchies and preferences (Wolbring 2008d; Wolbring 2012b). Ability Studies allows examination of the impact of ability expectations, and actions linked to such expectations, on social relationships and lived experiences. Ability Studies is broad ranging and can encompass ability expectation dynamics between human–human, human–animal, human–nature, human–post/transhuman, human–cyborg human, human–sentient machine, animal–sentient machine and nature–sentient machine. The subarea of investigating eco-ability expectations focuses on the ecological dynamics of human–human; human–animal and human–environment relationships (Wolbring 2013).

Ability Studies draws from the concept of ableism, which was coined by the disabled people's rights movement to indicate the cultural preference for species-typical physical, mental, neuro and cognitive abilities. This preference was/is often followed by the disablement/disablism of people who are judged as lacking the 'required' physical, mental, neuro or cognitive abilities (Wolbring and Yumakulov 2015). This form of ableism is a key concept used in Disability Studies (Campbell 2009; Goodley 2014; Wolbring 2012c). However, Ability Studies extends the use of the concept of ableism, beyond how it is used within the Disability Studies field. For example:

1   Ability Studies is not limited to people we call disabled people (i.e. people experiencing discrimination due to being labelled as impaired because they do not fulfill ability expectations). Ability expectations and ableism are also used to disable other social groups. Labelling women as being unable to be rational has been used to disable women in many instances, as seen in the Suffragette movement's fight for women's right to vote (Wolbring 2008d) and the claim that women are irrational beings is still used (Wolbring and Diep 2016). Imputed differences in cognitive abilities are used to justify racism, speciesism and anti-environmentalism (Wolbring 2008d).

2   Ability Studies is not limited to investigating the judgment of physical, mental, neuro and cognitive abilities of the human body. It also covers abilities such as competitiveness, the ability to consume and the ability to be productive. It also is not limited to human–human relationships.

3   Ability Studies does not look at ability expectations and ableism as purely negative phenomena. 'Ability expectations or ableisms can have positive (enablement/enablism) and negative (disablement/disablism) consequences' (Wolbring and Yumakulov 2015: Section 2). Indeed, one could make an argument that the concept of sustainable development was generated as an 'alternative positive ability expectation of how humans are to engage with their natural environment' (Section 2) to reign in the 'ability expectation of uncontrolled consumption of natural resources' (Wolbring and Yumakulov 2015: Section 2).

Various concepts are used in Ability Studies such as ability inequity and inequality whereby *Ability inequity* (version 1) is a normative term denoting an 'unjust or unfair distribution of access to and protection from abilities generated through human interventions' (Wolbring 2010: 99). *Ability inequity* (version 2) is a normative term denoting an 'unjust or unfair judgment of abilities intrinsic to biological structures such as the human body' (Wolbring 2010: 99). *Ability inequality* (version 1) is a descriptive term denoting 'any uneven distribution of access to and protection from abilities generated through human interventions, right or wrong' (Wolbring 2010: 99). *Ability inequality* (version 2) is a descriptive term denoting 'any uneven judgment of abilities intrinsic to biological structures such as the human body, right or wrong' (Wolbring 2010: 99). Other concepts include a) ability privilege, meaning that 'one has certain advantages if exhibiting certain abilities, and individuals enjoying these advantages are unwilling to give up these advantages' (Wolbring 2014: 119); b) ability expectation oppression, meaning one is oppressed by the ability expectations of others (Wolbring and Ghai 2015); c) ability expectation governance (Wolbring 2015; Wolbring and Ghai 2015); d) ability security, meaning that one has a chance for a decent life independent of one's abilities (Wolbring 2010); e) ability discrimination, meaning that one is oppressed because one is defined by ability differences and is judged wanted; and f) ability expectation creep/creeping ableism, meaning that what abilities we expect are changing often with a tendency to expect more abilities.

To conclude this section, the below conversation, scripted within the video game *Deus Ex: Invisible War*, sums up why Ability Studies is important. It makes the point that having certain abilities allows for people to have power and, furthermore, that influencing what is seen as an essential ability is a form of power. Essentially it makes the case that we need to govern ability expectations.

Conversation between Alex D and Paul Denton

Paul Denton: If you want to even out the social order, you have to change the nature of power itself. Right? And what creates power? Wealth, physical strength, legislation – maybe – but none of those is the root principle of power.

Alex D: I'm listening.

Paul Denton: Ability is the ideal that drives the modern state. It's a synonym for one's worth, one's social reach, one's 'election', in the Biblical sense, and it's the ideal that needs to be changed if people are to begin living as equals.

Alex D: And you think you can equalise humanity with biomodification?

Paul Denton: The commodification of ability – tuition, of course, but, increasingly, genetic treatments, cybernetic protocols, now biomods – has had the side effect of creating a self-perpetuating aristocracy in all advanced societies. *When ability becomes a public resource, what will distinguish people will be what they do with it.* [author's emphasis] Intention. Dedication. Integrity. The qualities we would choose as the bedrock of the social order. (*Deus ex: Invisible war (Wikiquote)*).

Ability expectations and education

Ableism as it relates to disabled people has been identified within the education system by many people, especially Disability Studies scholars (Biermann 2015; Hehir 2002; Hutcheon and Wolbring 2012; Kattari 2015; Wolbring and Yumakulov 2015). Some have used the ableism lens to question both inclusive education (Runswick-Cole 2011) and segregated education (Ferri and Connor 2005) and to highlight the move to online courses (Sutton 2016). Researchers have also used the ableism lens to identify how to teach about ableism (Lalvani and Broderick 2013; Livingston 2000) and to teach Disability Studies in general (Chinn 2016; Geurts and Hansen 2016; McKinney 2016; Woiak and Lang 2016).

However from an Ability Studies perspective, education-related ability expectations and forms of ableism are not only evident in regards to disabled people but ability expectations and forms of ableism are a general aspect of the education system. Education is one means through which one can obtain numerous abilities. Because ability expectations of people and by people constantly change (ableism creep/creeping ableism), education is seen as essential not only for children but also for adults (see UNESCO's work on adult learning, for example). Furthermore, one does not only obtain certain abilities through education in general, but educating people on certain topics such as sustainable development and citizenship education are also often linked to ability expectations.

According to UNESCO, education for sustainable development (ESD) is essential for sustainability to succeed. Within its list of requirements for education for sustainable development are various ability expectations of students (ST), teachers (TE) and the education system (ES). These include the ability to partake in participatory learning (ST) and to be able to exhibit higher-order thinking skills (ST); the ability to recognize what is locally relevant and culturally appropriate and which local needs could have an impact on international affairs (globalization) (TE, ES); the ability to provide lifelong learning opportunities (ES) and the ability to provide formal, non-formal and informal education (ES); the ability to be up to speed on the evolving nature of the concept of sustainability (TE); the ability to address content, taking into account context, global issues and local priorities (TE, ES); the development of the civil ability for community-based decision-making, social tolerance, environmental stewardship (ST, ES, TE), an adaptable workforce (ST, TE, ES); and the ability to be interdisciplinary (ST, TE, ES) (UNESCO 2013). Various other ability expectations in the discourse of education for sustainable development, such as ability expectations from teachers and students in secondary and higher education, are also evident. Ability expectations are also evident within the education for sustainable development framework under the header of indicators and competencies/skills. For example, a study concerning environmental education and education for sustainable development in the Swiss school system lists over 25 skills (abilities), 16 values (that often ask for the ability to act on them), 12 abilities we should do and experience and over 37 topics of knowledge one should have the ability to learn about (Jucker 2011, cited in Wolbring and Burke 2013). So far 'no consensus has been reached within ESD discourses as to the process of how to identify essential abilities and as to (a) which abilities should be taught through ESD, (b) which abilities are needed to teach ESD and (c) which abilities are needed to learn from ESD' (Wolbring and Burke 2013: 2327). For example, no consensus exists around whether competitiveness is an important ability to have or not. A debate is ongoing as to whether education for sustainable development covers enough or too much of the social or environmental aspects of sustainable development and whether it is too anthropocentric (human-centred) or not adequately eco-centered (Wolbring and Burke 2013). From an eco-ableism perspective, anthropocentric versus eco-centric approaches engender different ability expectations that humans could have of nature (Wolbring 2013).

Another area that explicitly asks the education system and its teachers to generate certain abilities in its students is the area of citizenship education:

The CRELL Research Network on Active Citizenship for Democracy has proposed the following detailed list of knowledge, skills, attitudes and values necessary for active citizenship:

- Knowledge: human rights and responsibilities, political literacy, historical knowledge, current affairs, diversity, cultural heritage, legal matters and how to influence policy and society.
- Skills: conflict resolution, intercultural competence, informed decision-making, creativity, ability to influence society and policy, research capability, advocacy, autonomy/agency, critical reflection, communication, debating skills, active listening, problem solving, coping with ambiguity, working with others, assessing risk.
- Attitudes: political trust, political interest, political efficacy, autonomy and independence, resilience, cultural appreciation, respect for other cultures, openness to change/difference of opinion, responsibility and openness to involvement as active citizens, influencing society and policy.
- Values: human rights, democracy, gender equality, sustainability, peace/non-violence, fairness and equity, valuing involvement as active citizens.
- Identity: sense of personal identity, sense of community identity, sense of national identity, sense of global identity.

(Wolbring 2012a: 152)

What can be said from all the various lists is that civic competence is a complex mix of knowledge, skills, understanding, values and attitudes and dispositions, and requires a sense of identity and agency (Hoskins and Crick 2010: 126).

In total, they selected 61 indicators for their composite indicator of active citizenship (Hoskins and Mascherini 2009).

The above is, in essence, a list of ability expectations: skills are abilities; expectation of knowledge requires the ability to obtain knowledge; the values that are listed require the ability to generate such a value for oneself and also have the ability to develop all the stated identities.

Ability Expectations and STEM

Ability expectations and STEM are linked in various ways. One way is whether and how disabled people are part of STEM education (Jenson *et al.* 2011; Leddy 2010). Some other ways are a) STEM advancements impacting on existing ability expectations; b) Existing ability expectations impacting on STEM advancements; c) STEM advancements enabling the generation of new ability expectations; d) STEM education impacting on ability expectations; and e) ability expectations impacting on STEM education.

The Sputnik example (Sleeter 1998) illustrates how existing ability expectations were impacted by STEM advancements, which in turn led to STEM advancements that did impact on STEM education and ability expectations. Sleeter argues that the appearance of the term 'learning disability' was a consequence of the U.S. government changing STEM education requirements in schools after Russia launched the satellite *Sputnik* (Sleeter 1986, 1987, 1998). This change led to various children, previously seen as having 'normal' ability, not being able to fulfill the new STEM requirements. The case has been made that the ability expectation of the U.S. of being 'number one' and the ability expectation of competitiveness might have contributed to the U.S. changing their STEM education requirements in schools in responses to the launch of *Sputnik* (Wolbring and Yumakulov 2015). Not being competitive is also used as an argument to push for more STEM education in other countries, such as the United Kingdom (British Ecology Society 2012).

STEM-enabled human enhancement and ability expectations

Human enhancement is one example of STEM advancements enabling the generation of new ability expectations. The ever increasing ability to generate human body enhancement products in many shapes and forms enables a culture of, demand for and acceptance of improving and modifying the human body (structure, function, abilities) beyond its species-typical boundaries (Ball and Wolbring 2014; Sparrow 2010; Wolbring 2008a, 2008d, 2012b; Wolbring and Diep 2016). The increasing availability of enhancement enabling products allows for an ability expectation creep, whereby ability enhancements enabled by STEM become the new ability expectation, whereby people will experience disablism because they are not enhanced (Wolbring 2006, 2008c, 2008d, 2010).

Human enhancement is also an example of ability expectations influencing STEM advancements. People's ability expectations are one driver for the advancement of STEM-enabled enhancement products. According to the summary report of an invitational workshop called *Good, Better, Best: The Human Quest for Enhancement* convened by the Scientific Freedom, Responsibility and Law Program of the American Association for the Advancement of Science, 'polls indicate that personal interest in or aversion to using human enhancement technologies depends on one's perceived social status, and how human enhancement would affect his/her competitive advantage' (Williams 2006: iii). The report highlighted the following pressures leading to rapid development of human enhancement technologies: 1) global competitiveness; 2) brain drain/depopulation economics; 3) national security concerns; and 4) quality of life/consumer lifestyle demands (Williams 2006). The report *Converging technologies for improving human performance: Nanotechnology, biotechnology, information technology and cognitive science* (Members of the 2001 NBIC conference 2003) mentioned the ability expectation of productivity over 60 times, the ability expectation of efficiency 54 times and the ability expectation of competitiveness 29 times (Wolbring 2008d).

A lively discussion exists around cognitive enhancements. A 2008 poll showed that 79 percent of the respondents felt that healthy people should be allowed to take cognitive enhancers and one-third of respondents said they would feel pressure to give cognition-enhancing drugs to their children (Maher 2008). Some parents of children labelled as cognitively impaired report feeling that the increasing availability of cognitive enhancers would put more pressure on themselves and their children (Ball and Wolbring 2014).

STEM-enabled enhancement advancements also impact on human–nature relationships. Within the article on human engineering and climate change:

> the authors propose human engineering that has the end goal of changing bodily abilities to enable them to fight the impacts of climate change. The authors propose that human engineering is a potentially necessary alternative to geo-engineering because they believe that efforts to change the ability expectations of humans (for example modifying aspirations towards consumerism through educational programs) is not working and geo-engineering might be too dangerous.
>
> *(Wolbring 2013: 100–101)*

STEM-enabled enhancement advancements also impact human–animal relationships. It has been suggested that cognitively enhancing animals to the level of greater sentience could be used as a means to fight speciesism, the negative treatment of, for example, animals by humans (Chan 2009).

Robots and ability expectations

Robots are one example of the impact on humans by STEM developments influenced by ability expectations. There are currently three types of robots: industrial robots, service robots and social robots, all of which have a potential impact on the abilities of humans to obtain employment, and consequently some 'human jobs' requiring particular abilities are seen to be in more danger of being taken over by robots than others (Wolbring 2016). Industrial robots, such as those being used on the car manufacturing assembly line, are the first type of robot deployed with the ability expectation to replace workers, but these are not the only ones. A 2016 BBC News item highlighted that Apple and Samsung supplier Foxconn had replaced 60,000 factory workers with robots (Wakefield 2016). Industrial robots are envisioned to have abilities that surpass humans and give companies the ability to save money as the robot is seen as cheaper than the human worker. Using the Ability Studies lens reveals how humans are increasingly in an ability competition with robots. Industrial robots are the furthest ahead in terms of replacing humans, but there are other robot types that are not far behind. Service robots are a class of robots being developed to compete with humans based on other abilities than those of industrial robots. These robots are envisioned as not only running hotels but also as replacing jobs such as recreational therapists.

Finally, the most recent developments are social robots. Social robots are complex machines that are envisioned to engage in meaningful, social and emotional interactions with humans and also with each other (Yumakulov *et al.* 2012a). Consequently, social robots gain abilities allowing them to compete with humans based on abilities that are different to those of service or industrial robots.

The developments within robotics have at least three ability expectation impacts on education. The first is that it is not clear what abilities one should still teach in schools in the immediate future. One argument is that the only safe jobs will be those based on cognitive abilities. However, in reality not everyone is cognitive-able to a level where they will outperform robots or where their jobs will not be seen as a target for robots. So, the ensuing development around robotics makes it essential that people obtain novel abilities, which are not able to be mimicked by robots. These developments are even more problematic for people labelled as cognitive impaired (Wolbring 2016).

Another impact is the envisioned educational use of social robots, for example, in the education of disabled people (Diep *et al.* 2015; Wolbring and Ghai 2015). Indeed, robots have been proposed as replacing special education aides and special education teachers in classes. Whilst special education teachers may think they are not replaceable because they believe that the emotional ability needed to connect to 'special education' students cannot be taken over by robots (Diep *et al.* 2015), the social robotics research literature sees robots developing the abilities to take over jobs requiring emotional interactive abilities.

A third impact is that the robotic discourse constructs a purely medicalized portrayal of disabled people, where disability equates to a biological deficit (Yumakulov *et al.* 2012b). This way of thinking goes against teaching strategies that focus on the social aspect of disablism and teaching strategies that try to decrease stigmas, stereotyping and 'otherism' (Chinn 2016; Geurts and Hansen 2016; Lalvani and Broderick 2013; Livingston 2000; McKinney 2016; Woiak and Lang 2016).

The Star Trek food replicator and ability expectations

Technology can transform human interactions with natural resources. The food replicator in *Star Trek* films where one says, for example, 'Coffee' and the machine builds a cup of coffee, synthesizing the beverage molecule by molecule (Wolbring 2008b), if it comes into existence, would change how we deal with natural resources and it could eliminate the need to grow food changing the landscape of many human endeavors. Not needing agriculture anymore will disrupt severely how humans interact. The field of molecular manufacturing is the science behind the vision of the food replicator. It focuses on designing, creating and building non-living matter by adding one atom to another atom (Wolbring 2008b). The term 'nanotechnology' was originally used to describe the manufacturing from atomic molecules by Richard Feynman (Feynman 1959); however, we use nanotechnology nowadays to indicate nanoscale processes and the original meaning of nanotechnology is now covered by molecular manufacturing. We are not there yet. However we have 3D printing of food which by itself is seen to have disruptive effects (Godoi *et al.* 2016; Lupton 2016), albeit effects that are different from those predicted for food replicators. Nanotechnology in its new meaning of nanoscale also is seen to impact the food industry and those who work in it.

> A recent OECD and Allianz report stated: Nanotechnology will not only change how every step of the food chain operates but also who is involved. At stake is the world's $3 trillion food retail market, agricultural export markets valued at $544 billion, the livelihoods of farmers and the well-being of the rest of us. Converging technologies could reinvigorate the battered agrochemical and agbiotech industries, possibly igniting a still more intense debate – this time over "atomically-modified" foods.
>
> *(Lauterwasser 2005: 17)*

This future change and its potential impact on the agricultural landscape can already be sensed in the creation of In-vitro-meat, where meat is grown from stem cells in an incubator (Hocquette 2016).

The examples of robots and food are given to illustrate the impact of STEM on occupation and the ability expectations linked to being able to work. Indeed, STEM has always had an impact on work. For example, the term Luddite came from English nineteenth-century weavers and textile workers who rioted, unsuccessfully, against their replacement by weaving machinery. But the scope and scale of how many jobs might be up for elimination as a consequence of modern STEM seems to be increasing and highlights the question of who is retraining whom in what new abilities.

Ability expectation governance

The European Parliament's Human Enhancement Study (2009) states:

> New human enhancement technologies and trends provide opportunities for individuals and for society. They also pose new risks and tend to create new needs and social demands. This tendency in itself puts a strain on solidarity and healthcare systems. The issues touch upon matters that are relevant at EU level, such as health budgets, research policies, and economic issues. Differences among member states will probably lead to tensions in the

future. In addition to interventions by nation states, EU policies will have to address these issues. Currently however, the EU has no platform for monitoring and discussing human enhancement issues. Arenas are lacking where the normative issues can be politically deliberated and the gap between the needs and the concerns of the broader public and the practitioners and experts bridged.

(Coenen et al. 2009: 142)

Many different governance discourses exist for scientific and technological innovation (e.g. democratizing science, anticipatory governance, responsible research and innovation, upstream engagement, participatory technology assessment). However, none have focused explicitly on ability expectation governance, and the phrase 'ability expectation governance' is not present in these governance discourses. Ability expectations play themselves out in various ways around governance issues, such as who has the power to push one's ability expectations or which ability expectations are discussed in which way if at all. Furthermore, another key ability expectation issue is that a person needs to have certain abilities to even partake in governance discourses. One needs particular knowledge to be part of governance discourses and the time and resources to obtain this knowledge. Marginalized groups who fight daily for survival often do not have the ability to obtain the knowledge and, as such, can't influence the governance discourse in a meaningful manner (Wolbring 2015; Wolbring and Diep 2016).

The social reality and social dynamic of ability expectations, as outlined by examples in this chapter and ability expectation governance, are also not a focus of education efforts. To illustrate how this type of education might raise awareness of these issues, this chapter concludes with an 11-step teaching exercise, designed to introduce ability expectations to learners.

Teaching ability expectations

Ability expectations are so pervasive that people will often not realize that is what drives them. The following is a suggestion for a set of exercises one could use in classes and elsewhere to make students and others realize how pervasive ability expectations are and the consequences of not engaging with ability expectation governance. These 11 exercises are envisioned to facilitate broad 'I see' experiences with regards to ability expectations.

Exercise 1

The exercise can start by asking the participants to list their top ten most cherished abilities.

This exercise will very likely generate a list of a variety of abilities, some directly linked to the body, such as hearing and seeing, and others not linked to the body, such as the ability to maintain friendships. If the initial list of ten abilities generates too many body-linked abilities, one can ask in a second round for abilities not linked to the body.

In a third round the following question can be asked, 'Which abilities do you assume you have without even thinking about it?' Based on the result one can point out some abilities the students or others might take for granted, such as the ability to have access to clean water, which is of course not a given for many people globally even in high-income countries, or access to a washroom (this is a topical issue globally with regard to both access to washrooms for disabled people and the transgender washroom discussion currently taking place). But one can use anything here as an example of what students or others might take for granted.

Then the question can be asked again to see what other abilities the students or others can now think of as a given.

The list of ability expectations of Exercise 1 can be collected and listed in order of decreasing frequency.

At the end of Exercise 1 one can have a discussion about: why the students or others consider certain abilities as more important than others (body and non-body related); whether they think that members of social groups other than those represented in class would generate a different top ten list; whether governments would have a different list; why they took certain abilities for granted.

Exercise 2

Once the list is generated, the students or others can be asked how they, others and society would perceive a person who does not have a given ability that the students or others just generated (starting with the most frequently mentioned ability).

The aim is to elicit an awareness that students or others might have different answers for different abilities; for example, for some abilities they might not view a person without the ability differently, for some it might change how they view the person (sad, let's do something about it, don't want to socialize with that person …).

Exercise 3

In Exercise 3 the concepts of hunter–gatherer societies, agrarian societies, industrial societies and knowledge-based societies can be introduced. The students can be asked to consider what abilities would be cherished in any of these societies.

This activity is designed to elicit societies that cherish different abilities. A hunter/gatherer society cherishes different personal abilities than an agrarian society, an industrial society or a knowledge-based society; for example, 'an agrarian society would require less of an ability to learn how to use weapons for hunting but would require that one learns skills essential for farming, such as how to use planting tools and learn about seeds' (Wolbring and Yumakulov 2015: Section 4).

This discussion can then be debated in relation to a global reality where each of these societies exist today somewhere on Earth and what this means for a global understanding of ability expectations.

Exercise 4

In Exercise 4 the questions can focus on why one is attending a university (or enrolled in a particular course of study) and which abilities participants assume they will gain from this. A discussion can then be facilitated about skills that may not be gained at their university or from their course of study (such as particular vocational skills), and whether these skills are considered less worthy.

Exercise 5

In Exercise 5 students or others can be asked 'what missing abilities would make you see a person as impaired or disabled?' The participants, opinions can lead to a consideration of the language they use. For example, if their discussion suggests that they feel that a person with individualized deficits should be 'fixed', they can be advised to use the term 'impairment'. If they see a person being 'fixed' by changes in the social structure, then they will be advised to use the term 'disabled'.

Exercise 6

In Exercise 6 participants can be asked about how they think sexism and racism are justified. The discussion can aim to elicit the idea that abilities are used to justify sexism and racism. If this does not occur, then content related to those aspects can be provided and discussed.

Exercise 7

Exercise 7 can focus on the abilities required for being an active citizen. Participants can be asked whether they think they have the essential abilities for being active citizens. They can then be given the following list (Hoskins and Crick 2010; Hoskins and Mascherini 2009) and discuss what these abilities mean for their own ability to be active citizens in a democracy.
   Do you have the ability:
   of political literacy,
   of conflict resolution,
   of intercultural competence,
   of informed decision-making,
   of creativity,
   to influence society and policy,
   of research,
   of advocacy,
   of being autonomous/being your own agent,
   of critical reflection,
   of communication,
   of debating skills,

of active listening,
of problem solving,
of coping with ambiguity,
of working with others,
of assessing risk,
of political trust,
of political interest,
of resilience,
of cultural appreciation,
of respect for other cultures,
to be open to change/difference of opinion,
to influence society and policy?
Do you know enough to have an informed ability to value:
human rights,
democracy,
gender equality,
sustainability,
peace/non-violence,
fairness and equity?

After this review it can be revealed that *all* of these have previously been stated as indicators of being an active citizen. A discussion can be facilitated after that on whether those people not having all these abilities could be seen as impaired.

The rest of the exercises cover various aspects of science, technology and innovation.

Exercise 8 Assistive technology

This exercise can start by asking participants about what they think an assistive device/assistive technology is.

The rationale for this exercise is that assistive technology is typically debated within a medical framework and people often do not think that everyone uses assistive devices (public transportation, car, wheelchair, shoes, dishwasher, airplane...). The answers should allow for a discussion concerning ability expectations of the body and which ability shortfalls can (or can't) be seen as impairments because they require assistive devices. The discussion should also allow for a consideration of social status hierarchies of assistive devices, which is likely to include the negative labelling of some assistive devices (confined to the wheelchair) but not others (car, airplane...).

Exercise 9 Robot

Exercise 9 can focus on the human–robot relationships and the issue of humans being 'out-abled' in different spheres of their life.

Participants can be asked to consider the following questions:

Which abilities should a robot have? Why?

Which abilities should a robot not have? Why?

What should happen if a robot out-ables you?

These questions should allow for a solid discussion of ability expectations from the angle of humans are being out-abled and what that means, in relation to the politics of impairment and disablement.

Exercise10 Eco-ableism/Geoengineering

In this exercise participants consider the relationship between ability expectations and the natural world. Participant discussion is prompted with the following questions:

What is the purpose of nature for humans?

What is the relationship between humans and nature?

Should humans expect anything from nature? If yes, what? If no, why?

What abilities are enabled by nature?

What ability expectations of humans enable/disable nature?

If humans have to change abilities in order to deal with changes in the environment, what should happen?

The ability issues that this discussion might engender can include:

Humans should change their ability expectations of how they live (e.g. level of consumption, what is consumed).

Humans should change the ability of nature to cope with human behaviour (geo-engineering).

Humans should modify their body to cope with environmental changes (human enhancement).

These questions and issues can be used as a basis for reflecting on ability expectation assumptions and the different 'solutions' that arise from them.

Exercise 11 Governance

Exercise 11 is intended to provoke participants to examine their own abilities in relation to those required to take part in governance discourses.

Do you think it is necessary for you to be part of governance discourses? If yes, why? If not, why not?

What abilities do you think you need in order to be part of governance discourses?

How would you obtain these abilities?

From whom would you obtain these abilities?

Answering these questions should allow the discussion to unearth what abilities we assume people should have to be part of, for example, science and technology discourses.

Future directions and conclusion

It is hoped that this chapter has enticed the reader to look at the world through the lens of ability expectations and engage with the concept of ability expectation governance. It is also hoped that this article might spark an interest in using ability expectations and its governance as a lens in the education system to facilitate broader systemic thinking about ability issues, and decrease the other-isms (such as disabled people and others seen as ability deficient versus the other) that result from a negative use of ability expectations. The reconceptualization that the Ability Studies framework allows creates a new community of practice, bringing together people and ideas from diverse areas. This community will be well placed to address the constantly changing challenges of societal ability expectations in a sustainable way.

References

Ball, N., and Wolbring, G. (2014) 'Cognitive enhancement: Perceptions among parents of children with disabilities', *Neuroethics*, Available online from: http://link.springer.com/article/10.1007/s12152-014-9201-8 [17 March 2017].

Biermann, J. (2015) 'Dimensions of ableism: educational and developmental ability-expectations', *Zeitschrift für Inklusion*, Available online from: www.inklusion-online.net/index.php/inklusion-online/article/view/271/254%20-%20Zugriff:28.06.2015 [17 March 2017].

British Ecology Society (2012) *Government must boost STEM skills for UK competitiveness*, Available online from: /www.britishecologicalsociety.org/blog/2012/07/24/government-must-boost-stem-skills-for-uk-competitiveness/ [viewed 17 March 2017].

Burke, B., and Wolbring, G. (2010) 'Beyond education for all: Using ableism studies lens and the BIAS FREE framework', *Development*, 53: 535–539.

Campbell, F. K. (2009) *Contours of ableism*, Palgrave Macmillan Basingstoke.

Chan, S. (2009) 'Should we enhance animals?', *Journal of Medical Ethics*, 35: 678–683.

Chinn, S. E. (2016) 'Teaching crip; or, what we talk about when we talk about disability pedagogy', *Transformations: The Journal of Inclusive Scholarship and Pedagogy*, 25: 15–19.

Coenen, C. *et al.* (2009) *Human Enhancement Study*, Available online from: http://www.europarl.europa.eu/RegData/etudes/etudes/join/2009/417483/IPOL-JOIN_ET(2009)417483_EN.pdf [viewed 17 March 2017].

Diep, L., Cabibihan, J.-J., and Wolbring, G. (2015) Social Robots: Views of special education teachers. ed. *Proceedings of the 3rd 2015 Workshop on ICTs for Improving Patients Rehabilitation Research Techniques*, 160–163.

Fabry, D. L., and Higgs, J. R. (1997) 'Barriers to the effective use of technology in education: Current status', *Journal of Educational Computing Research*, 17: 385–395.

Ferri, B. A., and Connor, D. J. (2005) 'Tools of exclusion: Race, disability, and (re)segregated education', *Teachers College Record*, 107: 453–474.

Feynman, R. (1959) *Plenty of Room at the Bottom*, Available online from https://pdfs.semanticscholar.org/1bc8/21e55e3b381eaba62bb02c861b9cb5273309.pdf [viewed 17 March 2017].

Geurts, K. L., and Hansen, J. (2016) 'Shifting students' imaginings of disability', *Transformations: The Journal of Inclusive Scholarship and Pedagogy*, 25: 183–188.

Godoi, F. C., Prakash, S., and Bhandari, B. R. (2016) '3d printing technologies applied for food design: Status and prospects', *Journal of Food Engineering*, 179: 44–54.

Goodley, D. (2014) *Dis/ability studies: Theorising disablism and ableism*, London and New York: Routledge.

Hehir, T. (2002) 'Eliminating ableism in education', *Harvard Educational Review*, 72: 1–32.

Hocquette, J.-F. (2016) 'Is in vitro meat the solution for the future?', *Meat Science*, 120: 167–176.

Hoskins, B., and Crick, R. D. (2010) 'Competences for learning to learn and active citizenship: Different currencies or two sides of the same coin?', *European Journal of Education*, 45: 121–137.

Hoskins, B. L., and Mascherini, M. (2009) 'Measuring active citizenship through the development of a composite indicator', *Social Indicators Research*, 90: 459–488.

Hoskins, B., d'Hombres, B., and Campbell, J. (2008) 'Does formal education have an impact on active citizenship behaviour?', *European Educational Research Journal*, 7: 386–402.

Hutcheon, E. J., and Wolbring, G. (2012) 'Voices of disabled post secondary students: Examining higher education disability policy using an ableism lens', *Journal of Diversity in Higher Education*, 5: 39–49.

Jenson, R. J., *et al.* (2011) 'Perceptions of self-efficacy among STEM Students with disabilities', *Journal of Postsecondary Education and Disability*, 24: 269–283.

Jucker, R. (2011) 'ESD between systemic change and bureaucratic obfuscation: Some reflections on environmental education and education for sustainable development in Switzerland', *Journal of Education for Sustainable Development*, 5: 39–60.

Kattari, S. K. (2015) 'Examining ableism in higher education through social dominance theory and social learning theory', *Innovative Higher Education*, 40: 375–386.

Keating, A., Ortloff, D. H., and Philippou, S. (2009) 'Citizenship education curricula: The changes and challenges presented by global and European integration', *Journal of Curriculum Studies*, 41: 145–158.

Kuenzi, J. J. (2008) *Science, technology, engineering, and mathematics (stem) education: Background, federal policy, and legislative action*, Available online from; http://digitalcommons.unl.edu/cgi/viewcontent.cgi?article=1034&context=crsdocs [viewed 17 March 2017].

Lalvani, P., and Broderick, A. A. (2013) 'Institutionalized ableism and the misguided "Disability Awareness Day"': Transformative pedagogies for teducation', *Equity & Excellence in Education*, 46: 468–483.

Lauterwasser, C. (2005) *Small sizes that matter: Opportunities and risks of nanotechnologies Report in co-operation with the OECD International Futures Programme*, Available online from: www.temas.ch/IMPART/IMPARTProj.nsf/6558781FF02F2AEBC125736400410F1E/$FILE/Allianz_study_nanotechnology_engl.pdf?OpenElement&enetarea=02 [viewed 17 March 2017].

Leddy, M. H. (2010) 'Technology to advance high school and undergraduate students with disabilities in science, technology, engineering, and mathematics', *Journal of Special Education Technology*, 25: 3–8.

Livingston, K. (2000) 'When architecture disables: Teaching undergraduates to perceive ableism in the built environment', *Teaching Sociology*, 28: 182-191.

Lupton, D. (2016) *'Both fascinating and disturbing': Consumer responses to 3D food printing and implications for food activism*, Available online from; https://papers.ssrn.com/sol3/papers.cfm?abstract_id=2799191 [viewed 17 March 2017].

Mackay, R., and Wolbring, G. (2013) Sustainable consumption of healthcare: Linking sustainable consumption with sustainable healthcare and health consumer discourses. ed. *3rd World Forum on Sustainability*, online.

McKinney, C. (2016) 'Cripping the classroom: Disability as a teaching method in the umanities', *Transformations: The Journal of Inclusive Scholarship and Pedagogy*, 25: 114–127.

Maher, B. (2008) 'Poll results: Look who's doping', *Nature*, 452: 674–675.

Members of the 2001 NBIC conference (2003) *Converging technologies for improving human performance: Nanotechnology, biotechnology, information technology and cognitive science*, Available online from: http://www.wtec.org/ConvergingTechnologies/Report/NBIC_report. pdf [viewed 17 March 2017].

Runswick-Cole, K. (2011) 'Time to end the bias towards inclusive education?', *British Journal of Special Education*, 38: 112–119.

Sleeter, C. E. (1986) 'Learning disabilities: The social construction of a special education category', *Exceptional Children*, 53: 46–54.

Sleeter, C. E. (1987) 'Why is there learning disabilities? A critical analysis of the birth of the field in its social context.', in: T. S. Popkewitz ed. *The foundations of the school subjects*, London: Palmer Press, (pp. 210–237).

Sleeter, C. E. (1998) 'Yes, learning disability is political; What isn't?', *Learning Disability Quarterly*, 21: 289–296.

Sparrow, R. (2010) 'A not-so-new eugenics: Harris and Savulescu on human enhancement', *Asian Bioethics Review*, 2

Sutton, H. (2016) 'Study finds increase in online graduate programs due to traditional classroom ableism', *Disability Compliance for Higher Education*, 21: 9-9.

UN General Assembly (1948) *Universal declaration of human rights*, Available online from: http://www.un.org/en/universal-declaration-human-rights/ [viewed 17 March 2017].

UNESCO (2013) *Education for sustainable development*, Available online from: http://unesdoc. unesco.org/images/0021/002163/216383e.pdf [viewed 17 March 2017].

UNESCO Conference on Education for Sustainable Development (2009) *Bonn Declaration on Education for Sustainable Development*, Available online from: http://unesdoc.unesco. org/images/0018/001887/188799e.pdf [viewed 17 March 2017].

United Nations (2007) *Convention on the rights of persons with disabilities*, Available online from: /www.un.org/disabilities/convention/conventionfull.shtml [viewed 17 March 2017].

Volman, M., and van Eck, E. (2001) 'Gender equity and information technology in education: The second decade', *Review of Educational Research*, 71: 613–634.

Wakefield, J. (2016) *Foxconn replaces '60,000 factory workers with robots'*, Available online from: http://www.bbc.com/news/technology-36376966 [viewed 17 March 2017].

Wikiquote *Deus ex: Invisible war*, Available online from: http://en.wikiquote.org/wiki/ Deus_Ex:_Invisible_War [viewed 17March 2017].

Williams, A. E. (2006) *Good, better, best: The human quest for enhancement Summary report of an invitational workshop convened by the Scientific Freedom, Responsibility and Law Program American Association for the Advancement of Science 1–2 June 2006*, Available online from: http://www.aaas.org/sites/default/files/migrate/uploads/HESummaryReport1.pdf [viewed 17 March 2017].

Woiak, J., and Lang, D. (2016) 'Theory meets practice in an introduction to disability studies course', *Transformations: The Journal of Inclusive Scholarship and Pedagogy*, 25: 96–113.

Wolbring, G. (2006) 'The unenhanced underclass', in J. M. P. Wilsdon (ed.) *Better humans? The politics of human enhancement*, London, UK: Demos Institute (pp. 122–129).

Wolbring, G. (2008a) 'Ableism, enhancement medicine and the techno poor disabled', in P. Healey and S. Rayner (eds.) *Unnatural selection: The challenges of engineering tomorrow's people*, Earthscan, (pp. 196–208).

Wolbring, G. (2008b) 'Lego atoms and base pairs', in T. Caulfield and S. Caulfield (eds.) *Imagining science art, science, and social change*. Edmonton, Alberta, Canada: University of Alberat Press, (pp. 84–91).

Wolbring, G. (2008c) 'The politics of ableism', *Development*, 51: 252–258.

Wolbring, G. (2008d) 'Why NBIC? Why human performance enhancement?', *Innovation; The European Journal of Social Science Research*, 21: 25–40.

Wolbring, G. (2010) 'Ableism and favoritism for abilities governance, ethics and studies: New tools for nanoscale and nanoscale enabled science and technology governance', *in*

S. Cozzens and J. M. Wetmore (eds.) *The yearbook of nanotechnology in Society, vol. II: The challenges of equity and equality.* New York: Springer, (pp. 89–104).

Wolbring, G. (2012a) 'Citizenship education through an ability expectation and "ableism" lens: The challenge of science and technology and disabled people', *Education Sciences*, 2: 150–164.

Wolbring, G. (2012b) 'Ethical theories and discourses through an ability expectations and ableism lens: The case of enhancement and global regulation', *Asian Bioethics Review*, 4: 293–309.

Wolbring, G. (2012c) 'Expanding ableism: Taking down the ghettoization of impact of disability studies scholars', *Societies*, 2: 75–83.

Wolbring, G. (2013) 'Ecohealth through an ability studies and disability studies lens' in M. K. Gislason ed. *Ecological Health: Society, Ecology and Health.* London, UK: Emerald (pp. 91–107).

Wolbring, G. (2014) 'Ability privilege: A needed addition to privilege studies', *Journal for Critical Animal Studies*, 12: 118–141.

Wolbring, G. (2015) Human enhancement verlangt die Auseinandersetzung mit Fähigkeitserwartungen in special issue "Schwerpunkt// Der optimierte Mensch The English version Human enhancement: The need for ability expectation governance available *Soziale Sicherheit CHSS» Social Security, Journal of the Federal Social Insurance Office, Switzerland*, Available online from: http://prism.ucalgary.ca/bitstream/1880/50371/1/eCHSS_1_2015_Wolbringenglishversion.pdf [17 March 2017].

Wolbring, G. (2016) 'Employment, disabled people and robots: What is the narrative in the academic literature and Canadian newspapers?', *Societies*, 6: Article 15.

Wolbring, G., and Burke, B. (2013) 'Reflecting on Education for Sustainable Development through Two Lenses: Ability Studies and Disability Studies', *Sustainability*, 5: 2327–2342.

Wolbring, G., and Ghai, A. (2015) 'Interrogating the impact of scientific and technological development on disabled children in India and beyond', *Disability and the Global South*, 2: 667–685.

Wolbring, G., and Yumakulov, S. (2015) 'Education through an ability studies lens.' *Zeitschrift für Inklusion*, Available online from: www.inklusion-online.net/index.php/inklusion-online/article/view/278/261 [viewed 17 March 2017].

Wolbring, G., and Diep, L. (2016) 'Cognitive/Neuroenhancement through an Ability Studies lens' in F. Jotterand and V. Dubljevic (eds.) *Cognitive Enhancement.* Oxford, UK: Oxford University Press, (pp. 57–75).

Yumakulov, S., Yergens, D., and Wolbring, G. (2012a) 'Imagery of disabled people within social robotics research' in S. Ge, *et al.* (eds.) *Social robotics*, Berlin Heidelberg: Springer (pp. 168–177).

Yumakulov, S., Yergens, D., and Wolbring, G. (2012b) 'Imagery of people with disabilities within social robotics research.', *Proc.ICSR, LNAI*, 7621: 168–177.

PART III

Global and cultural reflections on educational technology

8

'ALWAYS CONNECTED'

Transforming teaching and learning in education

Maggi Savin-Baden

Introduction

With the increasing use of technology across home, work and school most people are tethered to some form of digital device. Across the media there has been considerable criticism about students, and children's use of mobile devices, along with plentiful anecdotes across education about students being continually distracted by technology. There are many critiques, including authors such as Turkle (2005: 14), who has argued:

> The dramatic changes in computer education over the past decades leave us with serious questions about how we can teach our children to interrogate simulations in much the same spirit. The specific questions may be different, but the intent needs to be the same: to develop habits of readership appropriate to a culture of simulation.

Her argument in 2011 remains similar (Turkle 2011). There are others who see such a stance as negative and misplaced (for example, Bayne and Ross 2011). However, it is clear that this area of being 'always connected' requires further exploration. Being 'always on' or 'always connected' is defined as both a way of being and a set of practices that are associated with it. To be 'always connected' or 'digitally tethered' would generally be associated with carrying, wearing or holding a device that enables one to be constantly and continually in touch with digital media of whatever kind. Practices associated with digital tethering include the practice of being 'always engaged': texting at dinner or driving illegally while 'facebooking'. It is not clear if the worry and media hype is valid, or whether in fact it is having an unhelpful impact on learning and society in general.

Learning in the digital age

Debates around young people's use of digital technology have been likened to academic 'moral panic', with the suggestion that those in opposition are seen as being out of touch (Bennett *et al.* 2008). Yet what still seems to be occurring is an unhelpful dualism, promoted by both experts and in the media: the sense that managed and ordered technology is somehow good and messy, unmediated technology is bad. It is still unclear what kind of impact an increasingly connected environment is having on learning and what kinds of cultures this is creating within learning settings. However, it is clear that people's use of digital technology spans the age range from young children to older adults, but few have presented the research and literature across this age range.

Learning

The debates about learning and teaching, pedagogy and andragogy have been on the agenda for many years. Whilst there are those who still argue for knowledge-based lectures, others suggest Socratic approaches are more useful, and authors such as Fuller (2010) suggest that higher education should be places of creativity, filled with moments of experimentation. Further, for a number of researchers, Technology Enhanced Learning (TEL) is seen as a series of practices that have rather swept across higher education with relatively little critique, along with other terms such as engagement, quality and harnessing. Bayne (2014), for example, has argued that technology enhanced learning is more about technology than learning. Certainly the number of projects funded by the European Union over the last ten years would seem to suggest this is the case:

> 'TEL', far from being an unexceptionable and neutral term simply in need of clearer definition, is in fact a deeply conservative discourse which reduces our capacity to be critical about digital education, and fails to do justice equally to the disruptive, disturbing and generative dimensions of the academy's enmeshment with (digital) technology.
>
> *(Bayne 2014: 348)*

This stance towards technology is also seen in local university practices, where the focus is on the technology rather than on how learning *with* technology is most effective for students in terms of their individual approaches to learning. At a recent workshop on learning technology, staff from a range of universities spoke about their focus on software such as Pebble Pad, Blackboard, Echo360 and Mahara, to name a few. What was apparent was (still) the use of proprietary software imposed upon students with little sense of the need for staff to ask students how they learned best and if such software was useful. There was also relatively little critique from staff about this software in terms of the constraints it imposes on learning in higher education. It is suggested here that it is vital to shift away from easy to use, structured proprietary software, linear taxonomies and simplistic notions of learning styles.

For teachers and enablers of learning (from parent to evening class tutors), prompting criticality and creativity should be the central planks of education, but it is also important to be circumspect about some of the myths of the age. Technology is having an impact across the education section, from very young children to older people, and the following section begins to explore some important aspects that bear consideration.

Myths of the age: Toddlers, teenagers and traditionalists

Although there is a culture of always being connected, early years' centres, schools and universities still control what is seen as appropriate knowledge. Some of the recent technologies used for very young children include:

- Sproutling baby monitors capture and provide feedback about children's sleeping patterns.
- Teddy the Guardian is a teddy bear that locates and captures children's key vital signs, heart rate and body temperature, and is intended to be used to communicate this information to health professionals.
- KidFit is a wearable wristband fitness and sleep tracker for ages 5–11, able to capture and respond to children's physical activity (there is also a version for dogs).
- hereO is a watch with tracking that shows children's location, designed for ages 3–12.

Ones that are very popular with primary age children include Skylanders and Disney Infinity, which comprise plastic figurines that are positioned on a plastic base and then reflect a corresponding virtual avatar within the game which children control though a game controller. What these tagged toys indicate is the increasing digitisation of children's physical worlds.

Toys, tracking and learning today are perhaps more intertwined than many people would envisage and therefore it is important to understand them together. Tracking, whether through apps, sports watches or online shopping, is now commonplace and whilst many people are aware of this tracking, it is not (yet) perceived to be malicious or sinister. As consumers, both now and in the future, children are being influenced in their buying choices and guided to other retail spaces through related online marketing. These technologies are influencing early learning in the home and at preschool but as Plowman (2014) notes, children, and particularly preschool children, are largely invisible in studies about family life. The result is that there is still relatively little knowledge and understanding about how young children learn and are influenced by the wide range of connected, and often unsupervised, technologies in the home.

In terms of teenagers, there are not only a series of mixed messages but also polarities between those who consider monitoring teenagers' use of technology as a waste of time and those that see digital technology as negative and destructive. It seems that a balanced stance is required, whilst also recognising that in practice relatively little monitoring does in fact occur. Many young people can actually access anything they like on their phones and at school (texting in the toilet), whilst others take delight in finding ways around blocked sites at school.

As Crook (2012: 75) argues:

> The single issue that generated the most widespread and energetic discussion in these groups was the issue of schools blocking access to certain internet sites … It is clearly motivated by worthy ambitions to manage the personal security of students, to obstruct access to offensive material, and to sustain focus on central school tasks. However, it is not often viewed so charitably by students. Accordingly, it becomes a source of tension in this case between the felt 'Web 2.0 readiness' of students and the constraints felt necessary by schools. Such tension is reflected in a number of ways. It can sour relationships at all levels of the system— technical staff, librarians, teachers, managers and even the county education authority who were sometimes identified as the source of the imperative. Of particular concern was a species of double standard that was often perceived:
>
> Yes, when teachers ask you to get like multimedia files for PowerPoints and stuff you like say to them 'I can't get them because you've blocked the sites on the Internet' so, then they say 'Oh, you can do it at home', but that's not really fair because it's the school's fault for not like, for blocking them.
>
> *(Crook 2012: 75)*

In terms of older people in 2003, Selwyn *et al.* found that using was a minority activity amongst older adults but also highly stratified by gender, age, marital status and educational background. Yet some 15 years on, it seems that technology is seen as a means of older adults staying socially connected and in good health although it is not being widely adopted (see for example Essén and Östlund 2011). Much research in this area (Page 2014) still suggests that despite changes in interface design which make technology easier for users, developers still need to consider the needs and desires of older adults, and indeed older learners, more extensively. What is evident too is that learning innovations still tend to be technologically driven and it is clear that there needs to be a shift towards more user-led design and implementation, as well as an understanding of the impact that technology is having on learning innovations.

Learning innovation

There is increasing focus in the twenty-first century on what and how students learn, and on ways of creating learning environments to ensure that they learn effectively – although much of this remains contested ground. For example, are these new ways of learning just adaptations of old knowledge and practices moved into new formats? Do they merely deal with new knowledges and new practices?

Some of the recent innovations include the use of pedagogical agents, games and apps and virtual worlds.

Pedagogical agents

Pedagogical agents have a long history of use, beginning with Turing's (1950) work; he developed one of the first evaluation methods for pedagogical agents, which was a test for intelligence in a computer, requiring that a human being should be unable to distinguish the machine from another human being by using the replies to questions put to both. The recent research and the integration of pedagogical agents into educational settings suggest an increase in the value of pedagogical agents and the ways in which they might be adopted and adapted for teaching and learning. For example, a study by Veletsianos and Russell (2013) explored the nature and content of interactions when adult learners were offered the opportunity to communicate with pedagogical agents in open-ended dialogue with 52 undergraduate students and using a male and female agent. Data were collected over a 4-week period. The findings revealed six themes (388–389) that described the nature and content of agent–learner interactions. These results indicate that:

1   Even if agents are designed and positioned in a particular role (for example, expert/mentor), students may position them in a different or multiple roles.
2   The role of off-task and non-task interactions in agent–learner conversations is often seen as problematic, yet in this study it was apparent that non-task conversations were used to establish rapport and build relationships, and therefore attempts to prevent or discourage non-task conversations may be misguided.
3   Although students treated the agents in ways that seemed to indicate forms of human–human interaction, they also displayed apathy about sharing information about themselves.

The role of virtual mentors seems to be in guiding the learning process, for both children (Herring *et al.* 2017) and undergraduate students. For example, two recent studies have used autonomous agents for guiding learning and for understanding complex concepts. Beaumont (2012) argues that problem-based learning (PBL) requires students to use self-regulated learning, which invariably results in students asking facilitators for frequent guidance. As a result, he designed a web-based intelligent tutor system to provide guidance. This system presented students with guidance that helped them to improve their reading and analysis of the PBL scenarios and ultimately improved their understanding of the scenario and their ability to develop effective personal and group learning objectives from those scenarios. Hyashi (2012) investigated how an autonomous agent could be used to help students to explain concepts to one another – a capability that is very important. Students were required to explain a psychological concept to another student through an online chat system. The autonomous agent was used to provide feedback and suggestions to facilitate conversational interaction. The findings indicated that the autonomous agent could help to improve students' explanations as well as helping to develop their understanding of the concepts they were explaining. Thus it would seem that both of these studies essentially focused on both improving student engagement with learning and facilitating deep rather than surface approaches to learning. However, although Beaumont (2012) used autonomous agents in PBL, as yet research has not been undertaken to examine whether students can passively detect an agent presented as another student.

However, a study by Zakharov *et al.* (2007) focused on supporting learning by designing and then evaluating a pedagogical agent with a caring persona who would be interested in the learner's progress. The agent's behaviour was based on the earlier work of Kim and Baylor (2006a, 2006b) and adopted the mentor role, since they believed the passive affective support they wanted to provide via the agent was congruent with the role of a mentor. Thus the agent was designed to acknowledge the learner's emotions indirectly through its emotional appearance, while trying to keep the learner focused on the task as well. The study found that the agents' behaviour needed to appear more natural, and many students wanted to have greater control over the agents' behaviour and voice properties. In particular, user preference and the quality of agents' voice was found to be critical for maintaining the agents' rapport with the users and maintaining the flow of the learning process. These findings have been confirmed by later work by Savin-Baden *et al.* (2013) and Savin-Baden *et al.* (2015).

Learning apps and games

Games and apps are increasingly being used for online learning and in the classroom. Learning games have a clear educational purpose and are not intended to be played primarily for amusement. Epistemic games were developed by Collins and Ferguson (1993), who categorised them into structural analysis games, functional analysis games and process analysis games. The idea is that each type presents increasing levels of challenge, so that structural analysis games are the easiest and process analysis games the most difficult. Arnab *et al.* (2014) argue for the importance of a model of games-based learning. The model proposed is the Learning Mechanics–Game Mechanics (LM–GM) model, which is a model that locates pre-defined game mechanics and pedagogical elements to be used in a game. Whilst this complex model is a very useful starting point, it tends to draw on older theories and models of learning, which have been superseded by newer ones that tend to take greater account of the ways in which young people and students learn in the twenty-first-century. If this were to be developed by focusing on instantiations of problem-based learning that centre on critical pedagogy, rather than the outdated Bloom's taxonomy (Bloom 1956), it could help to shift current understandings of games-based learning away from linear, solid and content driven models of learning towards more creative approaches. However, it is vital to see games (serious and epistemic) through both their structure and the way in which modes of knowledge are located in the curriculum. By doing this, it will be possible to create games that increasingly move away from outcome-based models and instead towards creativity and uncertainty in learning. However, much of the focus on games to date has been on their usefulness in enhancing learning at university. For example, The Serious Games and Virtual Worlds research team at Ulster University explored the potential of video games technologies for undergraduate teaching of electronic and electrical engineering related subjects. The Circuit Warz project was conceived to investigate if creating a compelling, engaging, immersive, collaborative and competitive environment to teach electronic circuit theory and principles would increase student engagement (Callaghan *et al.* 2009). However, there is now an increasing focus on the role of the teacher in games-based learning. For example, Ketamo *et al.* (2013) suggest that the diffusion of games for learning are more likely to occur across higher education if teachers are included rather than excluded from the gaming process.

Apps such as Instagram, Snapchat, Wickr, Slingshot, Cyberdust and WeChat are popular apps that, whilst not used in schools and universities, do encourage sharing and peer-to-peer learning. Instagram is used to take pictures and videos, apply digital filters to them and share them on a variety of social networking sites. Snapchat, along with Wickr, Slingshot and Cyberdust offer photo and video sharing whilst WeChat provides multimedia communication and contact information. This peer-to-peer teaching and collaboration seems to result in increased identity status for those (teenagers) creating and teaching others, and support is provided for improving and developing media by peers, both offline and online. Such apps do seem to increase digital tethering and for some young people such tethering does seem to result in parental concerns about the ability of young people to self-regulate their screen time. For example, the KnowMo project (www.uv.uio.no/iped/english/research/projects/knowmo/index.html) investigated how teenagers and their parents engage with knowledge and learning across different arenas and found that there remains much diversity in strategies used to regulate screen time.

However, perhaps it is time that teachers, from schools to universities, recognise that young people and students have moved beyond bounded systems and instead use whatever apps, forums and sites that enable them to gain, create, recreate and repurpose knowledge. Whilst some university staff have developed the use of virtual worlds, as presented below, there is still space for further more creative and innovative developments to be made.

Virtual worlds

Virtual worlds are computer-based simulated 3D environments, which users navigate using an avatar and can therefore meet other avatars in-world. There are many virtual worlds ranging from Minecraft to World of Warcraft, as illustrated in Table 8.1:

These environments, such as Second Life, OpenSim and Jibe, allow users to purchase virtual land and construct objects on that land using inbuilt programming tools. A more recent version, High Fidelity, is open source software that allows users to share virtual reality on a server using a 2D screen or with a head-mounted display

TABLE 8.1 Popular virtual worlds

Virtual world	Descriptions commonly used	Key features
Second Life	Multi-user Virtual Environment (Immersive/Serious/Social/3D Virtual World/Environment)	Aimed at individual users focused primarily on social interaction Open and freely available, with premium advantages Customisable avatars (tools by which users navigate the world), either fantasy or humanoid with varying degrees of anthromorphism Predominantly user-generated content and objects (all members) Users are not provided with owned spaces, but can purchase Second Life islands and visit public islands, both owned by Second Life and by other users Ability to use world dependent on building, scripting and navigational skills No reward system or gaming structure
Twinity	Multi-user Virtual Environment (Immersive/Social/3D Virtual World/Environment)	Aimed at individual users focused primarily on social interaction Highly anthromorphic avatars, although fantasy characters also available Users provided with individual spaces and can visit pre-created virtual replicas of existing places Users can create or purchase content Participation-based reward system towards achievement of certain goals, but no specific rules or levelling systems
Blue Mars	Multi-user Virtual Environment (Immersive/Serious/Social/3D Virtual World/Environment)	Aimed at game developers, entrepreneurs, businesses and educators who wish to build 3D environments Open and freely available, with premium advantages Customisable avatars, typically humanoid with some fantasy options Participation-based reward system towards achievement of certain goals, but no specific rules or levelling systems

Name	Type	Description
Kaneva	Multi-user Virtual Environment (Immersive/Serious/Social/3D Virtual World/ Environment)	Aimed at individual users focused primarily on social interaction Humanoid avatars Integration with social networking, shared media and games Users provided with individual spaces and can visit public spaces
World of Warcraft	Massively Multiplayer Virtual World (3D Virtual World/Environment)	Aimed at individual users and groups focused primarily on gaming Subscription-based Fantasy characters Gaming virtual world with specific rules, reward systems and levelling systems
Minecraft	Massively Multiplayer Virtual World (user created) (Immersive/Serious/Social/3D Virtual World/ Environment)	Aimed at individual users focused primarily on building, often referred to as being akin to Lego The focus is on building and mining to protect oneself from monsters Single-player and multi-player options, freely available Game with reward system but no specific goals or levels Variety of 'modes' in which game can be played Ability to build and create specific objects Multiple non-player characters present in the game

such as Oculus Rift. Teachers, developers and students are able to depict virtual representations of particular settings, such as classrooms, historical buildings and geographical landscapes. This land can then be accessed by any avatar who gains permission, depending upon the settings of the land and the virtual world used. Virtual worlds have been popular in education since the late 2000s, and particularly so in problem-based learning and distance learning. Problem-based learning (PBL) has become a central learning approach in many curricula, but this collaborative style of learning is often perceived to be threatened by the movement towards online learning. The increasing adoption of PBL and the parallel growth in online learning each reflect the shift away from teaching as a means of transmitting information, towards supporting learning as a student-generated activity. For example, the Problem-based Learning in Virtual Interactive Educational Worlds (PREVIEW) demonstrator project investigated the creation and testing of PBL scenarios in Second Life (SL).

The aims of the PREVIEW project were to develop, deliver and test eight PBL scenarios within SL for paramedic and healthcare management education; ensure user-guided development; and share technology and good practice. Over a period of 9 months, two categories of PBL scenarios were initially designed: *Information-driven scenarios* and *Avatar-driven scenarios.* Information-driven scenarios presented information through virtual world content, such as video footage, images and audio with links to external content, such as relevant web pages. Avatar-driven scenarios use non-player characters, termed pedagogical agents, where the student interacts with the pedagogical agent to gather necessary information. The PREVIEW project sought to achieve its objectives by working with end users to create, trial and evaluate pedagogically informed learning scenarios that were to be simultaneously accessed by groups of learners with the principle aim of working together to achieve the desired learning outcomes. It explored the use of novel features such as pedagogical agents, together with different ways of presenting scenarios in two learning contexts: a Foundation degree in Paramedic Science and a BA in Social and Health Care Management. Specific developments emerged from the PREVIEW project (Conradi *et al.* 2009), which has since been developed further in response to the need for pedagogically driven scenarios that fit with a virtual world.

The Open University has also examined the pedagogical and methodological opportunities of such environments, as in the example below. Virtual Skiddaw is a virtual representation of a section of landscape in northern England, with six detailed sites designed for geological field visit explorations. The idea of the project was to foster practical fieldwork skills. The 3D virtual world was modelled on real topographic and geological data and has been designed to enhance and extend existing field teaching. Users control avatars to navigate the environment, working with virtual tools designed to support fieldwork in scientific disciplines and thus gaining additional practical experience (Argles *et al.* 2015). Such 'field trips' have also been used in a number of other disciplines. For example, Grant and Clerehan (2011) have used virtual worlds to provide language students learning Mandarin with 'real life' experiences such as ordering a meal in an in-world Chinese restaurant. Reeves and Minocha (2011) have shown the importance of co-creation of teaching and learning spaces in Second Life, so that the resultant spaces are ones in which students wish to learn. Equally important is the relationship between the pedagogy and the design of learning spaces; or, in Lefebvre's terms, the relationship between spatial practices and the representation of spaces.

Whilst there is increasing research into the use of pedagogical agents, games and virtual worlds, as portrayed here, there is still relatively little research into the long-term impact of new and innovative tethered technologies on learners' lives. Thus in terms of using these spaces, teachers will need to ensure students (whether undergraduate or postgraduate) are comfortable with the technology and provide activities that promote active learning through role-play and reflection with strong application to real-life settings.

The impact on learners' lives and experiences

It is argued here that in order to enhance learning and teaching through the use of educational technologies, and in particular virtual worlds, there needs to be a focus on participatory pedagogies. Participatory pedagogies are defined here as forms of learning and teaching that harness the use of digital media and participatory cultures and action (Savin-Baden 2015). In practice, these pedagogies are often hidden, enmeshed and transcend disciplines, structures and learning boundaries. The result is that they are both difficult to locate and delineate clearly, and are also often informal and difficult to understand in terms of their impact and value on education, culture and identity. Those adopting these kinds of pedagogies thus recognise the popular and cultural meanings of apps, social media and tools, and the ways in which young people adapt such media in both reflexive and non-reflexive ways for their own aims and purposes. They include such activities as learning through social networking, searching and retrieving information, researching information, using information, games, collaboration and shared interests. In unpacking participatory pedagogies, it is important to realise that encouraging young people to become reflexive, or more reflexive about their practices, behaviours and ethics is vital both in the development of their stance as media managers and producers, and in the development of voice, agency, personalisation and an ethical stance of their own. In practice some of the issues that need to be considered are the impact of being 'always connected', particularly in relation to over-reliance on technology. It is also important to consider the extent to which always being connected is changing social interaction and requires educators to implement more flexible pedagogies that include invention and production by students. Finally, issues such as privacy and surveillance are also challenging concerns when exploring the impact of digital tethering on learning.

Over-reliance on technology

Whilst there are many amusing stories of texting and emailing people in the same room, there is also a more serious side to the impact of technology on learning. Learning for many people relies on social interaction and yet digital multitasking in the classroom and particularly small group sessions can disrupt this. Such disruption can result in poor interpersonal communication, reduce interaction with diverse viewpoints and result in the devaluation of interactive learning altogether. Furthermore, over-reliance on search engines can reduce criticality, the development of rigorous research capabilities, and result in patch writing: the process of combining the work of others with one's own (Wisker and Savin-Baden 2009). It is not enough just to celebrate what is valuable in digital technology; it is also vital to recognise that over-reliance and over-use can reduce creativity and increase cyber-influence in ways that are pernicious. The decision not to use digital media (of whatever sort) should still perhaps be a choice in education, so that we do not ignore negative effects and become ensnared in uncritical digital spaces. To avoid such traps, there is a need to ensure that our pedagogies are flexible.

Flexible pedagogies

Barnett (2014: 10) has argued for 15 conditions of flexibility, which he believes will promote flexible provision in higher education; he writes:

> Flexible provision has the potential to enhance student learning, widen opportunities for participation in higher education, and develop graduates who are well-equipped to contribute to a fast-changing world. This report shows how these conditions of flexibility provide the foundations for the implementation of robust, well-informed and thought-through structures and strategies that will lead the sector into the future.

If flexible pedagogies are to be adopted that focus on human beings, as Barnett (2014) suggests, then the overly accepted behavioural norms that are the central plank of education worldwide need to be rejected in favour of something better. The ideals of Stenhouse (1975) and his important argument for learning intentions rather than objectives remain buried, and yet would seem to be much more appropriate, not only for flexible pedagogies but also perhaps more importantly for the digital age. Perhaps staff in schools and higher education are not ready for flexible pedagogies, nor really prepared to implement them unless they sit safely within a behavioural framework. Yet there are other more complex questions to be asked than how curricula might be designed flexibly. For example, is hacking the school computer system flexible pedagogy?

Implementing flexible pedagogies should ensure that students can bring all their learning capabilities to the classroom rather than being required to leave their sophisticated abilities developed out of the classroom behind – contained in some kind of hidden personal media scape. Students are making and creating opportunities and in arenas of which many staff are unaware. One example of this is vidding, whereby content is refashioned or recreated in order to present a different perspective, usually based on music videos and television programmes. Younger children are creating and orchestrating, using digital resources, to develop the capabilities of invention (Crook and Harrison 2014). Students can teach us much about learning at the borders and guide staff towards new understandings of learning, new notions of learning community and learning spaces. Whilst students may be innovative and creative, many too are perhaps unaware of the levels of surveillance and spying occurring.

Surveillance and spying

Surveillance is defined here as the monitoring of activities and behaviour in order to influence, manipulate and manage people's lives. In the context of digital tethering such monitoring occurs in online spaces and often is seen as more sinister and secretive than other kinds of surveillance. In 2008 Zimmer coined the term Search 2.0 as the loss of privacy which occurs through the aggregation of users' online activities. In practice, Search 2.0 enables companies to track and aggregate people's data in ways previously impossible, since in the past people's data were separated across diverse sites. Now, as a result of social networking sites, personal data can be mined and cross referenced, sold and reused, so that people are being classified by others through sharing their own data. Zimmer (2008) suggested that there should be better formal regulation and changes in the way social media are designed, but almost a decade later this is unlikely to occur; instead what we appear to be dealing with is liquid, participatory and lateral surveillance.

Despite the portrayal by the media, many students do in fact care about and wish to protect their personal information in cyberspace. However, the extent to which people are aware just how much of their personal information is stored and tracked is unclear. Facebook requires its users to provide their real identity, and all their information can be manipulated and classified through the company's huge database. Most students still, it seems, have open profiles and share email and phone numbers. However, what counts as privacy? Is it acceptable to use a webcam to spy on the person who is baby-sitting your child or film your roommate at university as a joke? Is lateral surveillance okay? Lateral surveillance, whereby a person tracks their children's' communications, monitors their lover's phone call and uses a webcam to spy on their neighbours, seems more sinister, as it has become a type of informal law enforcement and micro inquiry into others' lives. Thus, we market research, verify and check friends and colleagues, so that 'In an era in which everyone is to be considered potentially suspect, we are invited to become spies – for our own good' (Andrejevic 2005: 494). This might seem sinister, but the use of Chromebooks in schools ensures that Google can collate and mine school children's personal data as part of its Google for Education programme. For many years parents have signed forms allowing their children to be photographed in school; now they are signing away their privacy as they are mined and monitored. But what of the future?

Future issues

Whilst there remains much debate about the challenges of always being connected and the impact of this on institutions and student learning, there are also some broader and possibly pernicious developments that have emerged and need to be considered, namely digital immortality and virtual humans.

Digital immortality

The concept of digital immortality has emerged over the past decade and is defined here as the continuation of an active or passive digital presence after death. Advances in knowledge management, machine-to-machine communication, data mining and artificial intelligence are now making a more active presence after death possible. Despite the media interest in digital immortality, the research in this area remains small and discrete. However, digital immortality has moved beyond simple memorial pages (Frost 2014), and as early as 1997 the term thanatechnology was instituted by Sofka (1997) to represent this desire to preserve one's soul and assets digitally after death; it has since been developed further by Sofka and Gilbert (2012). There have also been cases where people have received 'beyond the grave' updates, either from dead friends (McAlear 2011), or companies dedicated to creating digitally immortal personas (LivesOn 2015). Facebook has now put in place measures to control the digital legacy of pages on their site (Buck 2013; Skelton 2012), and recent work by authors such as Adali and Golbeck (2014) illustrate that it is possible to generate accurate predictions of personality from online traces. Advances in data mining and artificial intelligence are now making a more active presence after death possible; thus, it would seem to be possible to create artificially intelligent systems that could generate new commentary on media events in the style of a particular deceased person, for whom an online profile had been created before death. However, there are still questions that remain about the the ideological underpinnings of digital immortality, since the search for such immortality is grounded in a human desire for control over life as well as death, and there still remains relatively little research in this area to date. The importance of this in terms of learning is that digital immortality could be used to develop virtual humans so that knowledge can be retained and built upon; thus digital immortality has both sinister and useful consequences.

Virtual humans

The evidence suggests that pedagogic agents, virtual tutors and virtual mentors have a role to play in the support of student and staff education, learning, access to information and personal support. For example, one recent development was the creation of an automated teacher at the University of Edinburgh (Bayne 2015) in the context of a Massive Open Online Course (MOOC). This Twitterbot...

> 'coded in' something of the teacher function to the MOOC, using it as a way of researching some creative and critical futures for a MOOC pedagogy in which the 'teacher function' might become less a question of living

teacher presence and more an assemblage of code, algorithm and teacher–student agency.

(Bayne 2015: 461)

It is clear that technical capability to develop agents now exists, and the majority of ongoing research and development is based around pedagogic, social and psychological design, with technical risks being minimal. For example, recent developments include:

- The film and game industry investing in the creation of realistic human characters – with a main focus on the body but also with a keen interest in creating believable behaviours of non-player-characters within games.
- The widespread adoption of semantic networks for information storage and processing, which mimic the way information appears to be stored in the brain.
- The emergence of virtual worlds, which allow embodied agents and by extension embodied cognition to be more readily investigated than through robotics.
- The emergence of simple natural language processing systems such as Artificial Intelligence Markup Language, and ongoing interest in passing the Turing Test.

Virtual humans are also seen in science fiction representations of virtual humans, which, whilst these are far from being currently achievable, they are what most members of the public think of when talking about virtual humans. Examples include *Caprica* (the *Battlestar Galactica* prequel, where Zoe Greystone has been creating a copy of herself, but she then dies leaving the digital copy to carry on her legacy), BBC's *Planet B* series (where the protagonist attempts to find his girlfriend who is dead in the real world but alive in the *Planet B* virtual world, with the help of a rogue avatar who has no human controller) and the Gleisner robots (human digital intelligences downloaded into physical robots) of Greg Egan's *Diaspora* (Egan 1997). However, in education virtual human technology is starting to be used to implement virtual mentors of differing levels of sophistication, such as virtual tutoring, personal career and resettlement mentoring, and counselling (Bhakta and Savin-Baden forthcoming), as illustrated in Table 8.2.

Conclusion

Whilst there are advantages and disadvantages to always being connected, it is important not to equate 'the digital' with something that is necessarily beneficial and transformative. Studies across the globe suggest that much of young people's learning is outside school, and certainly considerable amounts of school homework require access to information and sources that are invariably blocked by school systems. There are also mixed messages about the presence and use of social media in the classroom, in terms of about when and how it is acceptable to use digital technology. What is interesting, or perhaps worrying, is that children are often more aware of the impact of digital technology on themselves than parents are. Many of

TABLE 8.2 Types of virtual humans and possible uses

Type of Agent	Role	Context of use	Knowledge required	Conversation level	Personalisation level	Use Case
Knowledge Expert	Information provision	Interrogation of content through simple question and answer	Shallow	Keyword spotting, minimal dialogue management	Low	Resettlement information Health information Basic literacy development
Pedagogic Agent – Expert	Guide to using knowledge effectively	Context specific skill and knowledge development	Deep	Moderate dialogue management	Low/Medium	Learning a second language Skills development
Motivator	Learning prompter	Encouragement in learning, rather than imparting learning *per se*	Shallow	Advanced dialogue management, empathic	Medium/High	Skills development Personal development
Mentor	Personal support	Blend of motivator and expert, more attuned to individual user	Deep	Advanced dialogue management, empathic	High	Support learning Promotion
Guide	Guide to current and future planning	Personalised guide based on knowledge gaps	Deep	Advanced dialogue management, empathic	High	Career guidance Virtual aide
Counsellor	Support on sensitive issues and concerns	Reflective role rather than knowledge based	Medium	Advanced dialogue management, empathic	High	Personal well-being Counselling support

the current developments are both exciting and troublesome, but they also usher in new demands: the need to improve pedagogies so that they are flexible and rigorous and the need to understand what privacy really means. With a growing older population, technology for older people needs to be flexible and easy to use. There is also a need to ensure that toddlers and teenagers become questioning, critical individuals who can take a stance towards their own learning, instead of following the next social media suggestion about what is trending. However, for teachers it would seem that the promises and perils of always being connected prompt the troublesome question of what counts as learning, and who decides, in an age of digital fluency?

References

Adali, S., and Golbeck, J. (2014) 'Predicting personality with social behavior: A comparative study', *Social Network Analysis and Mining*, 4(1) 159–179.

Andrejevic, M. (2005) 'The work of watching one another: Lateral surveillance, risk, and governance', *Surveillance and Society*, 2(4) 479–497.

Argles, T., Minocha, S., and Burden, D. (2015) 'Virtual field teaching has evolved: Benefits of a 3D gaming environment', *Geology Today*, 31(6): 222–226.

Arnab, S., Lim, T., Carvalho, M. B., Bellotti, F., de Freitas, S., Louchart, S., Suttie, N., Berta, R., and De Gloria, A. (2014) 'Mapping learning and game mechanics for serious games analysis', *British Journal of Educational Technology*, 46(2). Available online from: http://dx.doi.org/10.1111/bjet.12113 [2 November 2015].

Barnett, R. (2014) *Conditions of flexibility: Securing a more responsive higher education system*, York, England: The Higher Education Academy (HEA). Available online from: www.heacademy.ac.uk/flexible-pedagogies-preparing-future [17 March 2015].

Bayne, S. (2014) 'What's wrong with 'technology enhanced learning'?', in S. Bayne, C. Jones, M. de Laat, T. Ryberg T and C. Sinclair (eds.) *Proceedings of the 9th International Conference on Networked Learning*, Edinburgh (pp. 347–350).

Bayne, S. (2015) 'Teacherbot: Interventions in automated teaching', *Teaching in Higher Education*, 20 (4): 455–467.

Bayne, S., and Ross, J. (2011) '"Digital Native" and "Digital Immigrant" discourses: A critique', in R. Land and S. Bayne (eds.) *Digital difference: Perspectives on online learning*, Rotterdam, Sense (pp. 159–170).

Beaumont, C. (2012) *Beyond e-learning: An intelligent pedagogical agent to guide students in problem-based learning*, (Unpublished PhD thesis), University of Liverpool, Liverpool, United Kingdom.

Bennett, S., Maton, K., and Kervin, L. (2008) 'The 'digital natives' debate: A critical review of the evidence', *British Journal of Educational Technology*, 39(5): 775–786.

Bhakta, R., and Savin-Baden, M. (2017) 'Virtual Humans: A literature review'. *Journal of Educational Computing Research* (submitted).

Bloom, B. (1956) *Taxonomy of educational objectives*, 2 vols, New York, Longmans Green.

Buck, S. (2013) How 1 billion people are coping with death and Facebook, *Mashable*. Available online from: http://mashable.com/2013/02/13/facebook-after-death/ [9 April 2015].

Callaghan, M., McCusker, K., Losada, J. L., Harkin, J., and Wilson, S. (2009) 'Engineering education island: Teaching engineering in virtual worlds'. ITALICS, *Innovation in Teaching and Learning in Information and Computer Sciences*, 8(3): 2–18.

Collins, A., and Ferguson, W. (1993) 'Epistemic forms and epistemic games: Structures and strategies to guide inquiry', *Educational Psychologist*, 28(1): 25–42.

Conradi, E. Kavia, S., Burden, D., Rice, D., Woodham, L., Beaumont, C., Savin-Baden, M., and Poulton, T. (2009) 'Virtual patients in virtual world: Training paramedic students'. *Medical Teacher*, 31(8): 713–720.

Crook, C. K. (2012) 'The 'digital native' in context: Tensions associated with importing Web 2.0 practices into the school setting', *Oxford Review of Education*, 38(1): 63–80.

Crook, C. K., and Harrison, C. (2014) 'Children as inventors: Orchestrating an informal pedagogic scenario with digital resources', *International Journal of Technology Enhanced Learning*, 6(1): 21–33.

Egan, G. (1997) *Diaspora*, London, Millennium.

Essén, A., and B. Östlund. (2011) 'Laggards as innovators? Old users as designers of new services and service systems', *International Journal of Design*, 5(3): 89–98.

Frost, M. (2014) 'The grief grapevine: Facebook memorial pages and adolescent bereavement', *Australian Journal of Guidance and Counselling* 24(2): 256–265.

Fuller, S. (2010) *The sociology of intellectual life: The career of the mind in and around the academy*, London, Sage.

Grant, S., and R. Clerehan (2011) 'Finding the discipline: Assessing student activity in second life', *Australasian Journal of Educational Technology*, 27 (5): 813–828.

Hayashi, Y. (2012) 'On pedagogical effects of learner support agents in collaborative interaction', in S. A. Cerri and B. Clancey (Eds.) *Proceedings of the 11th International Conference on Intelligent Tutoring Systems (ITS2012), Lecture Notes in Computer Science, 7315*, Heidelberg, Belin, Springer (pp. 22–32).

Herring, P. J., Kear, K., Sheehy, K., and Jones, Roger (2017) 'A virtual tutor for children with autism', *Journal of Assistive Technologies*, 11(1): 19–27. http://oro.open.ac.uk/46706/.

Ketamo, H., Kiili, K., Arnab, S., and Dunwell, I. (2013) 'Integrating games into the classroom: Towards new teachership', in S. de Freitas, M. Ott, M.M. Popescu and I. Stanescu (eds.) *New pedagogical approaches in game enhanced learning: Curriculum integration* (pp.534–537). IGI Global. Available online from: http://dx.doi.org/10.4018/978–1–4666–3950–8. ch007. [20 September 2016].

Kim, Y., and Baylor, A. L. (2006a) 'A social-cognitive framework for pedagogical agents as learning companions'. *Educational Technology Research and Development*, 54(6): 569–596.

Kim, Y., and Baylor, A. L. (2006b) 'Pedagogical agents as learning companions: The role of agent competency and type of interaction'. *Educational Technology Research and Development*, 54(3): 222–243.

Lefebvre, H. (1991) *The Production of Space*, 15th edn, Oxford, Blackwell.

LivesOn Available online from: www.liveson.org/ [19 March 2015].

McAlear, A. (2011) Grappling with tradition. 17 May 2011. Available online from: www. deathanddigitallegacy.com/2011/05/17/grappling-with-tradition/ [19 Mar 2015].

Page, T. (2014) 'Touchscreen mobile devices and older adults: A usability study', *International Journal of Human Factors and Ergonomics*, 3(1): 65–85.

Plowman, L. (2014) 'Researching young children's everyday uses of technology in the family home', *Interacting with Computers*, 27(1): 36–46.

Reeves, A., and Minocha, S. (2011) 'Relating pedagogical and learning space designs in Second Life', in A. Cheney, and R. Sanders (eds.) *Teaching and learning in 3D immersive worlds: Pedagogical models and constructivist approaches*, Hershey, PA: Information Science Reference (pp. 31–60).

Savin-Baden, M. (2015) *Rethinking learning in an age of digital fluency: Is being digitally tethered a new learning nexus?*, London: Routledge.

Savin-Baden, M., Tombs, G., Burden, D., and Wood, C. (2013) 'It's almost like talking to a person: Student disclosure to pedagogical agents in sensitive settings', *International Journal of Mobile and Blended Learning*, 5(2): 78–93.

Savin-Baden, M., Tombs, G., and Bhakta, R. (2015) 'Beyond robotic wastelands of time: Abandoned pedagogical agents and new pedalled pedagogies', *E-Learning and Digital Media*, 12 (3–4): 295–314.

Selwyn, N., Gorard, S., Furlong, J., and Madden, L. (2003) 'Older adults' use of information and communications technology in everyday life', *Ageing and Society*, 23: 561–582.

Skelton, A. (2012) 'Facebook after death: what should the law say?' *Mashable*. Available online from: http://mashable.com/2012/01/26/digital-assets-after-death/ [9 April 2015].

Sofka, C. J. (1997) 'Social support "Internetworks," caskets for sale, and more: Thanatology and the information', *Death Studies*, 21: 553–574.

Sofka, C. J., and Gilbert, K.R. (eds.). (2012) *Dying, death, and grief in an online universe: For counselors and educators,* New York, Springer Publishing Company.

Stenhouse, L. (1975) *An introduction to curriculum research and development,* London, Heinemann.

Turing, A. M. (1950) 'Computing machinery and intelligence', *Mind*, 433–460.

Turkle, S. (2005) (2nd edn). *The second self: Computers and the human spirit*, Cambridge, MA: MIT Press.

Turkle, S. (2011) *Alone together,* New York, Basic Books.

Veletsianos, G., and Russell, G. S. (2013) 'What do learners and pedagogical agents discuss when given opportunities for open-ended dialogue?', *Journal of Educational Computing Research*, 48(3): 381–401.

Wisker, G., and Savin-Baden, M. (2009) 'Priceless conceptual thresholds: Beyond the "stuck place' in writing", *London Review of Education*, 7(3): 235–247.

Zakharov, K., Mitrovic, A., and Johnston, L. (2007) 'Pedagogical agents trying on a caring mentor role', in R. Luckin', G Koedinger and J. Greer, (eds.) *Proceedings of 13th International Conference on Artificial Intelligence in Education AIED 2007*, Los Angeles, 59–66.

Zimmer, M. (2008) 'The externalities of Search 2.0: The emerging privacy threats when the drive for the perfect search engine meets Web 2.0.', *First Monday*, 13 (3).

9

LEARNING ANALYTICS

A firm basis for the future

Rebecca Ferguson

Introduction

Learning analytics is a fast-developing field of research that has emerged since 2011 and has been taken up worldwide, especially in Europe, North America and Australia. The field has its roots in data mining and in business intelligence. It also makes use of methodologies and theories developed in disciplines as diverse as artificial intelligence, computer science, education, learning sciences, linguistics, machine learning, philosophy, psychology, sociology and statistics (Dawson *et al.* 2014).

The Society for Learning Analytics Research (SoLAR) defines learning analytics as 'the measurement, collection, analysis and reporting of data about learners and their contexts, for purposes of understanding and optimizing learning and the environments in which it occurs' (Siemens *et al.* 2011: 4). Although much early work has focused on the data processing and analysis that make up the first half of this definition, the aim is to provide actionable insights that can make a practical difference to education. In the future, analytics could be used to tackle big problems such as gender and diversity issues, youth mobility, inclusion and drop out from education.

Learning analytics has recently emerged as a field in its own right, distinct from other work on technology-enhanced learning and broader work on analytics. This has been attributed to three principal drivers: big data, online learning and national concerns (Ferguson 2012):

1 **Big data:** The widespread adoption of institutional databases and virtual learning environments (VLEs) means that schools and universities now generate increasingly large amounts of data, and want to make use of these assets to improve learning and teaching.
2 **Online learning:** This increase in available data has been paralleled by an increase in take-up of online and blended teaching and learning. At the same time, more and more learners are learning informally using open educational

resources (OERs) and massive open online courses (MOOCs). There is therefore growing international interest in how to optimise learning in these settings.

3 **National concerns:** Countries and international groupings are now more able to compare statistics related to schooling. Well-known examples of systematic evidence gathering that enable such comparisons include the Programme for International Student Assessment (PISA) and the Trends in International Maths and Science Survey (TIMMS). As a result, countries are increasingly interested in measuring, demonstrating and improving performance in education and are looking for ways to raise educational standards in order to benefit their citizens and society as a whole.

As well as these drivers, the field also faces a variety of challenges. These include the rapid pace of change in technology-enhanced learning, the problems associated with implementing analytics within an educational institution, and confusion about what learning analytics are and what they can do.

As learning analytics are an example of technology-enhanced learning, they must respond to a rapid rate of change. 'Typically, we find that the doubling time for different measures – price-performance, bandwidth, capacity – of the capability of information technology is about one year' (Kurzweil 2005: 56). This fast pace of change means that if, in 2006, developers had begun to implement learning analytics without looking ahead, they would not have been able to plan for learning with and through social networks (Twitter registered its first members in July 2006), learning with smartphones (the first iPhones went on sale in 2007), or learning at scale (the term MOOC was introduced in 2008). Analytics take time to develop, so this work needs to be carried out with an eye to the future in which they will be implemented, rather than in relation to technology that will soon be outdated.

Analytics in 2016 draw on data from virtual learning environments, also known as learning management systems (LMS). However, these systems are not the only source of data. Already furniture, pens, writing pads – almost any tool used during learning – can be fitted with sensors. These can record many sorts of information, including tilt, force and position. Video cameras using facial recognition are able to track individuals as they learn in lecture theatres or online. These cameras monitor movements and can record exactly how learners work with and manipulate objects, as well as where they focus their gaze. In addition, sensors can be used to gather personal information about factors such as posture, attention, rest, stress, blood sugar and metabolic rate. In future, learning analytics could draw on combinations of these data sources in order to enhance teaching and learning.

Although technology changes quickly, educational institutions do not. They function as complex adaptive systems (Ferguson *et al.* 2015). That is to say, they exist as dynamic networks of interactions, made up of nested and clustered sets of similar subsystems. This means that educational institutions can prove extremely resistant to change. Changes that target only their subsystems are unlikely to succeed. Even when the focus is at the institutional level, learning analytics and other insights based on data may not be put into practice for many reasons. These reasons include a tendency to make decisions based on anecdote rather than on research, a focus on technical concerns, a failure to incorporate analytics within a process of evidence-based decision-making and the often low levels of management familiarity with statistical methods and analytics (Macfadyen and Dawson 2012; McIntosh 1979).

Take, for example, the following scenario from the Coalition for Evidence-based Education (CEBE 2017: Para 1) regarding a headteacher and her senior management team trying to decide what to do to help the struggling readers in their school:

> Her deputy has suggested that they should provide one-to-one tutoring, but she cannot be sure that the expense is worth it. The literacy leader is certain he has heard of a scheme that recruits volunteers from the community to do the same thing – he is positive he had read it in a magazine somewhere. The SEN co-ordinator thought it might be a problem with the way they are teaching all children to read, and maybe they should look for something that was more effective across the whole school. Now, to add to the confusion, her School Improvement Partner is on the phone, telling her about a really exciting pilot project running across the authority, which is using a new computer program to help those who are struggling.
>
> *(CEBE 2017: Para 1)*

The CEBE uses this example to illustrate the lack of an infrastructure to support decision-making where, rather than building on knowledge, important choices are swayed by 'politics, marketing, anecdotal evidence and tradition' (CEBE 2017: Para 3). Together, these factors mean that when educational institutions consider learning analytics, they often look for the 'low-hanging fruit' – data that are easy to gather and systems that are straightforward to implement. However, many tools that appear to offer these straightforward learning analytics solutions do little more than present a series of data visualisations. Although these make use of large sets of educational data, they are not necessarily 'actionable' in the way that learning analytics should be. They do not make it clear what actions should be taken in order to improve learning or teaching, they may distract attention from more immediate issues and they sometimes prove to be nothing more than an expensive way of telling teachers things that they already know.

In order to address these challenges and, in particular, to help deal with the rapid rate of technological change that influences the development of the field, two international studies have examined the current state of learning analytics and looked at what the future holds in store.

The first of these was the Visions of the Future study, run by the Learning Analytics Community Exchange (LACE) project (Griffiths *et al.* 2016b). This was a Policy Delphi study (Turoff 2002) that systematically solicited and collated informed judgments on learning analytics from experts and used these to identify the areas that these experts judged most important to the successful implementation of learning analytics in the next ten years. In order to do this, the study used eight 'visions of the future of learning analytics' as provocations that would prompt reflection and thoughtful responses (Ferguson *et al.* 2016b). Two examples of the visions used as provocations in the Policy Delphi study are provided below:

In 2025, classrooms monitor the physical environment to support learning and teaching

In 2015, learning analytics were mainly used to support online learning. By 2025, they can be used to support most teaching and learning activities, wherever these take place. Furniture, pens, writing pads – almost any tool used during learning – can be fitted with sensors. These can record many sorts of information, including tilt, force and position. Video cameras using facial recognition are able to track individuals as they learn. These cameras monitor movements and record exactly how learners work with and manipulate objects. All this information is used to monitor learners' progress. Individuals are supported in learning a wide range of physical skills. Teachers are alerted to signs of individual learner's boredom, confusion and deviation from task. Teachers and managers are able to monitor social interactions, and to identify where they should nurture socialisation and cooperative behaviour.

(Griffiths et al. 2016a: 11)

In 2025, individuals control their own data

In 2015, it was not clear who owned educational data, and it was often used without learners' knowledge. By 2025, most people are aware of the importance and value of their data. Learners control the type and quantity of personal data that they share, and with whom they share it. This includes information about progress, attendance and exam results, as well as data collected by cameras and sensors. Learners can choose to limit the time for which access is allowed, or they can restrict access to specific organisations and individuals. The tools for making these choices are clearly laid out and easy to use. In the case of children, data decisions are made in consultation with parents or carers. If they do not engage with these tools, then no data is shared and no benefits gained. Most educational institutions recognise this as a potential problem, and run campaigns to raise awareness of both the risks of thoughtless exposure of data and the benefits to learners of informed sharing of selected educational data.

(Griffiths et al. 2016a: 17)

The second study focused on the implications of learning analytics for educational policy (LAEP). It based its findings on state-of-the-art reviews of the literature, tools, policies and practices, on case studies and on focus group work with international experts (Ferguson *et al.* 2016a).

Together, these two studies revealed how learning analytics were being used and developed in 2016, and highlighted areas that would need attention in the future. On a national scale, these two studies showed how governments could influence the development of learning analytics. On a local scale, they pointed to five questions that institutions and individuals need to answer if they plan to implement learning analytics (see Table 9.1).

TABLE 9.1 Analytics implementation checklist

1	What do we want to achieve?
2	How will our analytics improve learning?
3	Where is the evidence?
4	Do staff and learners know how to use the analytics?
5	Who is in control and how is this regulated?

The following sections look at each of the areas on this checklist in turn, explaining what these questions imply and why they are important. These sections include quotes from participants in the LACE Visions of the Future study (VoF). The study had 133 participants from 21 countries. Participants included invited experts drawn from different sectors of education (schools, higher education and workplace learning) as well as volunteers who responded to publicity about the survey, all of which was targeted at learning analytics researchers, developers and practitioners. Within this chapter, four-digit numbers (for example, 2804) are used to identify individual respondents. The quotes are used verbatim, although capitalisation has occasionally been changed to align with sentence structure.

What do we want to achieve?

As one VoF respondent phrased it, 'It all starts with the pedagogical perspective' (2804) – that is, with a theorised approach to teaching and learning. If analytics are to support these activities, then it is important to know why we are engaging in them and what we want to achieve. We also need to examine our basic assumptions about knowledge, including whether it is stable or changing, whether it is made up of discrete facts or interrelated concepts, whether it exists outside the self and can be transmitted or is constructed by the self (Knight *et al.* 2014).

Many VoF respondents linked their view of learning analytics to their understanding of what education is for. They associated education with change, growth, transformation and the development of society. Respondent 3462 believed that 'We have a social duty to facilitate and provide opportunities for learners to achieve their full potential', while 6064 felt that 'Education overcomes historical injustices'.

Such views suggest that, in future, we shall need to move beyond the present focus on the use of learning analytics to reduce course drop-out rates or to improve performance in certain subjects. Georgia State University in the USA, for example, is already using analytics to eliminate achievement gaps based on race, ethnicity and economics (Georgia State University 2015) while the University of Technology Sydney (UTS) is using them to support the development of twenty-first-century skills and competences that underpin lifelong learning (Ferguson *et al.* 2016a).

For example, a major research project at UTS uses various technologies to carry out automated analysis of student writing, in order to provide formative feedback on essay drafts. Another project at the same university makes use of the CLARA self-assessment survey tool. CLARA was developed to make students aware of the habits of mind they bring to their learning (their 'learning dispositions'). The tool generates visualisations for each student that represent their current 'learning power'. It also suggests interventions that are based on those learning profiles. These automated visualisations and suggestions are used to support coaching and mentoring of students by trained peers and by staff.

As well as considering the purposes of education, VoF respondents also made explicit what they meant by learning: 'an essentially social activity which relies on mutual trust and confidence' (0649), 'a human, socially embedded, communal activity' (7473). Respondent 5297 picked out the types of activity involved in learning: 'Education is about collaboration, about human interaction, about creativity, about innovation and about spontaneity' (5297). Together, these comments drew attention to the human and social elements of the learning process.

An idea expressed by many was that human interaction is a crucial part of the learning process – 'we need a human teacher to guide and scaffold us' (6818). These respondents stressed that analytics cannot be understood without interpretation that makes reference to their context. Humans, specifically teachers, are needed to make sense of analytic output and to make use of it to support learning.

Social definitions of learning also made the point that focusing only on the data produced by individuals produces an impoverished picture of their learning. Analytics need to be able to provide feedback on how people construct knowledge together, as the SNAPP tool does when it analyses the social networks in online learning groups (Bakharia and Dawson 2011). Work on social learning analytics and discourse analytics is already exploring these possibilities (Buckingham *et al.* 2012; McNamara *et al.* 2014).

Some respondents worried that learning analytics could be used to remove essential but challenging elements of the learning process. 'Learning is not only about success, it is about learning from failure' (3614); 'there is a time for learners to be confronted in order for transformation and growth to occur' (3462). Sometimes ambiguity, conflict and uncertainty are elements that prompt the construction of knowledge. A potential danger of personalised learning is that it does not present learners with the most difficult problems and a discipline's overarching challenges. If a system automatically adjusts its difficulty level so that learners are always working within their comfort zone, then they may never be asked to deal with and benefit from challenge.

Overall, respondents were ambitious with regard to what learning analytics may be able to achieve in the future. Their visions did not focus simply on institutional concerns such as increasing retention and improving grades. Instead, they presented a wider view of the role of education. Education was seen as a route to individual transformation and the development of society, a way of developing skills and competencies for every stage of life and of reducing the impact of demographic and economic inequalities. Respondents also stressed the need to take into account pedagogic perspectives that emphasise the importance of interaction and communication to the construction of knowledge.

How will our analytics improve learning?

It is clearly difficult to express a dynamic process of transformation, innovation and spontaneity in terms of measurable items. Some VoF respondents felt that learning is not open to observation in this way and that it is difficult to define success in measurable terms that hold true in different contexts. Others felt that it is dangerous to equate learning with measurable outcomes because this would 'reduce learning to the acquisition of those skills that can be measured and advised by the sensors and apps' (8698). However, others referred to existing or ongoing research that shows relationships between activities and progress towards learning goals or changes in learning behaviour (see for example Pistilli *et al.* 2012; Rienties and Toetenel 2016).

Unless it becomes possible to measure changes to the human body that reliably indicate learning is taking place, analytics will continue to rely on proxies for learning such as performance on tests before and after a period of learning. Respondent 6446 suggested that 'work should focus on understanding how the learning process really works', developing a nuanced model that applies to individual learners rather than to learners in general. Respondent 4762 proposed the development of a new proxy for learning – 'correlation between what somebody learns and the visual perception of how s/he is learning'. Others observed that learning does not take place only in the classroom, so learning analytics cannot only be designed for closely controlled environments but need to take into account the wider experience of learners.

This wide range of possible learning contexts means that 'it demands enormous quantity of data to monitor individual learning' (2428). However, many respondents were optimistic that data problems can be dealt with, pointing to existing work and experience. As Respondent 0649 noted, it is 'hard to believe that there will be enough processing power to do this, but I guess people always say that when something is ten years away'.

Smart houses, wearable technology, the Internet of Things (a network of devices that can collect and exchange data) and face recognition are increasingly familiar parts of everyday life, so the data collection and data-crunching necessary for learning analytics should not prove to be impossible and may be closer than 'ten years away'. 'There already exist tools that monitor what is happening in blended learning scenarios and provide teachers – and learners – advice, in different ways' (8698). However, data collection and data crunching alone do not necessarily improve learning, so choosing a set of proxies for learning and collecting information about them is only part of the challenge.

The question 'How will our analytics improve learning?' therefore leads to a much broader question – 'What does it mean to improve learning?' We are so used to seeing improvement represented in terms of test results and examination performance that it is easy to forget that these are only proxies that help us to assess the effects of complex processes of cognitive and social change. New ways of collecting and processing data may open up new ways of identifying and supporting learning gains. As we make progress with the development of learning analytics, we also need to develop our understanding of what it means to learn.

Where is the evidence?

The complexity of the problem means that learning analytics solutions must often make a range of assumptions about which combinations of data provide evidence that learning has, or has not, taken place in a certain context. It is difficult to interrogate these assumptions if there is a 'black-box' situation in which data are input and results generated without users receiving any information about the intervening process. Even when the underlying algorithms are open to scrutiny, users may not have the time or the expertise to check them, or to recheck them when conditions change.

This is dangerous, because it is then difficult to check that the results are reliable (similar data always produce similar results), valid (the results are meaningful) and generalisable (the same analytics will be valid in a variety of contexts). Without a robust quality assurance process in place, users will find it difficult to judge the value of any analytics solution.

Validating analytics will involve linking behaviours and measurable outcomes clearly with pedagogy and with learning benefits, as well as employing an appropriate and robust scientific method. 'The use of LA applications in real practice has to be conscious of the limitations of any analysis, and apply them in a way that is coherent with the limitations of the approach' (8698). Validating analytics will also mean selecting and representing data carefully, using an appropriate conceptual framework and taking context into account when reporting results.

> Research in this space should be tied to pedagogical outcomes. If certain monitoring provides tangible learning benefits, then it should be explored further. If we are just collecting data because we can, and then trying to fit it to arbitrary behavioural outcomes, then the work is futile.
>
> *(2625)*

Validation will also need to build on previous work in learning analytics and in related fields, and will involve scientific cooperation and discussion to share and build on results. Overall, the research should build into a reliable evidence base. Reviewers will need to ensure there is no hype or misrepresentation of results, and that no conflict of interest is involved. They also need to examine underlying assumptions. If, for example, an algorithm is developed to recommend future qualification paths and career paths based on data from previous students, it could perpetuate inequalities if it fails to take into account past discrimination that has limited the success of particular groups.

Even once the quality assurance process is in place, educators and learners will need training in order to be able to question the analytic process and its assumptions, to avoid analytics that have not been validated and to make use of analytics in an appropriate way. 'Lots of professional learning would be required to ensure that all this information is interpreted and used appropriately' (4352).

'Where is the evidence?' is a question we need to keep in mind whenever analytics are in use. In many areas of our life, technology has become so complex that it can only be understood or fixed by trained experts. There is a real danger that learning analytics could follow the same route, using processes and algorithms that are incomprehensible to most teachers and learners. It will be important to develop processes at national and local levels to ensure that learners and teachers are involved with the development and validation of the analytics that influence their lives.

Do staff and learners know how to use the analytics?

Embedding analytics effectively within teaching practice will mean that analytics need to be covered in initial educator training, and within continuing professional development. This training will enable educators to make use of these new tools, to interpret the additional information appropriately and to use the data in meaningful ways.

Staff need to be aware of what analytics can and cannot do, and they need to be able to challenge overblown claims with confidence. They also need opportunities to engage in discussion about the goals and purposes of learning analytics.

A national report on learning analytics in Australia identified capacity building as an issue across the country, and suggested that this capacity building would require not only programmes of professional development, but also academic courses and secondment opportunities (Colvin *et al.* 2015). This training would be designed for classroom teachers and lecturers, but would also include training for educational leaders and managers in order to enable 'innovation, organizational ability and adaptivity' (Colvin *et al.* 2015). A similar study in Europe found it will be necessary to identify the skills required to work in this field, and then to train and support educators to use analytics to support achievement (Ferguson *et al.* 2016a).

Learners will have less need than staff to know about the nuts and bolts of learning analytics. However, as their data are collected and analysed, they will need to be increasingly aware of their rights and responsibilities in this area. Having control over your data, or choosing to assign that control to others, is inextricably bound up with the need for knowledge about the value of that data and the purposes for which it could be used. Respondent 7137 considered that 'It is essential that people are better equipped to understand their rights and how to control how it is used. Putting the owners of the data more central to the process makes it easier for people to accept its value'.

In the opinion of Respondent 5140, 'every single person must be enabled to decide who, when and how to proceed with the data'. In order for that to be possible, or even partly possible, learners and other stakeholders 'need to be educated to deal properly with the choices concerned' (7936). This does not necessarily require technical training, but they do need to have the ability to ask the right questions. 'Although not all consumers of these services will have the skill necessary to understand the computer science and computation, it is necessary that they have the access to question the processes and assumptions under which the data is input, messaged, and output' (6616).

Society is increasingly reliant on data and algorithms (the sets of instructions that are used to process these data). This means that it is particularly important to ask, 'Do staff and learners know how to use the analytics?' because this knowledge is relevant in many areas of life, not simply in an educational context. Algorithms are used to decide which online news and advertisements we see, which insurance package we are offered, whether our job applications can proceed to the next stage, and whether our applications for finance are successful. In order to understand the society in which we live, and in order to make an informed critique of many areas of life, we need a firm grounding in analytics and how they work.

Who is in control and how is this regulated?

The issue of understanding rights and responsibilities is associated with the important issues of data ownership and control. Large datasets are valuable and can be sold and traded. An individual or organisation with control of educational data potentially also has the power to make a range of decisions about the learning and teaching process, and about how learners and teachers should act.

These issues are bound up with regulation of the field and how this regulation should be developed and enforced. Key areas for regulation identified by the VoF and LAEP studies were the protection, ownership and storage of data and the development of standards. Study participants also considered that policy would be needed in the areas of education, privacy, ethics and assessment.

Some VoF respondents saw control of personal data as crucial. They considered this control to be a fundamental human right that should not be dealt with piecemeal at the local level, but should be a matter for the United Nations. 'It must be handled as a human right in the 21st century that every single person should have the power to decide, when + how + for what purpose + for which timeframe + … his/her personal data can/cannot be used' (5140). This would imply a 'Legal framework governed by an international authority. Perhaps key concepts included in the fundamental human rights declaration' (0650).

In the absence of such far-reaching change, there is still a need for some degree of control of data. For example, student data could be sold to third parties, and the 'potential for misuse by e.g. insurance companies is very high' (1643). There is 'the threat of profit-motivated businesses trying to take control of this information, "decommonising" it and selling it back to the individuals concerned' (7936)'. There is also the possibility that data could be used to monitor the process of learning and teaching in negative ways. 'If tracking and monitoring are used to foster and support education and learning, it might be desirable. If it is used to monitor and control and to enforce power it is not desirable' (5297).

In practice, many stakeholders currently share control of data for many purposes. Educational data are already used at national and international levels, as in the case of the PISA studies that track pupils' scholastic performance worldwide. Respondent 2692 noted that 'It's unlikely that governments or institutions will relinquish their control over learner data'. However, if governments controlled all data then educational institutions would lose the power to make informed choices. Nuanced contextual decisions based on local data would become impossible. 'I think it is vital that educational establishments have control over the methods and tools that they use with their students' (9792).

Schools and universities use data about students and teachers in order to exercise their own power – 'there will be times when the institution needs to be able to decide where to share information about progress, attendance and exam results, for example, as part of a disciplinary process' (7076).

External bodies, particularly commercial companies such as virtual learning environment (VLE) providers, are also likely to have access to analytic data. For example, Blackboard already offers an Analytics Suite that offers to 'support tactical decisions with statistics' and Desire2Learn offers Brightspace Insights to 'turn raw data into knowledge'.

VoF respondents had concerns about commercial companies gaining access to student information, worrying that data could be handed over to companies without sufficient consideration of how those data might be used in an intrusive way to monitor behaviour and activities. Respondents were also worried that commercial power could be used to limit data access: 'Experience suggests that money talks and the large international companies that supply education succeed by keeping some of the analytics and data generated hidden behind intellectual property barriers' (4820).

Moving from the corporate to the individual level, control of data could be placed in the hands of a variety of stakeholders. One choice would be the learner. 'The key is to establish the notion that each of us own our own data: the companies do not. If this can be recognised, it moves the needle from our data being co-opted and sold back to us to a vision where the ultimate good can be achieved' (6616). However, learners do not necessarily have the time and the inclination to make a string of decisions about how their data can and cannot be used in a variety of contexts, how it should be stored, who should have access and how long it should be retained. Agreeing to the terms of data use could become a tiresome process, completed without consideration, in the same way as users agree to terms of service without reading them and accept the use of cookies on their computers without investigating their purpose.

Another choice of data controller would be the teacher. 'One of the purposes of LA is to empower the teachers to provide better learning for the individual learners. To know earlier what the learners problems are and to be able to address those problems' (5297). However, teachers have no more time than learners do to spend on considering data collection and storage. Realistically, there are potential problems with data management no matter who is in control, and whether or not the data are used for learning analytics:

> I am not sure who *should* make use of such data: with care and education, it might be of direct value to learners. Teachers are likely better placed to make use of the data, but it is all too easy for it to be a tool for asserting

power. It is even worse to put that control in the hands of system designers and programmers, thus embedding their assumptions and beliefs (or, just as likely, making use of whatever turns out to be easiest to program and capture).

(7473)

The possibility of embedding assumptions and beliefs, consciously or unconsciously, within analytics is bound up with the issue dealt with above of training staff and learners to use analytics, and encouraging them to discuss and reflect on this process. It is also bound up with issues of ethics, the 'systematizing, defending, and recommending concepts of right and wrong conduct' (Ferguson *et al.* 2016b: 7).

There was widespread agreement amongst VoF respondents that there needs to be some form of regulation of ethical issues related to learning analytics, and that control of data has ethical implications. In parallel with the need for regulation in this area, there is also a need for awareness of how data are being used and how analytics function.

Many VoF respondents were vague about what the ethical concerns associated with learning analytics actually are, while stressing the need for an ethics policy, norms of good practice or 'a robust ethical framework, supported by legislation' (7076). Potential problems specifically mentioned include gaming the system, untrustworthy analytics, the creation of a two-tier educational system where only some have access to valid analytics, and the possibility that we could be 'typecasting/stereotyping and even discriminating against certain individuals or groups on the basis of data' (3462).

A body of literature in the field explores these issues in more depth. Ethical challenges include the location and interpretation of data; informed consent, privacy and the de-identification of data; and the classification and management of data (Slade and Prinsloo 2013). Slade and Prinsloo (Prinsloo and Slade 2013, 2015, 2016; Slade and Prinsloo 2014) have explored a range of these ethical issues, particularly those concerned with institutional surveillance, the right to opt out of the data-gathering process and the responsibility of educational institutions to ensure appropriate support and guidance for students. Organisations are already beginning to address these issues by putting in place checklists and codes of practice (Drachsler and Greller 2016; Rodríguez-Triana *et al.* 2016; Sclater 2016; Sclater and Bailey 2015).

The use of 'clear and understood ethical guidelines' (4361) provides one way of dealing with these issues. An alternative approach would be for governments to specify that 'institutional rules and regulations must exist and should meet certain criteria' (5140). This seems feasible, but Respondent 5140 also noted that if a government regulates the use of personal data 'this would influence the independency of Universities in teaching and research'.

Whether the emphasis is on action at the institutional or national level, work on ethics needs to be concerned not only with limitations on unacceptable conduct. If learning analytics can help institutions to provide the best possible support and guidance for their students, then institutions need to be willing to face the challenges in their students' interests. At the same time, analytics will not work well unless they are based on accurate, complete and up-to-date information. Students therefore will have a responsibility to curate, correct and update their data – not just in their own interest, but also in the interest of other students in their cohort.

Learning can be a small-scale activity, involving an interaction between two individuals. Education is a larger enterprise, shaped by political and societal pressures, in which most individuals play only a small role. Learning analytics typically require large datasets, and so they also tend to function at this wider level. It is therefore important to ask 'Who is in control and how is this regulated?' in order to protect individual interests and to ensure that learning analytics are used to optimise, rather than to control, learning.

Future directions

Learning analytics offer the potential for great changes to education. One of the eight LACE visions of the future provocations suggested that, in 2025:

> Activity towards a learning goal is monitored, and analytics provide individuals with feedback on their learning process. This includes suggestions, including peer learners to contact, experts to approach, relevant content, and ways of developing and demonstrating new skills. Formative assessment is used to guide future progress, taking into account individuals' characteristics, experience and context, replacing exams that show only what students have achieved. Texts and other learning materials are adapted to suit the cultural characteristics of learners, revealed by analysis of their interactions. As a result, learners are personally engaged with their topics, and are motivated by their highly autonomous learning. The competences that they develop are valuable in a society in which collection and analysis of data are the norm.
>
> *(Griffiths et al. 2016a: 3)*

Research and development work is currently underway in all these areas, and most of the experts who were invited to take part in the VoF study saw this as a feasible future.

However, this is only one future amongst many. It will require engagement from a wide range of stakeholders to move education towards the desirable visions, and away from those in which use of data becomes obtrusive and unhelpful. The five-point checklist outlined in this chapter provides a straightforward starting point whether you are developing, deploying or just considering learning analytics. Addressing these five questions provides a firm basis for moving forward – what do we want to achieve, how will our analytics improve learning, where is the evidence, do staff and learners know how to use the analytics, who is in control and how is this regulated?

Acknowledgements

The Visions of the Future (VoF) study was funded by the European Commission Seventh Framework Programme as part of the LACE project: Grant number 619424. The LAEP study was funded by the European Joint Research Centre in Seville.

References

Bakharia, A., and Dawson, S. (2011) 'SNAPP: A bird's-eye view of temporal participant interaction', in *LAK11: 1st International Conference on Learning Analytics and Knowledge (27 February – 1 March)*, Banff, Canada.

Buckingham Shum, S., and Ferguson, R. (2012) 'Social learning analytics', *Educational Technology & Society*, 15(3): 3–26.

Center for Evidence-based Education. Available online from: www.cebenetwork.org/picture-evidence-based-education.

Colvin, C., Rogers, T., Wade, A., Dawson, S., Gasevic, D., Buckingham Shum, S., Nelson, K., Alexander, S., Lockyer, L., Kennedy, G., Corri, L., and Fisher, J. (2015) *Student retention and learning analytics: A snapshot of Australian practices and a framework for advancement*, Sydney, Australia: Australian Government: Office for Learning and Teaching, Available online from: he-analytics.com/wp-content/uploads/SP13-3249_-Master17Aug2015-web.pdf.

Dawson, S., Gašević, D., Siemens, G., and Joksimovic, S. (2014) 'Current state and future trends: A citation analysis of the learning analytics field', in *LAK 14*, Indianapolis, IN, ACM, 231–240.

Drachsler, H., and Greller, W. (2016) 'Privacy and analytics: It's a DELICATE issue a checklist for trusted learning analytics', in *Sixth International Conference on Learning Analytics & Knowledge*, Edinburgh, ACM.

Ferguson, R. (2012) *The state of learning analytics in 2012: A review and future challenges*. Technical Report KMI-12-01, Milton Keynes, UK: Knowledge Media Institute, The Open University, Available online from: http://kmi.open.ac.uk/publications/techreport/kmi-12-01.

Ferguson, R., Macfadyen, L. P., Clow, D., Tynan, B., Alexander, S. and Dawson, S. (2015) 'Setting learning analytics in context: Overcoming the barriers to large-scale adoption', *Journal of Learning Analytics*, 1(3): 120–144.

Ferguson, R., Brasher, A., Clow, D., Cooper, A., Hillaire, G., Mittelmeier, J., Rienties, B., Ullmann, T. D., and Vuorikari, R. (2016a) *Research evidence on the use of learning analytics – Implications for education policy (EUR 28294)*, Seville, Spain: Joint Research Centre.

Ferguson, R., Brasher, A., Clow, D., Griffiths, D., and Drachsler, H. (2016b) 'Learning analytics: Visions of the future, in *Sixth International Conference on Learning Analytics & Knowledge*, Edinburgh, ACM.

Ferguson, R., Hoel, T., Scheffel, M., and Drachsler, H. (2016b) 'Special section on ethics and privacy in learning analytics', *Journal of Learning Analytics*, 3(1).

Georgia State University (2015) 'Georgia State University – Dr. Tim Renick', Available online from: www.youtube.com/watch?v=9Z-hp5NrSBg.

Griffiths, D., Brasher, A., Clow, D., Ferguson, R., and Yuan, L. (2016a) *Visions of the future of learning analytics: Horizon Report*, LACE Project.

Griffiths, D., Brasher, A., Clow, D., Ferguson, R., and Yuan, L. (2016b) *Visions of the future: Horizon Report*, Bolton, UK: LACE project, Available online from: www.laceproject.eu/d3-2-visions-of-the-future-2/.

Knight, S., Buckingham Shum, S., and Littleton, K. (2014) 'Epistemology, assessment, pedagogy: Where learning meets analytics in the middle space', *Journal of Learning Analytics*, 1(2): 23–47.

Kurzweil, R. (2005) *The singularity is near*, London: Duckworth.

Macfadyen, L. P., and Dawson, S. (2012) 'Numbers are not enough. Why e-learning analytics failed to inform an institutional strategic plan', *Educational Technology & Society*, 15(3): 149–163.

McIntosh, N. E. (1979) 'Barriers to implementing research in Higher Education', *Studies in Higher Education*, 4(1): 77–86.

McNamara, D. S., Graesser, A. C., McCarthy, P. M., and Cai, Z. (2014) *Automated evaluation of text and discourse with Coh-Metrix*, Cambridge: Cambridge University Press.

Pistilli, M. D., Arnold, K. E., Bethune, M., and Caasi, R. (2012) 'Using academic analytics to promote student success', *EducauSE Review Online*, (July/Aug).

Prinsloo, P., and Slade, S. (2013) 'An evaluation of policy frameworks for addressing ethical considerations in learning analytics', in *Third International Learning Analytics & Knowledge Conference (LAK13)*, Leuven, Belgium, 8—April.

Prinsloo, P., and Slade, S. (2015) 'Student privacy self-management: Implications for learning analytics', in Blikstein, P., Merceron, A. and Siemens, G., eds., *LAK '15*, Poughkeepsie, NY.

Prinsloo, P., and Slade, S. (2016) 'Student vulnerability, agency and learning analytics: An exploration', *Journal of Learning Analytics*, 3(1).

Rienties, B., and Toetenel, L. (2016) 'The impact of learning design on student behaviour, satisfaction and performance: A cross-institutional comparison across 151 modules', *Computers in Human Behavior*, 60: 333–341.

Rodríguez-Triana, M. J., Martínez-Monés, A., and Villagrá-Sobrino, S. (2016) 'Learning analytics in small-scale teacher-led innovations: Ethical and data privacy issues', *Journal of Learning Analytics*, 3(1) 43–65.

Sclater, N. (2016) 'Developing a Code of Practice for learning analytics', *Journal of Learning Analytics*, 3(1): 16–42.

Sclater, N., and Bailey, P. (2015) *Code of practice for learning analytics*, Jisc, Available onine from: www.jisc.ac.uk/guides/code-of-practice-for-learning-analytics.

Siemens, G., Gašević, D., Haythornthwaite, C., Dawson, S., Buckingham Shum, S., Ferguson, R., Duval, E., Verbert, K., and Baker, R. S. J. d. (2011) *Open learning analytics: An integrated and modularized platform (concept paper)* SOLAR.

Slade, S., and Prinsloo, P. (2013) 'Learning analytics: Ethical issues and dilemmas', *American Behavioral Scientist*, 57(10): 1510–1529.

Slade, S., and Prinsloo, P. (2014) 'Student perspectives on the use of their data: Between intrusion, surveillance and care', in *European Distance and E-learning Network Research Workshop, 27–28 Oct*, Oxford, UK.

Turoff, M. (2002) 'The Policy Delphi', in Linstone, H. A. and Turoff, M., eds., *The Delphi method: Techniques and applications* (80–96).

10

TEACHER EDUCATION

MOOCs for the developing world

Clifford Omodele Fyle

Introduction

According to a UNESCO monitoring report, by 2030, the world will need at least 27 million teachers in order to ensure that every child receives a primary school education (UNESCO 2014). This need for teachers is most acute in developing countries in sub-Saharan Africa, the Arab States, and South and West Asia. In order to meet these massive needs, distance-oriented education (Banks *et al.* 2009; Perraton 2010) including various technology-enhanced models, methods, and modes (Burns 2011) have been put forward as possible solutions. Specifically, mobile technologies, and web-based models that include computer-mediated communication platforms, webcasts and webinars, OERs and online courses are examples of the most recent generation of these models.

Notably, over the past few years, Massive Open Online Courses (MOOCs) have been gaining attention as a disruptive force that could change the face of higher education around the world (Armstrong 2012). In addition, their promise as well as implications and possible usefulness for education in developing countries has received considerable attention (Bates 2012; Daniel 2012).

However, the design, development, and facilitation of MOOCs are still in the early stages and what constitutes a successful and effective MOOC has yet to be determined. So, the purpose of this chapter is to contribute to the discourse by focusing on the issues and factors that should be considered before and during the design of teacher education MOOCs for use by learners in developing countries. First, MOOCs in terms of the required pedagogical affordances for effective teacher education will be discussed. Second, the various types and levels of teacher education will be reviewed in light of the appropriateness of MOOCs as learning and teaching platforms. Third, the technological affordances of MOOCs and their suitability for teacher education in developing world contexts will be examined.

Finally, quality assurance and accreditation issues will be reviewed and discussed in terms of their relevance to teacher education MOOCs targeting developing world audiences.

MOOCs and the required pedagogical affordances for teacher education

The pedagogical affordances of MOOCs can be described as those 'unique features sets and characteristics' they encapsulate that 'add value to the learning experience, over and above what might be expected without the technology' (Burden and Atkinson 2008: 121). In order to understand these affordances, it is apt to review them within the contexts of what constitutes a good teacher preparation programme and the attributes a good teacher must have. In this regard, in a recommendation concerning the status of teachers, UNESCO and the ILO adopted a recommendation on the status of teachers that outlined the various elements of a teacher education preparation programme (UNESCO/ ILO 1966). These elements include general studies, the main elements of philosophy, psychology, and sociology as they apply to education, the theory and history of education including comparative education, experimental pedagogy, and school administration and the methods of teaching various subjects. In addition, students should undertake studies related to their intended fields of practice, and engage in the practice of teaching and conducting extracurricular activities under the mentorship of fully qualified teachers. With respect to what constitutes good teaching, after a review of the literature, Burns (2011) outlined five attributes of a good teacher, which tally well with the UNESCO/ILO recommendations. These include a strong level of domain content knowledge, the adoption of a structured approach to instructional activities, a strong pedagogical content knowledge, having knowledge of how students learn, and having a strong sense of self-efficacy.

So, MOOCs must afford learners in teacher education programmes the features, tools, resources, and interactions that will enable the acquisition of the various aforementioned elements of good teaching. These can be outlined as follows:

1   MOOCs must be able to facilitate the acquisition and mastery of domain content knowledge and skills that includes general education as well as focused knowledge of a student's major specialism.
2   MOOCs must facilitate the acquisition of knowledge and skills related to the design and delivery of structured instructional activities.
3   MOOCs must provide opportunities for students to reflect on both the knowledge and skills they acquire, and on their in-the-field teaching practice experiences.
4   MOOCs must provide a platform for social interactions between learners and teacher educators, practicing teacher mentors, other experienced teachers, and their peers.

Closely aligned to the pedagogical affordances required for successful teacher education MOOCs would be issues relating to the ways MOOCs can be used to facilitate different types of teacher education.

The appropriateness of MOOCs for different categories of teacher education

Teacher education is a complex business that requires a multifaceted and multi-layered approach due both to the many different learning needs of the world's children as well as the diverse set of competencies that need to be acquired by teachers. In order to determine the appropriateness of MOOCs for teacher education, it is first necessary to delineate the various types and categories of teacher education specifically as they relate to developing world contexts. After this has been done, the acquisition of requisite knowledge, skills, and attitudes, and their attendant assessment methods can be discussed generally, as well as specifically in relation to their relevance and impact on teacher education MOOCS designed and developed for the developing world.

Teacher education categories and types

Perraton (2010), in a report on the role of open and distance learning in teacher education, categorized teacher education into initial training and continuing professional development. The initial training of teachers could take the form of either pre-service or in-service teachers (Perraton 2010). Pre-service teachers requiring initial training would be those that have had no training prior to getting a job as a teacher in a school. In-service teachers requiring initial training on the other hand are those individuals who already have jobs as teachers, but who never had any initial formal training as teachers. The continuing professional development of teachers can be categorized into teachers who already have a teaching qualification but need upgrading, teachers who need reorientation education due to curriculum change and teachers' career development.

The acquisition of knowledge, skills and attitudes

The acquisition of knowledge, skills, and attitudes through eLearning environments such as MOOCs could be attained by using didactic presentation methods that embody text, audio, or videos, by more interactive discursive one-to-many or many-to-many interactive methods that use channels such as webinars, forums, and live chat technologies, or a combination of both. The specific presentation methods used would not only depend on the material being learned, but also on the nature of the type of MOOC environment being used in the facilitation of this process. In this regard, the two general types, which have been widely discussed in the literature are cMOOCs and xMOOC (Daniel 2012; Kennedy 2014; Siemens 2012). CMOOCs or connectivist MOOCs emphasize the creation of knowledge while xMOOCs or extended MOOCs focus more on the sharing of knowledge (Siemens 2012). CMOOCs have more of a constructivist orientation focusing more on network-based learning and interactions between learners. While xMOOCs lend themselves well to content presentation and the acquisition of knowledge and skills by individual learners.

Assessment in MOOCs

One of the areas of MOOC design where the most experimentation is occurring is with respect to the process of assessment (Sandeen 2013). The 'massive' characteristic of MOOCs combined with its 'open' characteristics makes it different from traditional forms of brick-and-mortar and online and distance education courses which are limited in scale and invariably operate within closed environments. So, for this reason, the nature of MOOCs has led to a number of different assessment methods that can be used to assess student work in efficient, but yet effective ways.

Assessment in MOOCs has been categorized and explained in a variety of ways in the literature (Alber and Debiasi 2013; Chauhan 2014; Sanchez-Vera and Prendez-Espinosa 2015). Alber and Debiasi have listed and described various MOOC document types, which they deem most appropriate for automated assessments. These document types include selection tasks, text, mathematical formulas, and programming assignments. Sanchez-Vera and Prendes-Espinosa on the other hand categorized assessment methods according to MOOC type, with xMOOCs lending themselves well to assessing content using multiple-choice tests and exams and cMOOCs being used more for the assessment of tasks and resources using rubrics as well as for peers assessing each other.

Chauhan reviewed emerging assessment technologies and models that can be built into MOOCs to support and measure the achievement of learning outcomes. These trends include:

- Learner Analytics which are driven by the analysis of student behaviour and use of various MOOC components to inform the design of future assessments (Breslow *et al.* 2013).
- Personal Learning Networks (PLN) which use social media tools to encourage learner participation by creating and sharing knowledge (Kop *et al.* 2011).
- Mobile Learning where a connectivist pedagogy is used in conjunction with mobile technologies to access content and create and share knowledge (Rodriguez 2012).
- Digital Badges (http://openbadges.org/) which is a project launched by the Mozilla Corporation with the aim of rewarding the achievements of learners and thereby encouraging and nurturing lifelong learning.
- Adaptive Assessments which use MOOC features that customize automated assessment and feedback to individual learners based on their ability and learning progress (Meyer and Zhu 2013).

- Automated Assessments which can be used to provide prompt grading and feedback to learner provided assignments (Balfour 2013).
- Recognition of Prior Learning (RPL) where learners present portfolios of previous work and complete summative assessments to demonstrate their learning so that they can earn a certificate or credit (Conrad *et al.* 2013).

Finally, Sanchez-Vera and Prendes-Espinosa also reviewed a number of alternative proposals that could be used as part of carefully designed assessment schemes in MOOCs. These proposals include:

- Mixed peer assessment approaches (Sanchez-Vera and Prendes-Espinosa 2015) which combine peer assessment with assessments by experts.
- Network-based grading (Downes 2013) where learners are assessed on collaborative tasks using a network metric.
- Portfolios which are useful for understanding the learning process used by the student and for providing him or her with feedback.
- 'The mantle of the expert' (O'Toole 2013), where under the facilitative supervision of a teacher, groups of students are designated as expert assessors according to their spheres of expertise.
- The Semantic Web (Berners-Lee *et al.* 2001), which implies that information published can be understood and processed by both humans and machines on the World Wide Web. In this regard, students for example will be able to undertake assessments and through the use of the Semantic Web and its ontologies could receive feedback.
- Learner analytics which has been defined as 'the measurement, collection, analysis and reporting of data about learners and their contexts, for purposes of understanding and optimizing learning and the environments in which it occurs (Long and Siemens 2011: 34).

MOOCs as appropriate teaching and learning platforms

The appropriateness of MOOCs as teaching and learning platforms for teacher education would depend on how they are being used to support the various types and levels of teacher education. For example, the current design of MOOCs that use various content presentation and automated assessment methods would lend themselves well to the acquisition of content knowledge required in both the initial training and aspects of the professional development of teachers. Peer assessment methods currently being used by MOOCs such as Coursera could also work in the acquisition of skills related to the design and development of instructional activities required for teachers in initial teacher preparation programmes. However, the assessment criteria and peer pairing would have to be carefully thought out with an additional component of teacher–educator mentors monitoring the quality of the products being designed and developed. The challenge arises in figuring out effective and efficient ways to reinforce various aspects of the in-the-field teaching experiences required for initial teacher preparation programmes within the MOOCs. Reflection pieces and field reports could be peer-assessed, but the most effective feedback would come from experienced teacher educators. The review and provision of such feedback would not lend itself well to automated methods.

The same issues arise with the supporting of various aspects of the continuing professional development of teachers. Successful teacher professional development requires a social and community-centered approach (Barab *et al.* 2001; Cochran-Smith and Lytle 2001; Murphy and Laferriere 2003). According to Barab *et al.* (2001) this approach should foster a culture of sharing and provide sustained support for teachers as they review and reflect on their beliefs and practices. Teachers for instance needing reorientation education due to curriculum change may have belief and conceptual change issues that may need to be addressed. These require sustained interventions and can take time, sometimes months and years to bear results (Loucks-Horsley and Steigelbauer 1991; McCarthy 1993). Target teachers may need to be continually presented with the new concepts and content in different ways over a period of time before they begin to experience a disconnect between their current beliefs and this new information (Jensen 2005; Nuthall and Alton-Lee 1993).

According to Gaible and Burns (2005), teacher professional or career development (TPD) can be categorized into standardized TPD, site-based TPD and self-directed TPD. Standardized TPDs invariably include the use of training-based approaches where knowledge and skills are presented via face-to-face, broadcast, or online modes. This model is useful for exposing teachers to novel ideas, concepts and instructional methods. Site-based TPDs invariably occur in schools, resource centers, or teacher education colleges. They include the use of facilitators or master teachers and are useful for mastering pedagogic content and technology skills, and focusing on specific issues that teachers encounter in their particular schools or local environment. Self-directed TPDs entail teachers specifying their individual professional goals and selecting the plans and activities that would enable them to achieve those goals. The scope of self-directed TPDs varies depending on individual teacher needs. However, they are most useful to more experienced teachers who have a desire to augment and enrich their knowledge and skills than to less experienced teachers requiring basic or intermediate knowledge and skills.

In terms of their current designs, the appropriateness of MOOCS for teacher professional development related to career improvement would depend on what elements of the different categories the focus is on. While they could be used to serve elements of the three categories of TPD, MOOCs would best lend themselves in terms of usefulness to facilitation of standardized TPDs and certain aspects of self-directed TPDS and less so to site-based TPDs.

In order for MOOCs to fulfill the need for social interaction in communities that include teachers, their peers, teacher–educators and mentors, the parameters of current MOOC designs would have to be extended. In other words, MOOCs designed for teacher professional development would have to include more sophisticated online forums and other technology-oriented social structures and features that would support effective forms of social-constructivist learning. In addition, the standard course design structures and their embedded instructional strategies would need to be adjusted to support the learning that can only take place over longer periods of time with sustained interventions.

In sum, the appropriateness of MOOCs for different categories of teacher education would depend on whether they are being used for the initial training of teachers or for the professional development of existing teachers; the type of knowledge, skills and attitudinal content being presented or facilitated; and the kind of assessment strategies being used. It is important to note that the decision-making process regarding whether a MOOC is appropriate or not for a particular category of teacher education would also depend on a consideration of its suitability in terms of its inherent technological aspects.

The technological affordances of MOOCs and their suitability for teacher education in developing world contexts

The suitability of MOOCs in terms of their technological affordances for developing world contexts depends on the needs of the learner, the technological infrastructure in his or her location and the preparedness of the learner in terms of the requisite elearning readiness skills. The needs of the learner depend on the type and nature of knowledge and skills he or she requires. Certain types of knowledge and skill acquisition lend themselves better to MOOCs than others in terms of efficiency and effectiveness. For example, the acquisition of foundational conceptual knowledge and skills during a pre-service teacher preparation programme could be totally carried out through a MOOC. These could be delivered through videos and in text and audio formats through the Web. Conceptual knowledge and skills could be reinforced and assessed in a variety of ways using automated formative and summative assessment tools, peer assessments tools and discussion forums, chat rooms, etc. However, the acquisition of practical in-classroom skills necessitates that teachers spend substantial amounts of time out in the field in actual schools. These practical skills require substantial interaction between the trainee teacher and students and trained teachers in the physical school classroom. Some of this skills training could be reinforced through activities that take place in a MOOC. It could take the form of interaction with more experienced teachers, mentor teachers, and teacher educators who comment on trainee teacher reflections and have engaging and fruitful dialogues on their in-the-field classroom experiences. However, this component of learning and skills reinforcement of practical in-classroom skills acquisition in the MOOC would not suffice.

The application and use of MOOCs by learners depend on the nature and sophistication of technological infrastructure in place in his or her location. MOOC providers, Edx.org (Edx.org Help page) and Coursera.org (Coursera.org Help page) simply state that the requirement for participation in their MOOC is access to an Internet connection. Udacity.com (Udacity.com FAQs), however, provides more detailed general technical requirements stating required browser versions and Internet connection speeds, minimum specifications for computer operating systems, as well as specific ones for activities such as the playing of videos and online proctoring. So, in general, it can be safe to say that in order to participate fully in a MOOC regardless of the provider, the learner must have access to technology that meets certain basic specifications. These include having access to a computer device (desktop, laptop, tablet, mobile), having a computer device that has browsing software and word-processing software for courses that require this, and having access to an Internet connection with reasonable download and upload speeds. In other words, for active participation in MOOCS, a learner anywhere in the world must have a fairly up-to-date computer device and access to some form of broadband Internet.

However, it is important to note that the quality and sophistication of the technological infrastructures available to learners in developing contexts are still very limited. In addition, the level of ICT penetration is still very low (International Telecommunications Union 2015). As of 2015, the fixed- (wired-) broadband subscription rate in countries under the developing world umbrella was only 7.1 per cent and just 0.5 per cent in the least developed countries. For active mobile-broadband subscriptions in 2015, the rate of penetration was only 39.1 per cent and 12.1 per cent in the least developed countries. In addition, the percentage of households with Internet access in the developing world was only 34.1 per cent and 6.7 per cent in the least developed countries. This means that a teacher education MOOC would be out of the reach of a substantial number of teachers in the developing world, particularly those who are located in the 'least developed countries' of the world (UN-OHRLLS 2012), where even for those who could afford to purchase or have access to computer devices, broadband infrastructures may not exist, or in many cases will be patchy.

The preparedness of the learner in terms of the requisite elearning readiness skills is also an important factor for successful learning and participation in MOOCs. After a review of the literature, Dabbagh (2007) outlined a number of attributes a successful learner should have to participate in elearning environments. He or she should be skilled in the use of online learning technologies, particularly communication and collaborative technologies; have a strong academic self-concept, and good interpersonal and communication skills; have a basic understanding and appreciation of collaborative learning and develop competencies in related skills; acquire self-directed learning skills through the deployment of time management and cognitive learning strategies.

In sum, even when learners in developing countries have access to required technological infrastructures, they may not have the requisite aforementioned elearning readiness skills that will enable them to participate fully in MOOCs. And the reason for this is due to the limited exposure and experience of these learners to the Internet and specifically elearning environments compared to their counterparts in developed countries. To ensure that trainee and in-service teachers in developing countries receive the most optimal standards of tuition and training via MOOCs, the concepts and practices of quality and accreditation are critical.

Quality assurance issues in teacher education MOOCs

The training that teachers receive either initially before the beginning of their careers or on a professional development basis once they are employed in the profession must be of equivalent quality irrespective of the learning environment used. In other words, the quality of the training must be the same regardless of whether the training was received face-to-face in a brick-and-mortar environment, in a blended learning format, or through a distance or elearning platform. The term 'quality' has been generally defined by the International Organization for Standardization as 'the totality of features and characteristics of a product or service that bear on its ability to satisfy stated or implied needs' (ISO 1986: 3.1). In terms of teaching and learning, the Quality Assurance Agency defines academic quality in terms of 'how and how well the higher education provider supports students to enable them to achieve their award' (QAA 2015: 3).

The process of ensuring, maintaining and sustaining academic quality is known as quality assurance, which has also been conceptualized as the 'process of maintaining standards reliably and consistently by applying criteria of success in a course, programme or institution' (NAAC 2007: 82). The concept of 'standards' is a key component in the quality assurance process in the sense of it being 'a measure of processes, performances and outcomes that can be quantified or assessed on a continuum' (Ashcroft and Foreman-Peck 1996: 21).

In a review of quality assurance systems, Nielsen (1997) outlined conditions necessary for the development of quality teacher education in distance learning environments. Nielsen characterized these conditions in terms of internal and external constraints, which must be overcome in order to assure quality. The internal constraints encompassed the relevance and quality of the curriculum and learning materials; the effectiveness of the learning processes; the quality of student assessment systems; and the effectiveness of the system management and control which covered administrative procedures, processes and systems such as the recruitment and registration of students to the production and distribution of learning materials and the training of tutors.

The external constraints included the background and motivation of students; funding support for the distance education programmes particularly in the least developed countries; lack of organizational support for not only teachers in remote areas, but also collegially in the school and the local community; the level of physical, technological and socio-organizational infrastructure development; and cultural differences in terms of the language of instruction, the disadvantaged status of minority languages and the absence of reading cultures in the communities that learners live.

The designers, developers and facilitators of teacher education MOOCs would need to be aware of and incorporate the various aspects of quality assurance as they specifically relate to the training of high quality teachers. The manner in which they do this would depend on the purpose of the MOOCs. It would depend on whether the MOOC content forms part of an institution's curriculum, and/or whether adherence to particular standards and performance indicators have national or cross-border implications. In this regard, it is important to note that different countries and institutions may align their programmes and courses to different standards and quality assurance procedures. Therefore, MOOC designers must take this into consideration by reviewing those most relevant to the MOOC purpose and context.

Quality in elearning and distance education

In reflecting on the meaning of quality in open and distance learning (ODL), Lentell (2006) made the case that ODL programmes should not be addressed in terms of inputs such as best practices and procedures. Rather a determination should be made in terms of outcomes such as 'did this ODL programme achieve its objectives?' However, there are a variety of other views on the concept of quality as it relates to elearning and distance education (Ehlers 2012; Nichols 2002; Ossiannilsson *et al.* 2015; Uvalić-Trumbić and Daniel 2014). The International Council for Open and Distance Education (ICDE) recommends that criteria used for determining the quality of elearning should be made mainstream by developing a common set of standards (Ossiannilsson *et al.* 2015). Ehlers on the other hand disagrees and suggests that different criteria need to be used because there is a fundamental change in the way teaching and learning occurs in distance and elearning environments. Nichols, also in agreement, argues for the use of different criteria due to the multiplicity of digital tools being used. While Uvalić-Trumbić and Daniel suggest that because xMOOCs generally 'replicate traditional university courses,' the quality principles they adhere to can be used to enhance the quality of MOOCs.

A number of quality assurance frameworks have been developed to assess and continually monitor the quality of elearning and distance education courses and programmes in developing countries (Latchem 2016). The AVU Quality Assurance (QA) Framework for Open, Distance and eLearning Programmes was developed by the African Virtual University in 2014 and covers institutional policies and mission; programme design and development; course design and development, learning infrastructure and resources; learner support and progression; learner assessment and evaluation; and community capacity building, development and engagement.

The Quality Assurance of Multimedia Learning Materials (QAMLM) was developed by the Commonwealth Educational Media Centre for Asia with support by the Ministry of Human Resource Development in India and the Ministry of Higher Education in Malaysia (CEMCA 2009). It comprises a set of quality indicators developed in collaboration with practitioners, professionals, and industries involved in the field of quality audit.

The Open University of Sri Lanka in collaboration with the Commonwealth of Learning developed quality assurance protocols in the form of a toolkit that contains a set of standards and protocols (COL, 2009). The purpose of these standards

TABLE 10.1   Ten key areas exemplifying standards and performance indicators for a distance higher education system

Key area	Number of standards identifed	Number of performance indicators identifed
Vision, mission and planning	21	54
Management, leadership and organizational culture	27	79
The learners	7	19
Human resource and development	7	22
Programme design and development	13	33
Course design and development	13	33
Learner support	15	49
Learner assessment	12	38
Infrastructure and learning resources	8	35
Research consultancy and extension services	7	20

Adapted from Quality Assurance Toolkit for Distance Higher Education Institutions and Programmes (COL 2009).

and performance indicators are two-fold. Firstly, they are meant to be used by institutions to conduct self-evaluations of the performance of their processes. The results of these self-evaluations will enable institutions to carry out necessary quality improvement changes. Secondly, they can be used by external agencies to conduct audits and monitor institutional processes for continual learning and improvement. These standards and performance indicators were grouped into ten key criteria (Table 10.1), which represent what are deemed to be the most important features of a distance higher education system, and another six key areas (10.2), which are deemed to be the most pertinent elements necessary for offering distance higher education programmes.

MOOCs can be categorized under the umbrellas of elearning and distance education since they are designed, developed and facilitated using elearning platforms and also because they are delivered invariably at a distance. It is therefore necessary for MOOC developers to understand the concepts of quality and quality assurance as they relate to elearning and distance education.

MOOCs and quality

In a review of the literature on MOOCs and quality, Hayes (2015) laid out a number of considerations which must be accounted for in the design, development, and facilitation of MOOCS. These considerations include the following:

- Quality should be considered in terms of MOOC type rather than generally because up to eight different types of MOOCs serving different learning purposes have been identified (Clark 2013).
- Quality determines the effectiveness and success in the learning course or programme. In this regard, decisions need to be made regarding whether quality in a MOOC can be assessed in the same way as a traditional university course or

whether to account for smaller sequences of learning tailored to an individual learner's goals (Ehlers *et al.* 2013).

- Some criteria may be similar to those made for traditional courses but may have to be interpreted in different ways because of their implementation in the online environment (Creelman *et al.* 2014). For example, when assessing quality in MOOCs, should drop-outs be considered a sign of poor quality or just an issue of individual choice?
- Depending on type, MOOC quality may have to be determined differently because MOOCs can be deemed to be process-driven rather than outcomes-based because of non-exclusivity of enrollment in the course. In this regard some students may enroll but have no intention of completing the course.
- A determination would have to be made regarding the learner audience (Pomerol *et al.* 2015). In other words, what kind of learner is the MOOC trying to attract and for what purpose?

To bring structure to these considerations among others, The Commonwealth of Learning (2016) has developed a set of guidelines that institutions of learning can use to support the determination of the kinds of measures that are useful for assuring the quality of MOOCs. These guidelines were developed using the 3P Model (Biggs 1987) as a framework. The guidelines were categorized into three dimensions of quality namely presage, process and product measures.

The 'presage' measures deal with steps institutions must take before and during the process of developing MOOCs. They include identifying the goals for creating and facilitating the MOOC; establishing key performance indicators; considering resources to be used, taking a systems-oriented approach to the development of the MOOC; using instructional design frameworks to consider the overall design and structure of the MOOC; developing an evaluation plan that includes both the formative and summative phases.

The 'process' dimensions lay out the steps institutions should take during the implementation phase of the MOOC. They include monitoring student learning

TABLE 10.2 Six key areas exemplifying standards and performance indicators for a distance higher education Programme

Key area	Number of standards identifed	Number of performance indicators identifed
Institutional planning and management	33	97
Programme design and development	13	33
Course design and development	13	33
Infrastructure and learning resources	7	22
Learner support and progression	15	49
Learner assessment and evaluation	12	38

Adapted from Quality Assurance Toolkit for Distance Higher Education Institutions and Programmes (COL 2009).

activities and behaviours; developing systems for analyzing and implementing find-ings acquired from data collection on learning, for continuous improvement of the MOOC; and making use of data and feedback for the provision of ongoing staff support and guidance.

The 'product' dimensions can be used to evaluate and report on the MOOCs performance. They include collecting data on key performance indicators (KPI) and reporting on these to the various stakeholders; undertaking a SWOT analysis, which involves determining and assessing the strengths, weaknesses, opportunities and threats with the engagement of key personnel involved in the MOOC. This process and the experiences shared by key personnel will facilitate future planning and development.

MOOCs and accreditation

To implement the aforementioned quality assurance considerations, guidelines, and frameworks relating to teacher education, elearning and distance education, and gen-erally to the intrinsic nature of MOOCS, it may be necessary to work with accredi-tation agencies. The level of this necessity will depend on whether the certifications acquired on course completion are needed for external recognition by employers or as confirmation by institutions as mastery of prerequisite knowledge and skills.

Accreditation has been defined as 'the process or outcome of evaluating whether something, for example, an institution or Programme, qualifies for a certain status' Woodhouse 2013: 3). Accreditation may be of importance to the institution for a number of reasons. First, perhaps because of the requirement for the granting of or renewal of its operational status as a recognized educational entity; second, it may be of importance to students, for example, in terms of their eligibility for certain scholarships; and finally, it may be of importance to graduates in terms of whether they have attained the right standard of qualifications for certain occupations.

Accreditation may be achieved in one or two ways (Ingvarson *et al.* 2006). The institutions may be asked by the accreditation agency to provide evidence that its graduates have achieved the standards. Alternatively, the accreditation agency may directly test the graduates of teacher education programmes using standards specified for graduands. In addition, accreditation can take place at three levels: the institutional level, the programme level, and the course level (Kocdar and Aydin 2015). Course level review processes and quality rubrics include the Chico Rubric (California State University 2003), Quality Matters Rubric (Maryland Online Inc. 2014), and OLC Quality Scorecard (Online Learning Consortium 2014).

In determining whether a MOOC should be accredited or not and how this accreditation should occur, a number of questions may need to be asked (Eaton 2012). These questions include:

1   Through what lens should MOOCs be examined for quality? Should the same lens as used in traditional higher education be used (for example, curricular, faculty and student support) or something thing else?

2   Do MOOCs require additional rethinking of expectations of teaching and learning? For instance, MOOCs deliver instruction in different ways in the form of non-credit offerings to a mass audience; different approaches to teaching, learning in the form of greater reliance on learners, peer-to-peer grading, and auto-grading; and different ways of evaluating learning with the use of data analytics.

3   To what extent do current accreditation processes review the key elements of MOOCs?

4   If decisions were made to accredit MOOCs, what additional toolkits would accreditors require that they did not previously have for their work with traditional higher educational institutions?

5   If decisions are made NOT to accredit MOOCs, what other alternative forms of quality review should take place?

In addition, in the case of teacher education MOOCs for developing world contexts, questions relate to the appropriateness of existing accreditation frameworks for training quality teachers as well. Also the relevance of all the aforementioned questions and issues for institutions and learners in developing countries should be considered.

A set of proposals has been presented by the Commonwealth of Learning (2016) that accreditation agencies can use when dealing with MOOCs. These proposals focus on whether MOOC courses offered provide details of expected learning outcomes and the nature of the measurement of those outcomes. Considering how complex and varied MOOCS are, it is proposed that accreditation agencies should rethink existing quality metrics and frameworks; use a range of measures that incorporate multiple dimensions such as input, process and output variables; contextualize MOOCS within the broader purpose of education; position the learner at the center of considerations of quality; and focus on both accountability and improvement.

UNESCO (2005) has also developed a set of guidelines for all the stakeholders involved in the quality provision of cross-border higher education. The guidelines were drawn up for the protection of students and other stakeholders from low-quality, educational offerings as well as from those providers such as degree and accreditation mills, who bring the education industry into disrepute. Also, they were meant to act as a stimulus for the development of higher education across national borders. These two sets of proposals can be particularly useful for teacher education MOOC designers operating in developing countries that do not have adequate quality assurance and accreditation infrastructures.

However, for teacher education MOOCs with a focus on developing world contexts, accreditation proposals will need to account for both in terms of the MOOC composite quality as well as its constituent component parts. In other words, the MOOC developers will need to consider guidelines dealing with teacher education accreditation, guidelines dealing with elearning and distance education courses and programmes, and guidelines that focus on assessing quality and accrediting MOOCs specifically. In addition, the context and situation in developing countries must be built into whatever guidelines are being used.

Future directions

Future analyses, investigations and studies need to be conducted to clarify and streamline a number of issues relating to the design, development and implementation of teacher education MOOCs for developing world contexts. In terms of design, analyses need to be carried out to determine how the parameters of current MOOC design frameworks can be extended to incorporate the socialization and mentoring structures and strategies that form an integral part of teacher education. Methods of assessing quality in MOOC instruction also need to be evaluated and streamlined to account for the different types of MOOCs, their alignment with/ or inclusion in higher and further educational institutional programme offerings, and their practical appropriateness for teacher education in developing countries. And finally, in conjunction with studies on quality, accreditation processes need to be reviewed to understand how national and international governmental agencies can effectively measure and evaluate quality, and subsequently accredit institutions under their remits offering teacher education MOOCs.

Conclusion

The knowledge, skills, and attitudes that teachers need to acquire throughout their lifetime training and professional development as teachers is complex. As a result, when designing MOOCs for teacher education, care must be given to selectivity regarding what is most effective to be taught and its fit with existing teacher education programmes. Also, in this regard, there are various issues and design considerations that must be made during the possible design of a MOOC for teacher education that will be of benefit to learners in developing world contexts. A successful design would need to incorporate features and tools that would harness research-proven pedagogical principles. Consideration would also need to be given to the appropriateness of MOOCs for different kinds of teacher education. The acquisition of particular kinds of knowledge and skills can be achieved much more efficiently and effectively in MOOCs than others. In addition, the learners' access to the most appropriate technologies, as well as their preparedness in terms of the required elearning competencies, must be studied as these may vary from one developing world context to the other. Finally assessment, quality assurance and accreditation considerations will need to be made with respect to the qualities that make MOOCs uniquely different from previous elearning and distance education platforms.

References

Alber, S., and Debiasi, L. (2013) 'Automated assessment in massive open online courses. Seminar aus Informatik, University of Salzberg, 2013', *Alberta Journal of Educational Research*, 49(1): 71–83.

Armstrong, L. (2012, August). 'Coursera and MITx: Sustaining or disruptive?' Los Angeles, CA: Changing Higher Education. Retrieved from www.changinghighereducation. com/2012/08/coursera-.html.

Ashcroft, K., and Foreman-Peck, L. (1996) 'Quality standards and the reflective tutor', *Quality Assurance in Education*, 4(4): 17–25.

Balfour, S. P. (2013) 'Assessing writing in MOOCs: Automated essay scoring and calibrated peer review', *Research & Practice in Assessment*, 8(1): 40–48.

Banks, F., Moon, B., and Wolfenden, F. (2009) 'New modes of communication technologies and the reform of open and distance learning programmes: A response to the global crisis in teacher education and training', in 23rd ICDE World Conference on Open and Distance Learning, 8–10 June 2009, Maastricht.

Barab, S., Makinster, J. G., Moore, J., Cunningham, D., and The ILF Design Team. (2001) 'Designing and building an online community: The struggle to support sociability in the Inquiry Learning Forum', *Educational Technology Research and Development*, 49(4): 71–96.

Bates, T. (2012, August 5) 'What's right and what's wrong about Coursera-style MOOCs? Online learning and distance education resources'. Retrieved from www.tonybates. ca/2012/08/05/whats-right-and-whats-wrong-about-coursera-style-moocs/.

Berners, L., Hendler, J., and Lassila, O. (May 1, 2001), 'The Semantic Web', *Scientific American*. Retrieved from www.scientificamerican.com/article/the-semantic-web/.

Biggs, J. (1987) *Study process questionnaire manual*, Hawthorn: Australian Council for Educational Research.

Breslow, L., Pritchard, D. E., DeBoer, J., Stump, G. S., Ho, A. D., and Seaton, D. T. (2013) 'Studying learning in the worldwide classroom: Research into edX's first MOOC', *Research and Practice in Assessment*, 8: 13–25.

Burden, K., and Atkinson, S. (2008) 'Evaluating pedagogical affordances of media sharing web 2.0 technologies', Paper presented at ASCILITE 2008, Melbourne, Australia.

Burns, M. (2011) *Distance education for teacher training: Modes models, and methods*, Washington, DC: Education Development Center.

Chauhan, A. (2014) 'Massive Open Online Courses (MOOCs): Emerging trends in assessment and accreditation', *Digital Education Review*, No. 25.

Clark, D. (2013) MOOCs: Taxonomy of 8 types of MOOC. Retrieved from https:// donaldclarkplanb.blogspot.ie/2013/04/moocs-taxonomy-of-8-types-of-mooc.html.

Cochran-Smith, M., and Lytle, S. (2001) 'Beyond certainty: Taking an inquiry stance on practice', in A. Lieberman and L. Miller (Eds.), *Teachers caught in the action: Professional development that matters*, New York, NY: Teachers College Press (pp. 45–58).

Commonwealth Educational Media Centre for Asia (CEMCA) (2009) *Quality assurance of multimedia learning materials*, New Dehli: CEMCA.

Commonwealth of Learning (2009) *Quality assurance toolkit for distance higher education institutions and programmes*, Vancouver: Commonwealth of Learning.

Commonwealth of Learning (2016) *Guidelines for quality assurance and accreditation of MOOCs*, Burnaby, British Columbia, Canada: Commonwealth of Learning.

Conrad, D., Mackintosh, W., McGreal, R., Murphy, A., and Witthaus, G. (2013) *Report on the assessment and accreditation of learners using OER*, Alberta, Canada: Commonwealth of Learning. Retrieved from http://oasis.col.org/handle/11599/232.

Creelman, A., Ehlers, U-D., and Ossiannilsson, E. S. (2014) 'Perspectives on MOOC quality: An account of the EFQUEL MOOC Quality Project, INNOQUAL', *International Journal for Innovation and Quality in Learning*, 3. Retrieved from http://papers.efquel.org/index. php/innoqual/article/viewFile/163/49.

Dabbagh, N. (2007) 'The online learner: Characteristics and pedagogical implications', *Contemporary Issues in Technology and Teacher Education*, 7(3): 217–226.

Daniel, J. (2012) 'Making Sense of MOOCs: Musings in a maze of myth, paradox and possibility', *Journal of Interactive Media in Education*.

Downes, S. (2013) 'Assessment in MOOCs [Web log post]'. Retrieved from http://halfanhour.blogspot.com/2013/05/assessment-in-moocs.html.

Eaton, J. S. (2012) 'MOOCs and accreditation: Focus on the quality of "direct-to-students" education', *Inside Education*, (9)1, November 7, 2012.

Ehlers, U. D. (2012) 'Quality assurance policies and guidelines in European distance and e-learning', in I. Jung and C. Latchem (Eds.), *Quality assurance and accreditation in distance education and e-learning: Models, policies and research*, London, UK: Routledge (pp. 79–90).

Ehlers, U. D., Ossiannilsson, E., and Creelman, A. (2013), 'Week 1: MOOCs and Quality – Where are we – where do we go from here …?' Retrieved from http://mooc.efquel.org/first-post-of-the-series/.

Gaible, E., and Burns, M. (2005) 'Using technology to train teachers: Appropriate uses of ICT for teacher professional development in developing countries', Washington, DC: *info*Dev/World Bank.

Hayes, S. (2015) 'MOOCs and quality: A review of the recent literature', Gloucester, UK: Quality Assurance Agency (QAA). Retrieved from http://donaldclarkplanb.blogspot.se/2013/04/moocs-taxonomy-of-8-types-of-mooc.html.

Ingvarson, L., Elliott, A., Kleinhenz, E., and McKenzie, P. (2006) 'Teacher education accreditation: A review of national and international trends and practices', *Australian Council for Educational Research*. Retrieved from http://research.acer.edu.au/teacher_education/1.

International Organization for Standardization. (1986) ISO 8402, Geneva, Switzerland: ISO.

International Telecommunication Union (ITU) (2015) 'Measuring the information society', Geneva: ITU. Retrieved from http://www.itu.int/en/ITU-D/Statistics/Documents/publications/misr2015/MISR2015-w5.pdf.

Jensen, E. (2005) *Teaching with the brain in mind* (2nd ed.). Alexandria, VA: Association for Supervision and Curriculum Development. June/ICDEQualitymodels.pdf.

Kennedy, J. (2014) 'Characteristics of Massive Open Online Courses (MOOCs): A research review, 2009–2012', *Journal of Interactive Online Learning*, 13(1): 1–16.

Kocdar, S., and Aydin, C. H. (2015) 'Quality assurance and accreditation of MOOCs: Current issues and future trends', Paper presented at the Open Educational Global Conference, Banff, Calgary, Canada.

Kop, R., Fournier, H., and Mak, J. (2011). A pedagogy of abundance or a pedagogy to support human beings? Participant support on massive open online courses. *The International Review of Research in Open and Distributed Learning*, 12(7): 74–93.

Latchem, C. (2016) 'Open and distance learning quality assurance in commonwealth universities', Burnaby, British Columbia, Canada: Commonwealth of Learning. *Learning and Academic Analytics, Siemens, G., 5 August* 2011. Retrieved from www.learninganalytics.net/?p=131.

Lentell, H. (2006) 'Promoting quality in distance, flexible, and ICT-based education: Reflections on the meaning of quality in open and distance learning', Paper presented at meeting of the Commonwealth of Learning, Rio De Janeiro, Brazil.

Long, P., and Siemens, G. (2011) 'Penetrating the fog: Analytics in learning and education', *Educase Review*, September/October, 2011. Retrieved from http://er.educause.edu/~/media/files/article-downloads/erm1151.pdf.

Loucks-Horsley, A., and Steigelbauer, S. (1991) 'Using knowledge of change to guide staff development', in A. Lieberman and L. Miller (Eds.), *Staff development for education in the 90s*, New York: Teachers College Press (pp. 15–36).

McCarthy, H. (1993) 'From deadwood to greenwood: Working with burned out staff', *Journal of Staff Development*, 14(1): 42–46.

Maryland Online, Inc. (2014) Quality Matters rubric standards (5th ed.). Maryland, MD: Quality Matters. Retrieved from https://luonline.lamar.edu/_files/documents/luonline/qm-standards-2014-1.pdf.

Meyer, J. P., and Zhu, S. (2013) 'Fair and equitable measurement of student learning in MOOCs: An introduction to item response theory, scale linking, and score equating', *Research & Practice in Assessment*, 8(1): 26–39.

Murphy, E., and Laferriere, T. (2003) Virtual communities for professional development: Helping teachers map the territory in landscapes without bearings', *Alberta Journal of Education Research*, 49(1): 71–83.

National Assessment and Accreditation Council (NAAC) (2007) *Quality assurance in higher education: An introduction*, Bangalore: NAAC.

Nichols, M. (2002, December) 'Development of a quality assurance system for elearning projects', Paper presented at ASCILITE2002, UNITEC, Auckland, New Zealand. Retrieved from www.ascilite.org/conferences/auckland02/proceedings/papers/004.pdf.

Nielsen, H. D. (1997) 'Quality assessment and quality assurance in distance teacher education', *Distance Education*, 18(2).

Nuthall, G. A., and Alton-Lee, A. (1993) 'Predicting learning from student experience of teaching: A theory of student knowledge construction in classrooms', *American Educational Research Journal*, 30: 799–840.

Online Learning Consortium (2014) *OLC Quality Scorecard 2014: Criteria for excellence in the administration for online programs*. Newburyport, MA: Online Learning Consortium. Retrieved from http://onlinelearningconsortium.org/consult/quality-scorecard.

Ossiannilsson, E., Williams, K., Camilleri, A. F., and Brown, M. (2015) 'Quality models in online and open education around the globe: State of the art and recommendations', Oslo, Norway: International Council for Open and Distance Education. Retrieved from http://icde.org/admin/filestore/News/2015_January-.

O'Toole, R. (2013) 'Pedagogical strategies and technologies for peer assessment in Massively Open Online Courses (MOOCs)', Unpublished discussion paper. University of Warwick, Coventry. Retrieved from http://wrap.warwick.ac.uk/54602/. Open, Distance and E-Learning.

Perraton, H. (2010) *Teacher education: The role of open and distance learning*, Vancouver: Commonwealth of Learning. Retrieved from http://dspace.col.org/bitstream/handle/11599/290/Teacher_Education_Role_ODL.pdf?sequence=1&isAllowed=y.

Pomerol, J. C., Epelboin, Y., and Thoury, C. (2015) 'A MOOC for whom and for what purposes?', in *MOOCs*, Hoboken, NJ, USA: John Wiley & Sons, Inc.

Quality Assurance Agency (QAA) (2015) *The quality code: A brief guide*, London: QAA.

Rodriguez, C. O. (2012) 'MOOCs and the AI-Stanford like courses: Two successful and distinct course formats for massive open online courses', *European Journal of Open and Distance learning*. Retrieved from http://files.eric.ed.gov/fulltext/EJ982976.pdf.

Sanchez-Vera, M. M., and Prendes-Espinosa, M. P. (2015) 'Beyond objective testing and peer assessment: Alternative ways of assessment in MOOCs', RUSC. *Universities and Knowledge Society Journal*, 12(1): 119–130.

Sandeen, C. (2013) 'Assessment's place in the new MOOC world', *Research & Practice in Assessment*, 8: Summer.

Siemens, G. (2012) 'MOOCs are really a platform', *eLearnspace*. Retrieved from www.elearnspace.org/blog/2012/07/25/moocs-are-really-a-platform/.

UN-OHRLLS (2012) *The least developed countries: Things to know, things to do*, New York: Office of the High Representative for the Least Developed Countries, Landlocked Developing Countries and Small Island Developing States.

UNESCO (2005) *Guidelines for quality provision in cross-border higher education*, Paris: UNESCO.

UNESCO/ILO (1966) *Recommendation concerning the status of teachers*, Adopted by the Special Intergovernmental Conference on the Status of Teachers, Paris, 1966.

UNESCO Institute of Statistics. (2014) *Policy Paper 15/Fact Sheet 30: Wanted: Trained teachers to ensure every child's right to primary education.* Retrieved from http://unesdoc.unesco.org/images/0022/002299/229913E.pdf.

Uvalic´-Trumbic´, S., and Daniel, J. (2014) 'A guide to quality in post-traditional online higher education', Dallas, Texas: Academic Partnerships. Retrieved from www.icde.org/filestore/News/2014_March-April/Guide2.pdf.

Woodhouse, D. (2013) 'Global trends in quality assurance', *Quality Approaches in Higher Education*, 5(1): 3.7.

11

DIGITAL GAMES-BASED LEARNING

Time to adoption: Two to three years?

Wayne Holmes

Introduction

It is now more than 16 years since the publication of Marc Prensky's seminal book *'Digital Game-based Learning'* (2001), in which he argued persuasively that computer games will soon be 'how everyone learns'. More recently, in seven of the ten years up to 2014, the influential NMC Horizon Report on emerging technologies for teaching and learning (NMC 2004–2015) repeatedly identified digital games-based learning (DGBL) as a technology likely to be adopted 'within two to three years'. Meanwhile, from 2011, the Gartner Hype Cycle for Education (Gartner 2011–2015) tracked DGBL as it preoccupied developers, policy makers, researchers and many teachers. But then in 2015, despite many research studies reporting positive outcomes (reviewed in Boyle *et al.* 2016), DGBL slipped unceremoniously into the Hype Cycle's 'trough of disillusionment' while the Horizon Reports of that year did not mention DGBL at all.

Given the extensive research efforts and that many leading scholars have argued that DGBL can provide significant and possibly unique opportunities for learning (e.g. Gee 2004b), with some advocates even seeing it as a silver bullet for much that is wrong in education (Salen 2008), why does DGBL appear to be moving off the agenda? And why, in spite of all of the promise and hype, does DGBL remain relatively uncommon in classrooms (Takeuchi and Vaala 2014)? Unfortunately, this chapter does not have all the answers. Instead, the aim is to explore some core issues, building on insights from the learning sciences that influence whether or not DGBL is used successfully in classrooms. In order to provide a context, the chapter begins with an overview of digital games and the characteristics that make them candidate learning technologies.

Digital games

To understand digital games (computer games or video games) it is first useful to take a step back, to consider what is actually meant by games in general – although defining games is notoriously difficult. For Huizinga (1955), an early games theorist, games constitute a 'magic circle' which separates the experience from that of the real world; while for Caillois (1962), games are light-hearted, non-productive activities, which are bound in time and place and have uncertain outcomes. However, according to the philosopher Wittgenstein (1968), it is not actually possible to precisely define a game without some games falling outside of that definition. Instead, he argues that games should be understood as activities that are 'recognised as games' because they share some 'family resemblances'.

Here, drawing on Wittgenstein's approach, the family resemblances of digital games will be taken to include the following, all implemented in a digital technology: virtual make-believe environments, rules of play (limitations and constraints), tasks that require effort, explicit aims and objectives, feedback from actions, scored outcomes, virtual or real competition, lack of consequences for the real world and fun (Whitton 2014). The takeaway is that any digital game might share some or all of these family resemblances.

The many thousands of digital games now available may also be classified by genre. Most agree that core genres include 'action games' (such as the first-person shooter 'Doom'), 'adventure games' (such as 'Tomb Raider', featuring the character 'Lara Croft'), 'god games' (such as 'Civilization'), 'role-playing games' (such as 'World of Warcraft'), 'platform games' (such as those featuring the 'Mario Brothers' or 'Sonic the Hedgehog') and 'puzzle games' (such as 'Tetris' or 'Snake'). Digital games also come in many formats, including complex software packages (such as 'The Sims'), massively multiplayer online games that require many hours of game-play (such as 'Call of Duty'), 'casual games' that can be played in just a few minutes (including mobile phone apps such as 'Angry Birds' or 'Candy Crush') and digital physical games controlled with whole-body movements (such as 'Dance Central' or 'Wii Sport').

One reason often advanced for using digital games to support learning is that they are so popular. Surveys have consistently shown that around 90 per cent of children play digital games (Lenhart *et al.* 2015). However, it shouldn't be assumed that the popularity of digital games is universal. Some figures for the number of children who play digital games are based on them doing so for as little as one hour per month (Macchiarella 2013), while other research has shown that some children often prefer other activities, such as playing outside with friends or building with 'Lego' bricks; for those children, digital games are fun but not that important (Holmes 2011).

Before moving on to consider how the family resemblances of digital games are exploited in DGBL, a controversy that should not be avoided will be mentioned. Starting with one of the first digital games, 'Spacewar!', developed in 1962 at MIT, which involved the shooting of enemy spaceships, many popular digital games have involved increasingly graphic violence. Many such games have also been misogynistic or at least have reinforced gender stereotyping. While violent games have frequently been linked to aggressive behaviour (Anderson 2004), particularly towards women (Gabbiadini *et al.* 2016), the research remains contentious. This is partly because of the methodological challenges, with some identifying links between violent gameplay and real-life violence (Hall *et al.* 2015), while others suggest that any causal link is very weak (Przybylski 2014). It is unlikely that this debate will be resolved any time soon.

Digital games-based learning

DGBL, also known as educational games, learning games or serious games, has been the subject of academic research for at least 35 years, with Thomas Malone's PhD thesis, 'What makes things fun to learn? A study of intrinsically motivating computer games.' (1980), often being cited as one of the first academic studies. Since then, there have been many thousands of published studies and numerous systematic reviews (such as Boyle *et al.* 2016).

Even casual observation of children playing games inevitably leads to the conclusion that, as they do so, very often they are learning. For many, children's play is an essentially constructivist activity, the proto-natural form of learning, and learning is intrinsically playful (Bruner 1960). For Gee (1999), entertainment digital games are themselves 'learning machines', because their designs comprise various core principles of learning. This learning might be as simple as discovering how to use the game controller to move a character through the game's virtual space. It might involve learning about the benefits and disadvantages of cooperation, either with in-game avatars or with real people in shared game environments, or the learning of fine visual/motor coordination and faster decision-making. Although this learning 'may be more incidental than intentional, more broad than deep...it nevertheless does constitute learning' (Facer *et al.* 2003: 201).

However, DGBL usually aims to build on and move beyond these foundations, to address learning objectives more useful for, and often aligned with, the demands of formal education. It adapts and applies for educational purposes the mechanisms of digital games designed for entertainment. For example, by responding directly to the input of the player, allowing the player to take action and affect outcomes, digital games can encourage the player to explore a new idea or can reinforce learned behaviour. They can also be designed to adapt to the skills and needs of the individual, just as teachers do – increasing the challenge for players who move rapidly through the gameplay, reducing the challenge for players who are progressing more slowly. Digital game worlds can also be designed to simulate and render safe or make accessible features of the real world (for example, the inside of a volcano), giving learners a more authentic experience than is possible with books or other media. Players in authentic game environments are enabled to 'experience' things, rather than just read about them or watch them, situated in a virtual world that somehow connects to their real lives.

Another reason digital games are promoted as candidate learning technologies is that they can be highly motivating. Many possible motivational mechanisms have been identified (Iacovides *et al.* 2011), with a distinction often made between 'intrinsic' and 'extrinsic' motivation. At an intrinsic level, digital games can provide compelling narratives and dramatic tensions, using dynamic interactions, high-quality imagery and sounds. Some also offer optimal challenges, choice over actions and goals, adaptive and rapid feedback and an escape to an alternative reality. Playing digital games might also be pleasurable because doing so offers opportunities to discover new information and to acquire new skills and abilities, or because they can lead to a sense of achievement, mastery, empowerment and enhanced self-esteem when actions lead to results. Of particular interest is the pleasure gained from overcoming adversity, moving from the negative emotions of frustration or confusion to the joyful emotions of achievement when a gameplay challenge is overcome.

In fact, DGBL often claims to take this one step further. Digital games are candidate learning technologies because motivation to engage with the game, it is argued (e.g. Hoffman and Nadelson 2010), leads almost inevitably to learning, a claim that has been contested elsewhere. While Whitton (2007), for example, found no evidence of a connection between the enjoyment of entertainment games and games to support learning, Calvo-Ferrer's participants (2016) were more motivated by extrinsic factors (such as rewards external to the game). In short, the relationship between DGBL, motivation and learning is complex, such that the ability of games to motivate students is insufficient on its own to warrant their extensive use in classrooms. Instead, the impact of the games on the student's learning, in its widest sense, rather than simply their ability to motivate, ought to be prioritised.

In the last section, a controversy that surrounds digital games was mentioned: digital game violence. The impact of this contentious issue on DGBL should also be considered but again the debate is complex. Here, the precautionary principle (Van Der Sluijs *et al.* 2005) will be noted, which suggests that whatever the demonstrable effect on learning of a realistic or stylised violent digital game (e.g. Habgood and Ainsworth 2011), because any possible detrimental effects of such a game are unknown, teachers should think very carefully before including them in school classrooms.

The unfulfilled promise

Many reasons for the unfulfilled promise of DGBL have been proposed, not least the fact that using digital games to support formal learning for some remains controversial (Bourgonjon *et al.* 2013). While, as has been noted, some have argued for a games-based revolution in educational practices, others have rejected the notion that digital games may have a part to play in the classroom, fearing that this trivialises the serious project that is formal learning. In any case, if working within prevailing educational contexts rather than trying to fundamentally disrupt them, it can be challenging to find games that address the intended learning outcomes of existing curricula (while not being weighed down with unrelated or inappropriate content or gameplay), and that appeal to the varied interests of the students who are being invited to play the game (if a student does not enjoy playing a particular game, they are probably less likely to engage with it or to learn the intended outcomes from doing so).

Identifying DGBL that can be easily timetabled, that is not overly complicated and for which there are appropriate supporting materials, can also be difficult. And even when all of this is achieved successfully, orchestrating DGBL within the constraints of a typical classroom can still be very demanding of both the school and teacher (Dillenbourg and Jermann 2010). There is the need for robust infrastructure, computers and possibly Internet access, and for technical support and contingency plans (alternative classroom activities) for when the technology stops working mid-class – all of which can also impact on school budgets. Teachers also are often inexperienced in how DGBL works or might be used to support learning (Takeuchi and Vaala 2014) and thus would benefit from appropriate professional training, which again has serious cost implications. They also need opportunities to familiarise themselves with the game in question, because every game is different and so may affect learning differently, and to plan how that game and the learning that it might afford will fit into their teaching.

Teachers also need to be confident that the game does what it claims to do. This means that evaluations have to go beyond the simple and all too often poorly constructed quasi-experiments that tend to under-estimate the impact of the DGBL's novelty in the classroom and over-estimate its effectiveness (an inevitable consequence of researcher/developer-conducted evaluations, known as super-realisation bias, Cronbach 1980). Instead, smart evaluations should consider all the reasons a game might or might not be effective in a particular classroom, as well as what 'effective' in this context actually means. In any case, no matter how 'good' the game is shown to be, if no significant benefit is 'perceived', if teachers do not believe that it will reduce their daily workload or enhance student learning, if they fear it will compromise or undermine their usual classroom teaching, or if they are not confident in its pedagogical validity, DGBL is unlikely to become a feature of regular teaching practices.

Another set of reasons why DGBL has not obviously yet fulfilled its early promise centres on the fact that it is itself complex. As has been discussed, what actually constitutes DGBL is open to debate, with very different games being used with very different learners in very different contexts and for very different purposes. Another open question is whether DGBL is appropriate for typical learners, who are mostly well-served by existing pedagogical practices, or are better suited to specific groups of learners such as those who struggle in particular subjects or those who have disengaged (Holmes 2011).

Meanwhile, 'learning', which is after all the core aim, tends to be understood by many DGBL developers in simplistic terms. Rather than drawing on the learning sciences or education research, DGBL researchers and developers all too often assume that their personal experiences of learning and their limited knowledge of some education theory or psychology buzzwords (such as Vygotsky's 'zone of proximal development', 1978; or Csikszentmihályi's theory of 'flow', 1997) are sufficient to inform their approach to pedagogy – an assumption that should be challenged. Perhaps because they are usually enthusiastic digital game players and software developers, they too often tend to focus on the gameplay and the software development, those aspects of DGBL that perhaps they find most interesting, while the learning is more or less taken for granted. In any case, the rich history of learning sciences and education research is mostly ignored while learning is misunderstood 'as an activity relatively invariant across people, subject areas, and educational objectives' (Dede 2011: 236).

For example, as already mentioned, much DGBL research focuses on the impact of gameplay on student motivation, without much real understanding of the impact of motivation or of gameplay on learning. As a second example, some DGBL research references somewhat unquestionably so-called individual 'learning styles' that have long been heavily criticised by learning sciences researchers (Krätzig and Arbuthnott 2006). And finally, much DGBL research focuses exclusively on immersive constructivist games, while dismissing games that have been designed to give learners opportunities for deliberate practice, despite repetition and practice repeatedly being shown to be a prerequisite for robust learning (Richey and Nokes-Malach 2015).

Design approaches to DGBL

DGBL has been researched from various perspectives, for example, mobile games-based learning (Koutromanos and Avraamidou 2014), students learning to make digital games (Kafai and Burke 2015), digital games used to help bridge the gap between school and parents (Holmes 2011), DGBL literacy (Burn 2016) and so-called brain training games (although it is worth noting that most brain training games have been shown not to transfer any cognitive benefits beyond playing the game itself, Melby-Lervåg and Hulme 2013). Here, however, the focus will be on three DGBL 'design approaches': games designed for entertainment and repurposed for learning, games designed for structured practice and games designed for knowledge construction.

Entertainment games repurposed for learning

The first approach to DGBL that will briefly be reviewed involves the repurposing for the classroom of digital games that have been designed as entertainment. Examples of these so-called 'commercial-off-the-shelf' (COTS) games that have been used in classrooms include 'Myst', 'Spore' and 'Wii Play Motion' (there are many others). The fantasy computer game 'Myst' has been used as a stimulus in speaking and writing lessons for primary school students (Rylands 2010), the god game 'Spore' has been used to teach secondary school students about evolution (Schrader *et al.* 2016), while the 'Wii Play Motion' physical digital game has even been used to support the teaching of statistics to university students (Stansbury *et al.* 2014).

However, although each of these examples have reported notable successes, the use of COTS games in the classroom is far from straightforward. Even when teachers are experienced in using them, know how they are played and how they might contribute to desired learning outcomes, they can be difficult to use effectively. Their content might not be relevant, such that it has to be squeezed into the curriculum. And, if it is relevant, it might not be accurate – these games have been designed to entertain and thus often liberally interpret their subject matter (for example, Schrader *et al.* 2016, found that Spore included too many misconceptions about evolution for it to be especially useful in science classrooms).

Games designed for structured practice

Other DGBL has been designed specifically for use in classrooms, the most common of which usually aim to encourage the structured practice of previously learned educational content. These so-called 'edutainment' or 'drill and practice' games (Shuler 2012), such as the 'Maths Blaster' and 'Reader Rabbit' series, became very popular in many classrooms and family homes during the 1980s and the approach remains common (Takeuchi and Vaala 2014).

In this type of DGBL, the learning opportunity, which is often nothing more than answering a worksheet-style task in a digital context, often occurs *before* the game's gameplay. The playful opportunity is then the reward for a correct response and is usually unrelated to the learning (for example 'Neurogames', Kahn and Reed 2012, in which an animated squirrel is the reward for correctly answering a mathematics question). This is a behaviourist approach to learning with *delayed* rewards. In rather more sophisticated structured practice DGBL, the learning takes place *during* the gameplay but still that gameplay is usually but not always unrelated to the learning (for example, 'Timez Attack', West 2010, in which mathematics questions appear as unrelated obstacles to be overcome in order to progress within a virtual battle). This is a behaviourist approach to learning with more *immediate* rewards.

In fact, it is because these structured practice games build upon a behaviourist pedagogy that they are often pejoratively known as 'chocolate-covered broccoli', an attempt to conceal the 'unpleasant but nutritional' learning with the sugary coating of gameplay (Bruckman 1999). Nonetheless, although it is probably true to say that structured practice DGBL games too often 'combine the entertainment value of a bad lecture with the educational value of a bad game' (Squire and Jenkins 2003: 8), the evidence is that they can have a useful role in the classroom because they can encourage the 'deliberate practice' necessary for robust learning (Karpicke 2012).

This use of game-like rewards in response to correct answers has more recently been called a gamified approach to learning. More generally, 'gamification' is 'the use of game design elements in non-game contexts ..., a software service layer of reward and reputation systems with points, badges, levels and leader boards' (Deterding *et al.* 2011: 1). The reward mechanisms of entertainment games (rather than the games themselves or their gameplay) are repurposed to heighten the extrinsic motivation of those involved in a range of activities from exercise to shopping (although, in so doing, this might have a negative impact on intrinsic motivation, Mekler *et al.* 2013). Points, badges, levels and leader boards (PBL) aim to build upon the positive impact of social competition. For example, increasing levels of challenge can help to encourage the player to continue playing, a key aim being to 'level up' during gameplay to higher and higher levels, with leader boards enabling players to see when they have achieved a competitive score and letting other players know that they have done so. From a more pedagogical perspective, they can also provide players with a clear medium-term goal, which is known to support learning.

Incidentally, while PBL are used in many educational apps and online DGBL, a more holistic and sophisticated approach to the gamification of learning, using games-based quests and teamwork rather than the more mechanical PBL, has been developed for use in whole classrooms (World of Classcraft, Young 2013) and applied to an entire school to create highly immersive, game-like learning experiences (Quest to Learn, Shute and Torres 2012).

Games designed for knowledge construction

Interestingly, despite the advocacy, there are probably fewer examples of DGBL designed to support the active construction of knowledge than there are of DGBL designed to support the practice and consolidation of knowledge. And for those that do exist, the aim is most often to raise awareness of issues outside core curricula rather than to learn specific curriculum content. For example, a recent review identified 18 different digital games all of which had been designed to raise awareness and promote behaviours for individuals who have diabetes (to encourage self-management, to promote sensible eating habits and to increase the frequency of blood glucose checking) (Lazem *et al.* 2015). Other similar games (Romero *et al.* 2015) focus on promoting the so-called 'twenty-first-century skills' (including communication, collaboration and problem solving) which have long been known to be essential for all learners.

Something that often distinguishes DGBL designed for knowledge construction is the intimate relationship between the learning and the gameplay. Rather than the learning taking place before or during often unrelated gameplay (as with games designed for structured practice in which the gameplay is an immediate or delayed reward for the successful review of pre-learned knowledge), in games designed for knowledge construction, the learning is *immersed in* and takes place *through* the gameplay thus exploiting the exploratory nature of many digital games. Learning *through* the gameplay situates the learning content in the virtual context of the digital game's world and it does so by means of authentic gameplay tasks.

This might be considered a more constructivist approach. It aims to exploit the various family resemblances of entertainment digital games in order to provide learners with opportunities to construct knowledge about specific educational content. For example, to win the game you need to cross the chasm, to cross the chasm you need to build a bridge, to build the bridge you need to learn about Archimedes' 'law of the lever'. In such a game, players learn the physics in order to play and win the game; they do not play the game in order to learn the physics, even though that is the aim of the educational game developer. Arranging for the learning to take place *through* the digital gameplay (a process also known as 'intrinsic integration', Kafai 1996) also effectively situates that learning in a context potentially familiar to the learner or at least one to which they can relate.

An early example of DGBL designed for knowledge construction was 'Global Conflicts: Palestine' (Egenfeldt-Nelson 2006), an immersive first-person game. In this DGBL the student plays a freelance journalist new to Jerusalem in Israel who is tasked with gathering information about the Israel/Palestine conflict by undertaking various missions and speaking with the locals. A second example is 'Frequency 1550' (Huizenga *et al.* 2009), a mobile game developed to help students in their first year of secondary school to learn about fifteenth century Amsterdam by undertaking assignments around the medieval streets in order to discover various historical information, the gameplay goal being to gain citizenship of the city. A third notable example is 'The Mystery of Taiga River' (Barab 2013), which takes place in a 3D immersive world in which students are environmental scientists undertaking an investigation with the aim of saving a park where ecological problems are causing all the fish to die. The game provides students with opportunities to explore issues of water quality (pH, dissolved oxygen and nutrient run-off) and how to adopt a structured approach to weighing evidence and making valid decisions.

DGBL and educational practice

The various practical challenges around integrating DGBL successfully in classrooms have already been mentioned. However, an often forgotten issue still needs to be addressed. While classrooms are fundamentally social environments, all too often DGBL is designed to engage learners as separate individuals. Typically, each student sits with their own digital screen (desktop, laptop or tablet), playing their own bounded digital game (there are relatively few multiplayer DGBLs), and while there is often a classroom hubbub, it is unclear whether or how these fractured and unstructured conversations are contributing to the student's learning.

In short, the game developer has focused on the software and has not fully addressed the social interactions that might occur around the game, what has been called the game's 'affinity space' (Gee 2004a), and has not leveraged important socio-constructivist opportunities for learning. Indeed, research into a prototype platform game designed to be played by individual children (who were low-attaining in mathematics) has revealed that the game was most useful when, in addition to supporting individual learning, it was also a focal point for social interaction between the children and between the children and the supporting adults (Holmes 2013). Those children who sat next to each other as they played talked about what they were trying to achieve in the game, swapped hints about the gameplay and discussed how best to answer the mathematical problems. In other words, by encouraging a dialogue about the mathematics embedded in the game and by providing a pedagogically robust scaffold for that conversation, the game helped the children to construct and enhance their own mathematical understanding. Their collaboration and conversations around the game also provided the adults with opportunities to recognise individual needs so that they could give appropriate and timely guidance.

Gee (2011) formalises the distinction between the game as software, what he refers to as the 'small g game', and the social system of interactions that players engage in around the game, what he refers to as the 'Big G Game'. This meta level includes opportunities for dialogue with peers, for making connections to other aspects of the lesson being taught and for interactions extended beyond the classroom. The argument is that, while well-designed 'small g game' experiences involving the solving of complex problems can lead to learning, the 'Big G Game' 'acts as a force multiplier on the impact potential of bounded game–play experiences' (Barab et al. 2013: 2) leading to deeper learning and enhancing transfer of that learning to the wider context. Accordingly, although developers all too often focus wholly on the individual bounded 'game', it is in fact the entire meta-level 'Game' that must be considered when developing, implementing or evaluating the impact of DGBL.

The DGBL mentioned earlier, 'The Mystery of Taiga River', developed over more than a decade (Barab et al. 2013), exemplifies a 'Big G Game' approach. Beyond the game itself, 'Taiga River' involves a learning platform, on which the game is hosted and which connects several games together to provide a learning journey, a data and analytics dashboard to allow teachers and students to inspect and learn from their learning trajectories, social network functionality which might enable discussion and reflection and a gamification layer of carefully designed extrinsic rewards. It is this 'Big G' infrastructure that contextualises the 'small g game' into a flexible affinity space connected with the real-world and extending beyond the classroom.

However, although 'The Mystery of Taiga River' and its 'Big G' approach is self-evidently engaging and powerful, it is not without issues. To begin with, it has required many thousands of hours of development time, and hence has probably been relatively costly, yet it addresses only a very small part of the science curriculum (although the underlying game engine has been designed so that the game is modifiable for other curriculum areas). It can also be time consuming to implement in classrooms. It requires teachers to devote some hours to understanding both the 'game' and the 'Game' and how they might best be used to complement their teaching and to address their intended learning outcomes. And it can require a significant amount of student time (learning how to play the game, the gameplay itself and the important post-game debriefing, helping the students to make connections back to other classroom learning), which can be out of balance with the relative importance of this small area of the science curriculum.

There are various other issues that impact on the design and implementation of effective DGBL in educational practice. Focusing again on the sophisticated example of 'Taiga River' (if only to emphasise quite how difficult the DGBL project actually is), what happens if the students who are asked to engage with the game either do not like this particular gameplay, or prefer to protect game playing from the classroom (Facer *et al.* 2003) or do not like playing digital games much at all? Just because the designers have designed a game that they, as experienced gamers, find engaging, it should not be assumed that their enthusiasm will be shared by all students. For example, the reality is that many students prefer casual games (like 'Angry Birds') to adventure games (like 'Tomb Raider'), and they might be disadvantaged if an adventure game becomes the only opportunity to learn a specific area of curriculum content.

A last issue to be mentioned here refers to the fact that games like 'Taiga River' prioritise knowledge construction opportunities, exploration and discovery, effectively to the exclusion of structured practice opportunities. This begs the question of whether, by being so critical of games routinely dismissed as chocolate-covered broccoli, a necessary part of the learning process is being overlooked: 'it is not that behaviourism, or constructivism, is wrong; indeed, they are both right in their core ideas but they are incomplete and, on their own, make an inadequate basis for design' (Burkhardt 2006: 131).

DGBL and the learning sciences

A refrain in this chapter has been the complexity that surrounds digital games and how they might be used in and beyond classrooms, a challenge that is only amplified when the implications of the learning sciences on DGBL are considered (Connolly *et al.* 2014). Learning has been a core focus of psychological and neuroscientific research since at least Ebbinghaus's experiments on memory (1913). Since that time, research into the cognitive and social psychology of learning and the neuroscience of learning has been extensive and has involved constructs as wide ranging as executive function, metacognition, self-regulation, affect and social cognition. Here, having acknowledged that there have been numerous studies involving DGBL and each of these concepts, the earlier discussions of structured practice and motivation will be concluded from a learning sciences perspective.

DGBL, structured practice and the learning sciences

As has been noted, DGBL games that have been designed for knowledge construction tend to be more engaging, because they are more like immersive entertainment digital games, which is perhaps why they are frequently preferred by researchers and developers over games designed for structured practice. However, as has also been suggested, enabling the construction of knowledge on its own is insufficient for robust learning, and deliberate retrieval practice is also a prerequisite (Rummel *et al.* 2016). Robust learning involves 'deep, connected and comprehensive knowledge about a domain that lasts over time, accelerates future learning, [and] transfers easily to new situations' (Mazziotti *et al.* 2015: 2). It comprises three closely coupled types of knowledge: factual knowledge (knowing 'what'), procedural knowledge (knowing 'how') and conceptual knowledge (understanding 'why'); and it includes three closely coupled processes: knowledge and skills acquisition, consolidation and storage, and recall (mostly conscious recall, for declarative knowledge, and often unconscious recall, for skills).

The often ignored reality in much DGBL research and development is that, while constructivist opportunities might be more engaging and are essential for the acquisition of conceptual knowledge, deliberate practice is also necessary for being able to consolidate and store (encode into long-term memory) and then later recall and apply almost all types of knowledge. Put another way, while immersive games-based experiences might enable students to construct an in-depth understanding of a particular topic, a process which is a fundamental component of learning, if they do not also have opportunities to practise what they have learned, they are likely to soon forget it. The importance of structured deliberate practice for learning is also supported by neuroscience research, which has identified various possible neural mechanisms for learning (such as synaptic plasticity, Löwel and Singer 1992], and axonal myelination, Mabbott *et al.* 2009), each of which requires some form of repeated activity.

The design-based research mentioned earlier of a platform game to support children low-attaining in mathematics set out to build on this psychology and neuroscience research by combining knowledge construction and structured practice in the one DGBL (Holmes 2013). This game provided guided constructivist opportunities: problems that could only be solved by thinking mathematically, in which the child was able to discover and construct their own mathematical knowledge. These were also integrated with behaviourist opportunities: repeated practice to help the child encode their newly constructed mathematical knowledge into long-term memory, to help ensure that knowledge became automatic and without error, with the aim being to free their working memory for other cognitive demands.

DGBL, motivation and the learning sciences

As noted earlier, the relationship between DGBL, motivation and learning is complex. However, the learning sciences provide some insight. For example, cognitive neuroscience suggests that our brain's response to rewards in games increases when players are in the presence of their peers (Chein *et al.* 2011), which refers back to our earlier discussion of the impact on DGBL of social context. In addition, parallel research suggests that players actually respond to a competitor's loss as if it were their own gain (Howard-Jones *et al.* 2010), which emphasises the potential impact of competition on enjoyment and self-efficacy.

In the brain, motivation is associated with the generation of dopamine, a neurotransmitter which also has links to learning. Within limits, the larger the reward, the larger the motivational signal and the bigger the potential impact on learning. However, Howard-Jones (2011) explains that the anticipation of rewards can be as important or more important than the reward itself, and that perhaps counter-intuitively the use of uncertain rewards, anticipated rewards that might or might not be given depending on chance, actually increases the overall dopamine release. This additional dopamine helps explain why uncertain rewards can be enticing (a fact not lost on the developers of mainstream digital games) and provides a potential neurobiological explanation for our attraction to games involving an element of chance (consider, for example, sporting fixtures where the teams are well-matched and thus the result uncertain, which are typically much more engaging than one-sided games). Of particular importance, anticipation of an uncertain reward is also likely to generate an extended window of enhanced attention, an opportune teachable moment during which students are especially receptive to encoding long-term memories, which the design of DGBL or its use in classrooms might exploit (Holmes *et al.* 2013).

However, although children appear to prefer the inclusion of chance-based uncertainty in learning tasks (Howard-Jones and Demetriou 2009), the use of uncertain rewards is counter to much educational practice. In classrooms and other educational contexts, teacher consistency tends to be valued and uncertain rewards are usually thought to be unfair and de-motivating, which is perhaps why chance-based or uncertain rewards are rarely featured in DGBL. Nevertheless, the research briefly reviewed here demonstrates a clear link between increased motivation and improved deep learning in response to chance, such that researchers and developers should consider using uncertain rewards more often in DGBL.

Coda

Despite all of the research, advocacy and hype over 35 years, DGBL remains relatively uncommon in classrooms – and, for some, using digital games to support formal learning remains controversial. Nevertheless, there are many examples of 'well-designed' DGBL that have been shown capable of supporting 'some' aspects of learning in 'some' contexts. However, as has been argued in this chapter, if DGBL is to realise its demonstrable potential, a clearer understanding of digital games, learning and classroom practices in all their complexity is necessary. For example, researchers and developers need to consider combining core approaches to DGBL (games designed to support structured practice and games designed to support knowledge construction), rather than prioritising one to the exclusion of the other. They need to draw on insights from the learning sciences, by working with learning scientists, and move beyond simplistic understandings of what it actually means to learn and what conditions best support learning (for example, recognising the importance of retrieval practice and the impact of uncertain rewards on learning). And, if DGBL is to be seen by teachers as a useful complement to their usual teaching practices, DGBL designers and researchers also need to consider and accommodate the 'Big G' (the affinity space and the classroom context), in addition to the 'small g' of educational games. Only once all that is in place might DGBL be widely adopted within two to three years.

References

Anderson, C. A. (2004) 'An update on the effects of playing violent video games', *Journal of Adolescence*, 27: 113–122.

Barab, S. A. (2013) *Taiga River*. Available online from https://gamesandimpact.org/ taiga_river [1 October 2016].

Barab, S. A., Center for Games and Impact and E-Line Media (2013) *Game infused theory of change for impact.* Available online from https://gamesandimpact.org/ resources/game-infused-theory-of-change [1 October 2016].

Bourgonjon, J., Grove, F. D., Smet, C. D., Van Looy, J., Soetaert, R., and Valcke, M. (2013) 'Acceptance of game-based learning by secondary school teachers', *Computers in Education*, 67: 21–35.

Boyle, E. A., Hainey, T., Connolly, T. M., Gray, G., Earp, J., Ott, M., Lim, T., Ninaus, M., Ribeiro, C., and Pereira, J. (2016) 'An update to the systematic literature review of empirical evidence of the impacts and outcomes of computer games and serious games', *Computers in Education*, 94: 178–192.

Bruckman, A. (1999) *Can educational be fun - Chocolate covered broccoli* (unpublished presentation provided by the author). Presented at the Game Developer's Conference, San Jose, CA.

Bruner, J. S. (1960) *The process of education*, Cambridge, MA: Harvard University Press.

Burkhardt, H. (2006) 'From design research to large-scale impact: Engineering research in education', in J. van den Akker, K. Gravemeijer, S. McKenney, N. Nieveen (eds.), *Educational design research*, London: Routledge (pp. 121-150).

Burn, A. (2016) 'Liber ludens: Games, play and learning', in C. Haythornthwaite, R. Andrews, J. Fransman, E. M. Meyers (eds.), *The SAGE handbook of e-Learning research*, Thousand Oaks, CA: SAGE Publications Ltd. (pp. 127–151.

Caillois, R. (1962) *Les jeux et les hommes (Man, play and games)*, Champaign, IL.: University of Illinois Press.

Calvo-Ferrer, J. R. (2016) 'Educational games as stand-alone learning tools and their motivational effect on L2 vocabulary acquisition and perceived learning gains', *British Journal of Educational Technology*, 48(2): 264–278.

Chein, J., Albert, D., O'Brien, L., Uckert, K., Steinberg, L. (2011) 'Peers increase adolescent risk taking by enhancing activity in the brain's reward circuitry: Peer influence on risk taking', *Developmental Science*, 14: F1–F10.

Connolly, T. M., Hainey, T., Boyle, E., Baxter, G., and Moreno-Ger, P. (eds.) (2014) *Psychology, pedagogy, and assessment in serious games.* Hershey, PA: IGI Global.

Cronbach, L. J. (1980), *Toward reform of program evaluation: Aims, methods and institutional arrangements.* San Francisco, CA: Jossey-Bass Publishers.

Csikszentmihályi, M. (1997) 'Flow and education', *NAMTA Journal*, 22: 2–35.

Dede, C. (2011) 'Developing a research agenda for educational games and simulations', in S. Tobias and J. D. Fletcher (eds.), *Computer games and instruction*, Hershey, PA: Information Age Publishers (pp. 233–250).

Deterding, S., Dixon, D., Khaled, R., and Nacke, L. (2011) 'From game design elements to gamefulness: Defining gamification', in A. Lugmayr, H. Franssila, C. Safran and I. Hammouda (eds.), *Proceedings of the 15th International Academic MindTrek Conference: Envisioning Future Media Environments.* Tampere, Finland (pp. 9–15).

Dillenbourg, P., Jermann, P. (2010) 'Technology for classroom orchestration', in M. S. Khine, I. M. Saleh (eds.), *New science of learning: Cognition, computers and collaboration in education*, New York, NY: Springer-Verlag (pp. 525–552).

Ebbinghaus, H. (1913) *Memory: A contribution to experimental psychology*, New York, NY: Teachers College, Columbia University.

Egenfeldt-Nelson, S. (2006) *Case study of global conflicts: Palestine.* Available online from http://egenfeldt.eu/papers/case_study_global_conflicts.pdf [1 October 2016].

Facer, K., Furlong, J., Furlong, R., and Sutherland, R. (2003) *ScreenPlay: Children and computing in the home*, London: Routledge.

Gabbiadini, A., Riva, P., Andrighetto, L., Volpato, C., and Bushman, B. J. (2016) 'Acting like a tough guy: Violent-sexist video games, identification with game characters, masculine beliefs, & empathy for female violence victims', *PLOS ONE* 11.

Gartner (2011–2015) *The Gartner hype cycle for education*. Available online from www.gartner. com/doc/ 3090218 [1 August 2016].

Gee, J. P. (1999) 'Good video games and good learning', *Community College Review*, 27: 73–92.

Gee, J. P. (2004a) *Situated language and learning: A critique of traditional schooling*, New York, NY: Routledge.

Gee, J. P. (2004b) *What video games have to teach us about learning and literacy*, New York, NY: Palgrave Macmillan.

Gee, J. P. (2011) 'Reflections on empirical evidence on games and learning', in S. Tobias and J.D. Fletcher (eds.), *Computer games and instruction*, Hershey, PA: Information Age Publishers (pp. 223–232).

Habgood, M. P. J., and Ainsworth, S.E. (2011) 'Motivating children to learn effectively: Exploring the value of intrinsic integration in educational games', *Journal of the Learning Sciences*, 20: 169–206.

Hall, G., Hamby, S., and Hedges, L. (2015) *American Psychological Association task force on violent media technical report on the review of the violent video game literature*, Washington DC: American Psychological Association.

Hoffman, B., and Nadelson, L. (2010) 'Motivational engagement and video gaming: A mixed methods study', *Educational Technology Research and Development*, 58: 245–270.

Holmes, W. (2011) 'Using game-based learning to support struggling readers at home', *Learning, Media and Technology*, 36: 5–19.

Holmes, W. (2013) *Level Up! A design-based investigation of a prototype digital game for children who are low-attaining in mathematics* (Unpublished PhD thesis), University of Oxford.

Holmes, W., Howard-Jones, P., Tanimoto, E., Jones, C., Demetriou, S., Morgan, O., Perkins, P., and Davies, N. (2013) 'Neuroeducational research in the design and use of games-based teaching', in P. Escudeiro and C. Vaz de Carvalho(eds.) *Proceedings of the 7th European Conference on Games Based Learning* (pp. 235–243).

Howard-Jones, P., and Demetriou, S. (2009) 'Uncertainty and engagement with learning games', *Instructional Science*, 37: 519–536.

Howard-Jones, P.A., Bogacz, R., Yoo, J. H., Leonards, U., Demetriou, S. (2010) 'The neural mechanisms of learning from competitors', *NeuroImage* 53: 790–799.

Howard-Jones, P., Demetriou, S., Bogacz, R., Yoo, J. H., and Leonards, U. (2011) 'Toward a science of learning games', *Mind Brain and Education*, 5: 33–41.

Huizinga, J. H. (1955) *Homo ludens: A study of the play-element in culture*, Boston, MA: Beacon Press.

Huizenga, J., Admiraal, W., Akkerman, S., Dam, G. (2009) 'Mobile game-based learning in secondary education: Engagement, motivation and learning in a mobile city game', *Journal of Computer Assisted Learning*, 25: 332–344.

Iacovides, I., Aczel, J., Scanlon, E., Taylor, J., and Woods, W. (2011) 'Motivation, engagement and learning through digital games', *International Journal of Virtual and Personal Learning Environments*, 2: 1–16.

Kafai, Y. B. (1996) *Constructionism in practice: Designing, thinking and learning in a digital world*, Mahwah, NJ: Lawrence Erlbaum Associates.

Kafai, Y. B., and Burke, Q. (2015) 'Constructionist gaming: Understanding the benefits of making games for learning', *Educational Psychology*, 50: 313–334.

Kahn, M. M., and Reed, J. (2012) 'An evaluation of Neurogames®: A collection of computer games designed to improve literacy and numeracy', in T. Michael (ed.), *Technologies, innovation, and change in personal and virtual learning environments*, Hershey, PA: IGI Global (pp. 141–154).

Karpicke, J. D. (2012) 'Retrieval-based learning: Active retrieval promotes meaningful learning', *Current Directions in Psychological Science*, 21: 157–163.

Koutromanos, G., and Avraamidou, L. (2014) 'The use of mobile games in formal and informal learning environments: A review of the literature', *Educational Media International*, 51: 49–65.

Krätzig, G. P., and Arbuthnott, K. D. (2006) 'Perceptual learning style and learning proficiency: A test of the hypothesis', *Journal of Educational Psychology*, 98: 238–246.

Lazem, S., Webster, M., Holmes, W., and Wolf, M. (2015) 'Games and diabetes: A review investigating theoretical frameworks, evaluation methodologies, and opportunities for design grounded in learning theories', *Journal of Diabetes Science and Technology*, 10(2): 447–452.

Lenhart, A., Smith, A., Anderson, M., Duggan, M., and Perrin, A. (2015) *Teens, technology and friendships*, New York, NY: Pew Research Center.

Löwel, S., and Singer, W. (1992) 'Selection of intrinsic horizontal connections in the visual cortex by correlated neuronal activity', *Science* 255: 209–212.

Mabbott, D. J., Rovet, J., Noseworthy, M. D., Smith, M. L., and Rockel, C. (2009) 'The relations between white matter and declarative memory in older children and adolescents', *Brain Research*, 1294: 80–90.

Macchiarella, P. (2013) *Trends in digital gaming: Free-to-Play, social, and mobile games*, Dallas, TX: Parks Associates.

Malone, T. W. (1980) *What makes things fun to learn? A study of intrinsically motivating computer games*, (Unpublished PhD thesis), Stanford, CA: Stanford University.

Mazziotti, C., Holmes, W., Wiedmann, M., Loibl, K., Rummel, N., Mavrikis, M., Hansen, A., and Grawemeyer, B. (2015) *Robust student k: Adapting to individual student needs as they explore the concepts and practice the procedures of fractions* (workshop paper), Presented at the 17th International Conference on Artificial Intelligence in Education, Madrid.

Mekler, E. D., Brühlmann, F., Opwis, K., Tuch, A. N. (2013) 'Do points, levels and leaderboards harm intrinsic motivation?: An empirical analysis of common gamification elements', in *Proceedings of the First International Conference on Gameful Design, Research, and Applications, Gamification '13*, New York, NY: ACM (pp. 66–73).

Melby-Lervåg, M., and Hulme, C. (2013) 'Is working memory training effective? A meta-analytic review', *Developmental Psychology*, 49: 270–291.

NMC (2004-2015) *The New Media Consortium Horizon Report*. Available online from www.nmc.org/publication-type/horizon-report [1 October 2016].

Prensky, M. (2001) *Digital game-based learning*, St. Paul, MN: Paragon House.

Przybylski, A.K. (2014) 'Electronic gaming and psychosocial adjustment', *Pediatrics*: 2013–4021.

Richey, J. E., and Nokes-Malach, T. J. (2015) 'Comparing four instructional techniques for promoting robust knowledge', *Educational Psychology Review*, 27: 181–218.

Romero, M., Usart, M., and Ott, M. (2015) 'Can serious games contribute to developing and sustaining 21st century skills?' *Games Cultures*, 10: 148–177.

Rummel, N., Mavrikis, M., Wiedmann, M., Loibl, K., Mazziotti, C., Holmes, W., and Hansen, A. (2016) *Combining exploratory learning with structured ractice to foster conceptual and procedural fractions knowledge*, presented at the International Conference of the Learning Sciences, Singapore.

Rylands, T. (2010) The Myst game series explained. Available online from www.timrylands. com/html/myst.html [1 October 2016].

Salen, K. (Ed.) (2008) *The ecology of games, connecting youth, games, and learning (The John D. and Catherine T. MacArthur Foundation Series on Digital Media and Learning)*, Cambridge, MA: The MIT Press.

Schrader, P., Hasan, D., and Keilty, J. (2016) 'Breaking SPORE: Building instructional value in science education using a commercial, off-the-shelfhelf game', *Journal of Learning, Teaching, and Scholarship in a Digital Age*, 1: 63–73.

Shuler, C. (2012) *What in the world happened to Carmen Sandiego? The edutainment era: Debunking myths and sharing lessons learned*, New York, NY: The Joan Ganz Cooney Center at Sesame Workshop.

Shute, V. J., and Torres, R. (2012) 'Where streams converge: Using evidence-centered design to assess Quest to Learn', *Technology-Based Assessments for 21st Century Skills. Theoretical and Practical Implications from Modern Research*, 91–124.

Squire, K. D., & Jenkins, H. (2003) 'Harnessing the power of games in education', *Insight*, 3(1), 5–33.

Stansbury, J. A., Wheeler, E. A., and Buckingham, J. T. (2014) 'Can Wii engage college-Level learners? Use of commercial off-the-shelf gaming in an introductory statistics course', *Computers in the Schools*, 31: 103–115.

Takeuchi, L. M., and Vaala, S. (2014) *A national survey on teaching with digital games*, New York, NY: Joan Ganz Cooney Center.

Van Der Sluijs, J. P., Kaiser, M., Beder, S., Hosle, V., Kemelmajer de Carlucci, A., and Kinzig, A. (2005) *The precautionary principle. World commission on the ethics of scientific knowledge and technology*, Paris, France: UNESCO.

Vygotsky, L. S. (1978) *Mind in society: Development of higher psychological processes*, Cambridge, MA: Harvard University Press.

West, R. E. (2010) *Evaluation report of big brainz' timez attack*, Provo, UT: Brigham Young University.

Whitton, N. (2007) 'Motivation and computer game based learning', in R.J. Atkinson, C. McBeath, S.K.A. Soong, and C. Cheers (eds.) *ICT: providing choices for learners and learning. Proceedings ASCILITE Singapore 2007*, Singapore: Nanyang Technological University (pp. 1063–1067).

Whitton, N. (2014) *Digital games and learning: Research and theory*, London: Routledge.

Wittgenstein, L. (1968) *Philosophische Untersuchungen* (*Philosophical investigations*, translated by G.E.M. Anscombe, P.M.S. Hacker, and J. Schulte), Oxford: Basil Blackwell.

Young, S. (2013) *World of classcraft* Available online from worldofclasscraft.com/en [1 October 2016].

12

CYBERBULLYING

From 'old wine in new bottles' to robots and artificial intelligence

Conor Mc Guckin and Lucie Corcoran

Introduction

As we often remark to colleagues, just when we were getting towards a better understanding of 'traditional' face-to-face (f2f) (Mc Guckin *et al.* 2010) bully/victim problems among school pupils, along came cyberbullying! At this point in the history of aggressive behaviour among school pupils, there exists a wealth of literature regarding the phenomenon of school bullying (see also Smith 2014, for a recent introduction and review). Whilst we have known about the insidious bullying behaviours of Flashman in Hughes' (1857) novel *Tom Brown's School Days*, Bauman (2011) reports that whilst the first reported use of the term 'cyberbullying' is often ascribed to Bill Belsey (2003), earlier uses of the term can be found in a *New York Times* article about cyber addiction in 1995.

And so, that's the historical scope of our canvas in this area of human behaviour. We could probably even trace incidences of bully/victim problems among children back to the start of time and the early cave paintings of the Cro Magnon (Corcoran *et al.* 2015; Drogin and Young 2008). At a theoretical and conceptual level, much of the work in this area can be considered within the broader field of human aggression. A review of the theories, or the genetic determinants, of aggression is beyond the scope of this chapter. However, one theoretical proposition remains with us and will not go away: are we not born aggressive and with Freud's "Thanatos" death drive (Freud and Hubback 1922) – should we not just accept that we are animals and are born with aggressive tendencies – and that the society we have constructed is a 'gilded cage' where we convince ourselves that we are truly free, have free-will and are not aggressive? Could it be that by ignoring and denying our biology, are we beached on the shores of dogma, believing that good will win out against evil? Are research efforts and applied practice in the area of cyberbullying futile? As we progress through this chapter, whilst we remain cognisant of this theoretical possibility, we are adamant that it would be even more futile to ignore the very real issues that children and young people (CYP) are confronted with, both in and out of school. In fact, as adult members of an ethical society, we see it as our responsibility to ameliorate the insidious effects of cyberbullying. There is a useful quote from Linda Sanford (1991) that guides us in our work as educators and researchers, and it serves as our alarm clock every morning: it is possible not to be responsible for a problem yet still to be responsible for its solutions.

With this, it is our hope that you will enjoy reading and learning about the issues that have enthused us as educators and researchers, yet have saddened us as adults who are concerned about the happiness and educational attainment of CYP. This chapter provides a review of the research knowledge in the area of cyberbullying, from the first study in 2003 (Zych *et al.* 2015) to the state of the knowledge at the end of 2015 (Smith and Berkkun 2016) and through 2016. In doing this, we explore the issues that have intrigued the research and applied communities, and we attempt to 'stop and stand and stare' into the future – to identify what we think are the crucial developments that are just over the horizon.

Setting the scene: From f2f bully/victim problems to cyberbullying

Following the early and important examination of school-based victimisation in Scandinavia by Dan Olweus during the 1970s (Olweus 1978), the issue of bully/ victim problems among CYP quickly became an important focus for researchers, educators, psychologists and policy-makers. What had previously been ignored or mislabelled (e.g. character building, part of growing up) was now an important area of focused attention. The locus of much of this early work was in northern and western European countries, with other important work being conducted in Australia, and a smattering of activity in other countries (see also Smith *et al.* 1999 for an important cross-national review).

Only much later did we see a significant increase in the attention paid to this type of 'low-level aggression' by our colleagues in the US. A question we always pose to students is, was the US focused on a much higher level of aggression in schools (e.g. guns, knives) and only became more focused on bully/victim problems after the events that unfolded at Columbine High School on 20 April 1999? Whilst this question is complex, it does help us to understand and appreciate the multiple factors that have to be considered when we think about bully/victim problems among CYP in schools. There are often so many myths about this topic that the reality sometimes gets lost in the 'noise' of popular notions – for example, that 'sticks and stones may break my bones, but words will never hurt me' (*The Christian Recorder* 1862), or that girls are made of 'Sugar and spice and all things nice' (Opie and Opie 1977: 100–101). One thing that we have certainly learnt from the area of f2f bully/ victim problems is that girls and boys aggress to the same extent; it is just that they prefer different methods from each other – boys preferring more 'direct' and physical approaches, and girls favouring more 'indirect' and subtle approaches (e.g. rumours).

In our research we always seek to explore the personal factors that might le someone becoming a bully, a victim, a bully/victim (i.e. both bully and victim a same time), or a bystander (i.e. knowing that bullying is happening but choo perhaps because of fear, not to intercede). We categorise all pupils in a classr or school into one of these four behavioural categories, and sometimes sub-di the categories depending upon whether their experiences occurred 'sometimes more often' or 'more frequently'. Indeed, some researchers use different and more detailed categorisation approaches (e.g. participant role approach: Salmivalli *et al.* 1996). Sometimes we are asked by journalists why we categorise all pupils into these categories. The reason is because bully/victim problems happen in close knit social groups that meet regularly, like classrooms, workplaces, work teams and social groups. As well as this, we seek to understand the differences between boys and girls in terms of involvement and types of bullying behaviours, effects of being involved (e.g. self-esteem, physical health, psychological health, educational attainment) and issues like culture, level of community aggression and violence, the law, school climate and ethos, school policies and parental and community variables. For example, whilst most children report attitudes that are against bullying behaviours, they do not seem to use their potential to intervene – even in hypothetical situations – as 'upstanders and not bystanders' (Salmivalli 2010). This is perhaps because, like many of us, these bystanders fear that any action by them will either reinforce the bullying behaviour, or that they themselves will become a victim. Only by paying attention to all of these issues can we plan appropriately for evidence-informed prevention and intervention programmes (Mc Guckin and Minton 2014) that are community-wide and expand upon the notion of a Whole School Approach (Farrington and Ttofi 2009; Minton *et al.* 2013; Smith *et al.* 2004). An interesting and successful intervention approach that really helps CYP develop an 'upstander' approach is the KiVa program developed by Salmivalli *et al.* at the University of Turku in Finland (www.kivaprogram.net). At its very basis is a useful three-step, self-efficacy strategy that can be readily adapted to any educational process. At the first level, CYP learn about the issues and develop an attitude of 'I know' (i.e. I know that bullying is wrong and people should stand up for victims). At the next level, the issue is made more salient and, through examples and hypothetical situations, the CYP move from 'I know' to 'I can' (i.e. I could do that in a real situation). At the final level, the CYP move from the hypothetical to the real – 'I do'. Results demonstrate reductions in bullying behaviour and more positive attitudes from bystanders.

Traditional f2f bully/victim problems: A useful 'jumping-off point'?

A logical question that we often get asked by educators and parents is whether cyberbullying is just an extension of f2f bullying. When we started to research cyberbullying, neither we nor our international colleagues were sure of the answer. In the previous research regarding f2f bullying, the main researchers were from the fields of psychology and education. With the role of technology and the fact that cyberbullying was a 24/7 phenomena, the input of other disciplines was required (e.g. law, technology, sociology, communications). For the early research into cyberbullying, the main researchers extended their knowledge of f2f bullying by amending their definitions and measurement tools to talk of bully/victim issues that were mediated through the internet, text messages and smartphones. Whilst this was an obvious start, it was only later that we started to understand the real nuances associated with cyberbullying and the limitations of an *ad hoc* approach to researching a social and educational issue like cyberbullying. For example, whilst legal and school policy approaches were traditionally limited to the boundary of the school perimeter, cyberbullying events were mainly occurring outside of school hours and outside of school property, thus requiring a new understanding of home–school–community responsibilities (Purdy and Mc Guckin 2015). For parents and educators, they had no previous personal knowledge of this type of aggressive behaviour, growing up before the advent of much of Web 2.0 capabilities and new social media platforms. Also, initial hypotheses about those involved in cyberbullying incidents were later found to be limited – e.g. the 'revenge of the nerd' hypothesis (Vandebosch and Van Cleemput 2009).

Whilst well-meaning and a welcome start, we have to remember that these early studies became the 'evidence base' for the initial prevention and intervention programmes in the area. However, as professional educators and researchers, we must remember that we have a moral responsibility to ensure that such work is theoretically informed, methodologically robust and tested thoroughly (Mc Guckin and Corcoran 2016). If not, we are building upon quicksand, and that is simply not acceptable when we are dealing with the real issues that confront CYP, families, schools and communities.

An interesting debate on whether cyberbullying is indeed a new phenomenon or just an extension of f2f bullying can be seen in the debate between the two most important and influential researchers in the area (Olweus 2012; Smith 2012). Both of these giants of the literature present arguments about the relative merits of each side of the debate. Olweus takes the position that cyberbullying is an 'overrated phenomenon'. He bases this assertion on the fact that cyberbullying has relatively low prevalence, was not researched in any systematic manner by many research studies (e.g. poorly constructed definitions) and that its prevalence was not rising across time (2006–2010). Smith contends that these types of issues present cyberbullying researchers with both 'challenges and opportunities' for a research programme that would extend knowledge of the more traditional types of bully/victim problems. Indeed, Smith and Berkkun (2016) presented an interesting review of the research to date in the area of cyberbullying, demonstrating that the research community has accepted, and explored, these new challenges and opportunities.

The early cyberbullying research agenda and current collections of knowledge

Whilst there have been some issues with the initial research into cyberbullying, these are typical of any new research into an issue that we confront as educators and researchers. However, the thorough grounding in f2f research and knowledge that had been accrued at the start of the explorations into cyberbullying led to some very valuable outputs from EU sponsored projects and networks. For example, the CyberTraining project (2008) provided a well-grounded, research-based training manual on cyberbullying for trainers. The manual includes background information on cyberbullying, its nature and extent in Europe, current projects, initiatives and approaches tackling the cyberbullying problem, best practice Europe-wide, as well as practical guidance and resources for trainers working with the target groups of (a) pupils, (b) parents and (c) teachers, schools and other professionals. As well as country level chapters regarding the research evidence from that country, there are also chapters regarding contextual issues such as policy directives. Also included are many very practical resources, such as YouTube clips, that can be used as discussion points with groups of trainees. These resources are all backed-up with suggested schedules and materials for each training session. The manual concludes with a comprehensive compilation of supporting references, internet links and other resources for trainers. The newer project, CyberTraining-4-Parents (CT4P), built upon the CyberTraining project by extending support and resources towards parents and family members. CT4P provided 'face-to-face' training courses in each partner country as well as both moderated and self-directed online training courses targeted at an international audience of individual learners. The long-time sustainability of CT4P has been ensured with the self-directed courses remaining online for public use.

The outputs from the EU supported research network (COST Action IS0801: 2008–2012) have been incredibly useful in providing a solid foundation for research and action in the area (Smith and Steffgen 2013). This network has been responsible for much of the contemporary knowledge regarding cyberbullying, with members of the network still collaborating on new projects and seeking to develop critically informed prevention and intervention programmes. At an international level, there have been significant updates from projects such as EU Kids Online, Global Kids Online and Net Children Go Mobile.

Cyberbullying 101: Trying to define the area

For any researcher in the social sciences, but especially in education, the first task that is of fundamental importance is to 'operationally define' the area of concern. By this we mean that we need to define the key terminology in sufficient detail that at a scientific level, we can test the issue of concern. That is, we need to know what we are including (inclusion criteria) and excluding (exclusion criteria) from the definition. Whilst this sounds relatively easy, it is a lot more complex than it first appears. The biggest hurdle for us is that we are often using words that are common everyday words that everyone else uses – albeit that we probably mean something a bit more scientific by them. If we take 'bullying' as an example, you would soon find out that there is no 'agreed' definition that researchers, teachers, parents and CYP can converge upon. So, how did we get to an agreement that we were researching and talking about cyberbullying – that word did not just fall from the sky above? How did we decide that it was one word and not two, or that there was no hyphen in the word?

Of crucial importance here is whether the word and subsequent definition came from a group of 'all knowing adults' or from the CYP that were involved in such 'adult assumed' behaviours. In educational research, we value the notion of 'inclusion' as conceptualised in The Salamanca Statement and the Dakar Framework (UNESCO 1994, 2000) and 'pupil voice' methodologies (Noyes 2005) that allow CYP to participate in issues that affect them and, crucially, to be heard. We even develop novel methodological approaches so as to engage various groups of CYP (Carr-Fanning and Mc Guckin 2017), and develop models (Lundy 2007) that allow us to move beyond a simplistic notion of the inclusion of CYP and their 'voice' so that we are fully conceptualising Article 12 of the United Nations Convention on the Rights of the Child (United Nations 2010).

From f2f definitions to cyberbullying definitions

Despite some differences between researchers regarding the most apt definition for f2f bully/victim problems, the general consensus is that it is a form of social aggression characterised by (a) an intention to cause harm, (b) a repetition of the behaviour and (c) a power imbalance between the perpetrator(s) and victim(s). As a straightforward and logical extension to this definition, we might assume that the same characteristics, with the addition of the electronic context, would constitute the defining components of cyberbullying. However, there is still a lack of consensus regarding the terminology to be used and the core parts of a definition for cyberbullying (see Bauman et al. 2013; Corcoran et al. 2015). Take a second to consider the enormity of this – we have been researching the prevalence, involvement, correlates and developing prevention and interventions in an area that still does not have an agreed definition.

Whilst repetition refers to repeated actions on the part of the perpetrator(s) in an f2f setting, a victim of cyberbullying can experience repetitive victimisation through 'liking', 'sharing' and 'commenting' on content by other users. Indeed, exposure to aggression can be amplified in a cyber context with the possibility for abusive content to be accessed and created globally rather than restricted to the school grounds. Moreover, abuse can occur after school hours with the remote access to victims facilitated by various internet enabled devices. Intent to cause harm is also difficult to assess when the individual(s) creating or perpetuating the bullying content may not fully appreciate the emotional impact for the targeted person(s) as, in many cases, there is a physical separation at the time of the behaviour. Minton (2016) urges us to consider the importance of proximity (or lack thereof) in contributing to acts of such abuse. For example, Minton (2016) highlights advanced weaponry in warfare as a form of technological 'progress' which creates distance from an enemy/target, thus making violent acts more tolerable and likely. In the realm of cyberbullying, any one of the numerous social media platforms may be the weapon of choice. Some argue that such ease of access as well as the capacity to hide one's identity offers a form of power which is unique to the cyber context. Menesini (2012) argues that public access to content and anonymity should be considered important, but not defining, features of cyberbullying. In considering these differing characteristics, there is a case for considering an alternative approach to labelling and defining the area. For instance, whilst Olweus (2012) regards cyberbullying as a subtype of bullying (see above regarding our discussion of Olweus and Smith), others (including us, Corcoran *et al.* 2015; Grigg 2010) feel that a focus on 'cyber aggression' may be more appropriate – in that it is a broader concept that subsumes cyberbullying as understood by CYP. We now explore these differences in terminology.

Is it cyberbullying ... or cyber aggression?

Although we cannot overlook the well-documented overlap between victimisation in schools and victimisation online, it is perhaps time to recognise cyber aggression as a distinct, but related concept, one that encompasses a range of behaviours that extend beyond what would strictly fall within the parameters of bullying. Grigg (2010) has previously recommended a broader focus than simply cyberbullying, which includes abuses such as 'happy slapping' and 'stalking'. In addition to the association between f2f and cyber aggression, research has shown that similar outcomes are predicted by both forms of aggression. Involvement as an aggressor, victim or both in either the physical or cyber world has been found to predict reduced psychological well-being in terms of depressive symptoms, self-esteem, anxiety, suicidal thoughts and behaviours, as well as many other markers of ill-being (Wolke *et al.* 2016). Extending Grigg's (2010) recommendation, our research (Corcoran and Mc Guckin 2014) among 2,474 Irish second-level students aged between 12 and 19 years showed that the way in which we label and measure cyber-based abuse (as either cyber aggression and cyberbullying) can lead to marked differences in the reporting of victimisation and perpetration of such behaviours. The research found that the incidence of reported behaviours was higher if the behaviours were categorised as cyber-aggression rather than as cyberbullying. From this research, we have argued that it is perhaps time to regard cyber-based and school-based peer-to-peer aggression as similar and related, but distinct concepts.

From definitions to the law and to a better solution: Coping skills

The ongoing research and debate regarding the definitions of cyberbullying and cyber aggression are more than mere academic squabbles. Until agreed upon, there will continue to be problems for research that attempts to estimate the prevalence of the issue and the relationship between involvement in such problems and the variables that we are concerned with – from happiness to health and well-being to educational attainment. Indeed, whilst many educators and concerned adults call for legislation in the area, we can now see that if seasoned researchers find the issue difficult to define, what hope is there for a legal remedy? Indeed, we would always question the need for a legal solution to cyber-based aggression among CYP as it could lead to many vexatious claims – claims that could take a long time to progress through the legal system and weigh heavily for too long on the vulnerable shoulders of CYP. Also, with the focus on a legal solution, we argue that many adults and educators would move quickly towards this 'nuclear option' rather than a more considered attempt to help CYP 'cope' with the pressures associated with cyber aggression. With the rate of development of the technologies that can be used in this type of aggression among CYP, a legal solution would end up being out-of-date almost as quickly as it is developed, with the reality being that we would inadvertently criminalise many CYP. Unfortunately, many CYP unwittingly cross the line between the normal explorations and testing of adult boundaries associated with being young and the canon of criminal law that can seem outdated, yet still very real (Purdy and Mc Guckin 2015). The forms of aggression that we are concerned with may spring from either malice or normal developmental challenges (e.g. poor decision-making). Although legislation relating to cyberbullying has been developed in some jurisdictions as a deterrent (e.g. in some US states), in many jurisdictions there is in fact often existing legislation that already addresses specific cyberbullying behaviours, such as stalking and harassment. We concur with Szoka and Thierer (2009) that we should advocate for an 'educate first' approach, rather than prosecute first approach. As coping is one of the most important variables in the study of cyber aggression among CYP, let's take a look at what is known about it.

Coping with cyber-based aggression: Moving from worrying about the technology to helping children and young people cope

In our recent review of the literature regarding coping with cyberbullying, we queried why it seems like every phase of human and societal advancement brings with it a mix of both excitement and anxiety (Corcoran and Mc Guckin 2014). Whilst the experiences and feelings of CYP are real and should not be diminished, we wonder whether the issues related to cyberbullying have been contextualised in such a way that many adults and teachers feel out of their depth when confronted with the issue. Whilst the technological gap between CYP and adults may have created a perceived barrier in knowledge, we argue that this has blindsided many adults to the skills that they already have to counter the insidious behaviours associated with cyber-based aggression. Specifically, whilst some of the solutions to the issue are definitely technological in nature, most of the solutions are to be found in good parenting skills, basic communication skills, differentiated teaching and teaching methodologies, and other non-technical approaches to coping. When we talk with parents about the issues, we often pose the rhetorical question: 'What would your granny have advised?' – with the notional answer being that her advice would probably still be pertinent today. The continual and increasing development of consumer technology, and the fears associated with it, are not new. Whilst our parents could not work out how to use the VHS video cassette recorder when we were younger to record television programmes, and worried for our safety with the development of the portable audio cassette, we all survived to tell the tale. However, with these more modern approaches to interpersonal communication, the issues have become more focused, dangerous and problematic.

The types of concerns that are expressed about today's CYP meeting with physical and psychological harm as a result of online interactions, or anxiety about hindered academic attainment or psycho-social growth as a result of cyber activity, are somewhat different from the worries of past generations in relation to the technological developments of their day. This does then raise important questions in relation to how society copes with the risks associated with the cyber world. For instance, can we learn from the coping skills we employed in other aspects of life when faced with different challenges? It seems logical that we should be able to identify the types of strategies that tend to prove adaptive or maladaptive, those techniques which improve the situation, do little to help, or escalate an already difficult situation. If we are able to recognise successful coping styles relating to the physical world, then surely we should be able to assimilate these responses to a cyber context – shouldn't we? In other words, we may not need to go back to the drawing board when confronted with a cyber-based risk. We have blueprints that can be easily edited and updated. Of course, and as highlighted above, an important principle of prevention and intervention is that we decide upon a course of action based on theory and the research evidence where possible. For this reason, it is essential that we take a thoughtful and considered approach to countering cyber victimisation. So, although we can build on some of the knowledge applied to coping with life's stressors, and more specifically, coping with f2f bully/victim problems, it is also important to consider the ways in which cyber-based aggression may differ and present context-specific challenges. In this way, the most adaptive and advantageous strategies can be identified. We also highlighted the particular vulnerabilities associated with the group most likely to be involved in f2f and cyber-based aggression.

Recognising successful coping styles

The coping strategies of CYP are not always well-informed as they are at a particular developmental juncture where their thinking and decision-making is driven more by emotion and pleasure seeking than it is by analysis and foresight of potential consequences. Life experience and a more developed pre-frontal cortex will enhance decision-making and, in turn, coping strategies over time. Unfortunately, we know that social distance and rash responses to victimisation only provoke and escalate the cycle of victimisation. Considering the challenges of adolescence with the onset of puberty, the focus on peer acceptance and shift away from reliance on parents, the sometimes intense focus on the self and developing identity, victimisation may be particularly tough psychologically. Despite such vulnerability, it is also important to remember that risk does not always amount to harm. The adolescents of previous generations also faced risks in the form of early sexual activity, teenage pregnancy, exposure to alcohol and drugs and other physical risks such as driving too fast or being under the influence of alcohol. However, it must be recognised that the current generation live (at least) a portion of their lives online. As a result, their risky behaviours may be more public and may be recorded and reproduced. Similarly, their humiliation may be more public and permanent. So, whilst the same developmental principles apply, the risk of harm to CYP in the modern and contemporary world is somewhat predicated on the severity of the incident, the public nature of it, how others respond to it and how the young person copes.

Theories about coping

Before we review the research findings regarding how CYP cope with cyber-based aggression, we want to take this opportunity to set out the main theories about how we cope with life's challenges. Considering that our topic is just one of many that CYP will have to cope with, it is useful for us as adults and educators to understand the underlying principles and thoughts about coping.

There are a variety of perspectives on coping with life's strains and stresses (Lazarus and Folkman 1984; Pearlin and Schooler 1978; Roth and Cohen 1986). Although definitions of coping are varied, there are commonalities across definitions. Coping is generally regarded as a response to an experience which is taxing on the resources of the person, something that can potentially cause some degree of harm. Indeed, coping can be regarded as the response (or lack thereof) which may prevent or reduce harm to the person. This is a broad concept which can include both thoughts and behaviours. The coping style used by the person can serve to reduce the emotional distress (emotion-focused coping) of the experience or to bring about a solution to the source of the stress (solution-focused coping). A variety of coping strategies can be used at the same time, and strategies can be adapted over time to respond to the changing nature of a situation. Theorists provide differing terms and conceptualisations of coping. However, a number of important factors are consistent across various theories (see Hill's ABC-X model: 1949, 1958). First, the event or experience itself will be a central component which affects the person's response. Second, it is important how the event or experience is perceived or 'framed' by the person. Whilst one person may regard an online insult as hurtful and frightening, another person may find it amusing. Third, the person's ability or resources to deal with the event or experience when it occurs will be an influential factor. These three aspects of an experience in combination will decide the nature of the crisis the person is met with. When deciding how adaptive a particular coping style or strategy is, we could argue that effectiveness is based upon the psychological well-being of the individual and their ability to overcome or solve the stressful situation. So, we might say that no single coping style is necessarily maladaptive, only more or less adaptive depending on its appropriateness to the current situation. According to Lazarus and Folkman (1984), we should examine coping from a situation-specific perspective. Therefore, not only should we evaluate the coping strategies of the victim(s) in relation to cyber aggression specifically, but we should also assess strategies on a case by case basis, taking Hill's ABC-X model into account. Currently, there is a wealth of literature about coping in response to f2f bully/victim problems, but little evidence in relation to effective coping styles.

Research on coping with cyber aggression

The research on coping with cyberbullying has focused mainly on two aspects of coping: buffering the negative impact of victimisation and stopping the victimisation (Perren et al. 2012a, 2012b). We have highlighted (Corcoran and Mc Guckin 2014) the difficulty of identifying a set of adaptive coping strategies for CYP in this area. We argue that prevention and intervention attempts can be likened to conducting chemistry experiments with 'dirty test tubes' – that is, a variety of factors (intra-personal, inter-personal, situational) will dictate whether a coping strategy will be effective or ineffective – we do not live in a sterile world. Specifically, situational factors such as other concurrent stressors, self-related factors such as maturity, supports such as availability of family and strategies such as preferred coping responses (Schlossberg et al. 1995) will shape how successfully one copes with an incident of cyber-based aggression. Therefore, it is possible to provide evidence that an intervention/strategy will benefit some individuals, but virtually impossible to prove that a particular response will work for any specific individual. However, an important first step is to identify which coping strategies tend to be successful and which strategies tend to be ineffective or harmful. With just some knowledge of these, educators would be better prepared and more confident in their ability to help CYP in their care.

Research has identified a number of effective strategies in response to f2f bully/victim problems. For example, there is a generalised agreement across the literature that the notion of a 'dose effect' regarding friendships is exceptionally helpful, in that the more good friends a CYP has, the better insulated they are from bully/victim problems. Also, appropriate help seeking from 'one good adult' (Dooley and Fitzgerald 2012) is viewed by CYP themselves as a useful coping and support mechanism. Some researchers have explored responses to actual victimisation. Aggressive coping and retaliation are not found to be adaptive strategies, as such responses tend to contribute to further victimisation and reduced psychological well-being. Furthermore, avoidant coping or passive inaction are also found to be unsuccessful styles. By contrast, adaptive coping strategies, including active (as opposed to passive) problem solving strategies have been shown to be successful. Conflict resolution and advice seeking have also been found to be related to reduced victimisation and internalising thoughts.

Considering the unique contextual aspects of cyberbullying, researchers have also examined coping strategies in relation to this phenomenon. This is crucially important, in that we need to build upon the existing knowledge of f2f coping, without indiscriminately applying lessons learned from the traditional context to the cyber world. In reviewing the relevant literature in this area, it is evident that there is a reluctance among many CYP to report victimisation to parents or teachers, due to fear of losing technology-related privileges or receiving inadequate support. This is an important and consistent finding as this strategy by CYP removes an important social resource. Dooley and Fitzgerald (2012) have identified the availability of 'one good adult' as a protective factor for good psychological health among CYP. One of the consistent findings from all of the f2f and cyber literatures is that an appropriate and authentic response from any 'appropriate adult' to a request for help is one of the best interventions available (e.g. parent, sibling, relative, teacher, other school personnel). Interestingly, the need to be cautious in making recommendations for appropriate coping strategies is highlighted by the finding by Shelley and Craig (2010) that social support seeking may, in fact, be a harmful coping strategy for males but not females. This is an interesting scenario. In terms of the socialisation of CYP in society, we know that males may be at risk of further victimisation if they seek social support, in that they can be viewed as weak. And, even if they do seek social support and subsequently receive it, the quality of the support offered may lack the warmth that they require. Online social support seeking by CYP, whilst anecdotally interesting and somewhat intuitive, requires a lot more research examination and has been an issue that has yet to be fully explored (Gunther et al. 2016). Technical coping strategies can also allow a victim of cyberbullying to create social distance from an aggressor through blocking or reporting. Furthermore, technical strategies, such as saving content, allow for the preservation of evidence of the abuse. However, we have continually argued (Corcoran and Mc Guckin 2014) that technical strategies are not necessarily a solution; rather they are a step towards a solution. Whilst new consumer products that are socially driven and interactive will continue to be developed, CYP who are victims of aggression mediated through these technologies should not have to feel that the only solution is to turn the technology off. Rather, there is a wider responsibility for parents and adults to skill themselves in how to support CYP in developing appropriate pro-social communication skills and personal coping strategies so that they can fully enjoy the benefits of what a technology enhanced world can offer.

Reporting abuse to a service provider or sharing evidence of abuse with the police are important considerations. For adults and CYP alike, an important joint task is to explore the support mechanisms that are available from service providers – before any instances of aggression. Simply knowing what support is available and how to access it can enhance the feeling of safety. Whilst not all instances of cyberbullying will veer into the criminal sphere, we always advocate that adults consider informing their local police of what has been happening. The police are always interested in any issues pertinent to CYP and their safety. Like most abuse, the abuser often has more than one victim. By informing the police, the parent may be sharing information that is crucial to the police in their wider investigations of other incidents or in planning crime prevention strategies. By contrast, maladaptive responses to cyberbullying include avoidance, retaliation and aggression. Considering the social distance (physical and temporal), what has often been witnessed has been an escalation of the aggression by the aggressor in response to each of these maladaptive initial responses. From the safety of a bedroom, an aggressive retaliation may seem okay, but all this serves to do is increase the chance of a similar response. Hence, we are always encouraging teachers and adults to teach CYP about emotions and the difference between 'responding' (i.e. delaying the response by taking 'thinking time' as to how best to reply) and 'reacting' (i.e. immediate and perhaps emotionally driven response that may serve to escalate the issue). As technological developments follow Moore's Law (1965), in that the development and availability of connected communication devices approximate an exponential graph, the emotional development of CYP still rises on the graph with modest incremental changes – the same rate as when we were children. It is the gap between these two lines on the graph that we are concerned with. The development of CYP will never match Moore's Law. Rather, we need to accept that this gap is there and is very real, but can be usefully addressed with appropriate and – sometimes old-fashioned – coping skills. Also, similarly to f2f coping, passive or avoidant coping are found to be ineffective in a cyber context, in that neither of these addresses in an assertive manner the discomfort that is being experienced. Effective coping at an individual level seems to be characterised by gaining social support and focusing on possible non-aggressive solutions such as advice seeking and technical strategies.

Future directions

And so, here we are. But, where is 'here'? 'Here' is a very temporal concept. By the time that you have made it to the end of this chapter, we will be at a different 'here'. Having spent our time in this chapter considering the state-of-the-art literature in this fast moving area of modernity that our CYP live in, let us take time to do that very thing that we discussed and hankered for at the start of the chapter – the time to stop-and-stand-and-stare.

In the chapter we outlined the movement from initial definitions of cyberbullying to perhaps a more nuanced definition based upon cyber aggression. A serious question that we now consider in our research and practice is whether we have, in trying to help CYP, inadvertently researched the wrong set of issues. We might have been close to the nub of the issue, but surely this is not good enough when we are working with CYP? This should remind us to remain humble in our work with CYP, cognisant and chastened by our previous failures to protect these most vulnerable citizens, and seek to see ourselves as being 'as good as, but no better than' these cherished co-researchers and citizens. In the age of the internet and social media, children acquire digital footprints before they are born, with gleeful parents posting the neo-natal scan to social media for all to see. Despite what we may think, we are only at the start of the digital revolution. It is both exciting and fearful for each and every one of us. Should we be using iPads and Android tablets in the classroom – even before the research has matured, and when we have 600 years of experience with the printed word since the Guttenberg Press?

Humanity has survived the agricultural revolution and the industrial revolution – why can't we survive this new revolution? Going back to an earlier point – what would be different now, in a generic way, from the advice of our grandmother at the start of any of these previous revolutions? Probably nothing – it always comes back to the issue of helping CYP cope with the vices of modernity. Society learns. Theory and research learn. We learn. We were not born perfect, and we will not die perfect.

In education, we often assert that we cherish CYP, and we all attempt to do our best for them. However, we should remember the wise words of the Roman poet Juvenal: 'Quis custodiet ipsos custodes?' 'Who will guard the guards themselves?' (1982, 347–348). As we move forwards with educational research, we need to constantly challenge each other and our conceptions about the lives and capacities of the CYP that we seek to help.

At the end of 2015, we were actively planning a new book in this area. The premise of the book was that even though we had learnt a lot about f2f bully/victim problems from 30 years of international research and applied practice in schools and education, we were, largely, unprepared for the huge issues that would come along with the internet and Web 2.0 technologies – never mind the internet of things (IoT) and the rapid developments in Artificial Intelligence (AI) and robotics. We had planned 'the' book of 2020 – the one that would predict and plan for the interplay between (a) CYP and their pseudo-cyborg status, (b) emerging technology, (c) AI and robotics, (d) aggression, (e) new coding abilities of CYP and the "dark web" and (f) the advances of issues (e.g. eugenics, ectogenesis) and movements (e.g. transhumanism).

At the end of 2015, as often happens to researchers in the fields of psychology, education and the social sciences, world events overtook us and our research agendas. The events at the Bataclan Theatre in Paris on 13 November, 2015, where 89 people were killed in a coordinated terrorist attack in the theatre, served to remind us all that the world is getting smaller and more local. Since the end of World War II, we have been aware in psychology and education that we are often seen to be reactionary disciplines, whereby society sees our duties as being about understanding these new social issues and the development of appropriate educational responses for our younger generations. For example, see the response to issues regarding influence, conformity and compliance after the events of World War II. Since the events of Paris at the end of 2015, our research and social agenda has seen further development of the research community, the initial psychologist–educator dyad interested in f2f bully/victim problems to the now incredibly wide family of disciplines and researchers trying to understand the processes regarding the radicalisation of CYP in relation to fundamentalist religious groups.

We have arrived at a very opportune point in our knowledge of cyberbullying. From the initial 'rabbit in the headlights' position that we were in just a few years ago, knowledge regarding definitions, involvement, correlates and prevention and intervention strategies are at a more mature stage. I can remember a recent lecture where I had drawn the typical pyramid structure of Maslow's hierarchical theory for the students. Upon returning from our mid-lecture coffee break, I found it funny to see that my chalkboard representation of Maslow's theory had acquired a new base – one much more important than the theoretical 'food, water and shelter' – labelled 'Wi-Fi' – such is the importance of access to Wi-Fi and the continual developments arising from the prophetic and parsimonious Moore's Law for these post-Millenial 'Generation Z' citizens.

To conclude with, we reiterate that the central message from the research in this area is that CYP are vulnerable and will continue to be vulnerable to any new developments in inter-personal communication technology. The cheapest and best preventative method that we have in this area is something that all adults and educators have knowledge and experience of – the development of children's emotions and the strategies that can help them to cope with the issues they confront on a daily basis.

References

Bauman, S. (2011) *Cyberbullying: What counsellors need to know*, Alexandria: ACA.

Bauman, S., Cross, D., and Walker, J. (2013) *Principles of cyberbullying research: Definitions, measures, and methodology*, New York: Routledge.

Belsey, B. (2003) The world's first definition of 'cyberbullying'. Available online from www. cyberbullying.ca [12 May 2017].

Carr-Fanning, K., and Mc Guckin, C. (2017) 'Developing creative methods for children's voice research: Potential and pitfalls when constructing verbal and visual methods for research with children with Attention Deficit Hyperactivity Disorder', in *SAGE Research Methods Cases*, London, United Kingdom: SAGE Publications, Ltd.

Corcoran, L., and Mc Guckin, C. (2014) The incidence of bullying and aggression in Irish post-primary schools: An investigation of school and cyber settings. *Proceedings of Annual Conference of the Educational Studies Association of Ireland*, Sheraton Hotel, Athlone, Ireland, 10–12 April 2014.

Corcoran, L., Mc Guckin, C., and Prentice, G. (2015) 'Cyberbullying or cyber aggression?: A review of existing definitions of cyber-based peer-to-peer aggression', *Societies*, 5: 245–255.

COST Action IS0801 (2008–2012) Cyberbullying: Coping with negative and enhancing positive uses of new technologies, in relationships in educational settings. European Cooperation in the field of Scientific and Technical Research – COST –Available online from http://sites.google.com/site/costis0801.

CyberTraining (2008) CyberTraining – A research-based training manual on cyberbullying. EU Lifelong Learning Programme: [Project No.142237-LLP-1-2008-1-DE-LEONARDO-LMP].

CyberTraining-4-Parents (2010). CyberTraining-4-Parents – Cyberbullying and e-literacy training courses for adult educators working with parents. EU Education and training\ Life long learning (2007–2013)\GRUNDTVIG \ Multilateral projects (Project number: 510162-LLP-1-2010-1-DE-GRUNDTVIG-GMP).

Dooley, B., and Fitzgerald, A. (2012) *My world survey: National study of youth mental health in Ireland*, UCD School of Psychology, Dublin: Headstrong – The National Centre for Youth Mental Health.

Drogin, E. Y., and Young, K. (2008) 'Forensic mental health aspects of adolescent cyber bullying: A jurisprudent science perspective', *Journal of Psychiatry & Law*, 36: 679.

Farrington, D. P., and Ttofi, M. M. (2009), 'School-based programs to reduce bullying and victimization', *Campbell Systematic Reviews* 2009:6, 10.4073/csr.2009.6.

Freud, S., and Hubback, C. J. M. (1922) *Beyond the pleasure principle*, London: The International Psycho-analytical Press.

Grigg, D. W. (2010) 'Cyber-aggression: Definition and concept of cyberbullying', *Australian Journal of Guidance and Counselling*, 20: 143–156.

Gunther, N., Dehue, F., and Thewissen, V. (2016) 'Cyberbullying and mental health: Internet-based interventions for children and young people', in C. Mc Guckin and L. Corcoran (eds.), *Bullying and cyberbullying: Prevalence, psychological impacts and intervention strategies*, Hauppauge, NY: Nova Science (pp. 189–200).

Hill, R. (1949) *Families under stress*, New York: Harper & Row.

Hill, R. (1958) 'Social stresses on the family', *Social Case Work*, 49: 139–150.

Hughes, T. (1857) *Tom Brown's school days*, New York and London: Harper & Brothers.

Juvenal. (1982) *The sixteen satires. Trans. Peter Green*, London: Penguin Books.

Lazarus, R. S., and Folkman, S. (1984) *Stress, appraisal, and coping*, New York: Springer Publishing Company.

Lundy, L. (2007) '"Voice" is not enough: Conceptualising Article 12 of the United Nations Convention on the Rights of the Child', *British Educational Research Journal*, 33: 927–942.

Mc Guckin, C., and Corcoran, L. (2016) 'Intervention and prevention programmes on cyberbullying: A review', in R. Navarro, Y. Santiago, and E. Larrañaga (eds.), *Cyberbullying across the globe: Gender, family and mental health*, London: Springer International Publishing (pp. 221–238).

Mc Guckin, C., and Minton, S. (2014) 'From theory to practice: Two ecosystemic approaches and their applications to understanding school bullying', *Australian Journal of Guidance and Counselling*, 24: 36–48.

Mc Guckin, C., Cummins, P. K., and Lewis, C. A. (2010) 'f2f and cyberbullying among children in Northern Ireland: Data from the Kids Life and Times Surveys', *Psychology, Society, & Education*, 2: 67–48.

Menesini, E. (2012) 'Cyberbullying: The right value of the phenomenon. Comments on the paper "Cyberbullying: An overrated phenomenon?"', *European Journal of Developmental Psychology*, 9: 544–552.

Minton, S. J. (2016) 'Physical proximity, social distance, and cyberbullying research', in C. Mc Guckin and L. Corcoran (eds.), *Bullying and cyberbullying: Prevalence, psychological impacts and intervention strategies*, Hauppauge, NY: Nova Science (pp. 105–118).

Minton, S. J., O'Mahoney, M., and Conway-Walsh, R. (2013), 'A "whole-school/community development" approach to preventing and countering bullying: The Erris Anti-Bullying Initiative (2009 – 2011)', *Irish Educational Studies*, 32: 233–249.

Moore, G. E. (1965) 'Cramming more components onto integrated circuits', *Electronics*, 38: 114–117.

Noyes, A. (2005) 'Pupil voice: Purpose, power and the possibilities for democratic schooling', *British Educational Research Journal*, 31: 532–540.

Olweus, D. (1978) *Aggression in schools: Bullies and whipping boys*, London: John Wiley & Sons.

Olweus, D. (2012) 'Cyberbullying: An overrated phenomenon?', *European Journal of Developmental Psychology*, 9: 520–538.

Opie, I., and Opie, P. (eds.) (1997) *The Oxford dictionary of nursery rhymes (2nd Edn.)*. Oxford: Oxford University Press.

Pearlin, L. I., and Schooler, C. (1978), 'The structure of coping', *Journal of Health and Social Behaviour*, 19: 2–21.

Perren, S., Corcoran, L., Cowie, H., Dehue, F., Garcia, D., Mc Guckin, C., … Völlink, T. (2012a) *Coping with cyberbullying: A systematic literature review: Final report of the COST IS 0801 working group 5*. Available online from https://sites.google.com/site/costis0801/books-and-publications-1 [25 May 2017].

Perren, S., Corcoran, L., Cowie, H., Dehue, F., Garcia, D., Mc Guckin, C., … Völlink, T. (2012b) 'Tackling cyberbullying: Review of empirical evidence regarding successful responses by students, parents, and schools', *International Journal of Conflict and Violence*, 6: 283–293.

Purdy, N., and Mc Guckin, C. (2015) 'Cyberbullying, schools and the law: A comparative study in Northern Ireland and the Republic of Ireland', *Educational Research*, 57: 420–436.

Roth, S., and Cohen, L. J. (1986) 'Approach, avoidance, and coping with stress', *American Psychologist*, 41: 813.

Salmivalli, C. (2010) 'Bullying and the peer group: A review', *Aggression and Violent Behavior*, 15: 112–120.

Salmivalli, C., Lagerspetz, K., Björkqvist, K., Österman, K., and Kaukiainen, A. (1996) 'Bullying as a group process: Participant roles and their relations to social status within the group', *Aggressive Behavior*, 22: 1–15.

Sandford, L. (1991) *Strong at the broken places. Overcoming the trauma of childhood sexual abuse*, London: Virago.

Schlossberg, N. K., Waters, E. B., and Goodman, J. (1995) *Counseling adults in transition: Linking practice with theory (2nd ed.)*, New York: Springer.

Shelley, D., and Craig, W. M. (2010) 'Attributions and coping styles in reducing victimization', *Canadian Journal of School Psychology*, 25: 84–100.

Smith, P. K. (2012) 'Cyberbullying: Challenges and opportunities for a research program – A response to Olweus (2012)', *European Journal of Developmental Psychology*, 9: 553-558.

Smith, P. K. (2014) *Understanding school bullying*, London: Sage Publications.

Smith, P. K., and Steffgen, G. (eds.), (2013) *Cyberbullying, technology and coping*, Oxfordshire: Psychology Press.

Smith, P. K., and Berkkun, F. (2016) 'How research on cyberbullying has developed', in C. Mc Guckin and L. Corcoran (eds.) *Bullying and cyberbullying: Prevalence, psychological impacts and intervention strategies*, Hauppauge, NY: Nova Science (pp. 11–27).

Smith, P. K., Morita, Y., Junger-Tas, J., Olweus, D., Catalano, R., and Slee, P. (eds.) (1999) *The nature of school bullying: A cross-national perspective*, London: Routledge.

Smith, P. K., Pepler, D. J., and Rigby, K. (eds.) (2004) *Bullying in schools: How successful can interventions be?* Cambridge: Cambridge University Press.

Szoka, B. M., and Thierer, A. D. (2009) *Cyberbullying legislation: Why education is preferable to regulation*. Available online from https://ssrn.com/abstract=1422577 [25 May 2017].

The Christian Recorder (1862) The African Methodist Episcopal Church, March.

United Nations (2010) *The UN Convention on the Rights of the Child*, United Nations, June 2010.

United Nations Economic and Social Council (UNESCO) (1994) *The Salamanca statement on principles, policy and practice in special needs education*, Spain: UNESCO World Conference on Special Needs Education: Access and Quality.

United Nations Economic and Social Council (UNESCO) (2000) *The Dakar framework for action: Education for all: Meeting our collective commitments*, Senegal: UNESCO World Education Forum, 26–28 April.

Vandebosch, H., and Van Cleemput, K. (2009) 'Cyberbullying among youngsters: Profiles of bullies and victims', *New Media & Society*, 11: 1349–1371.

Wolke, D., Lereya, T., and Tippett. N. (2016) 'Individual and social determinants of bullying and cyberbullying', in T. Völlink, F. Dehue, and C. Mc Guckin (eds.), *Cyberbullying: From theory to intervention. Current issues in social psychology series* (series editor: Arjan Bos), London and New York: Routledge (pp. 26–53).

Zych, I., Ortega-Ruiz, R., and del Rey, R. (2015) 'Scientific research on bullying and cyberbullying: Where have we been and where are we going', *Aggression and Violent Behavior*, 24: 188–198.

INDEX

 Taylor & Francis eBooks

Helping you to choose the right eBooks for your Library

Add Routledge titles to your library's digital collection today. Taylor and Francis ebooks contains over 50,000 titles in the Humanities, Social Sciences, Behavioural Sciences, Built Environment and Law.

Choose from a range of subject packages or create your own!

Benefits for you

» Free MARC records
» COUNTER-compliant usage statistics
» Flexible purchase and pricing options
» All titles DRM-free.

Benefits for your user

» Off-site, anytime access via Athens or referring URL
» Print or copy pages or chapters
» Full content search
» Bookmark, highlight and annotate text
» Access to thousands of pages of quality research at the click of a button.

REQUEST YOUR **FREE** INSTITUTIONAL TRIAL TODAY

Free Trials Available
We offer free trials to qualifying academic, corporate and government customers.

eCollections – Choose from over 30 subject eCollections, including:

Archaeology	Language Learning
Architecture	Law
Asian Studies	Literature
Business & Management	Media & Communication
Classical Studies	Middle East Studies
Construction	Music
Creative & Media Arts	Philosophy
Criminology & Criminal Justice	Planning
Economics	Politics
Education	Psychology & Mental Health
Energy	Religion
Engineering	Security
English Language & Linguistics	Social Work
Environment & Sustainability	Sociology
Geography	Sport
Health Studies	Theatre & Performance
History	Tourism, Hospitality & Events

For more information, pricing enquiries or to order a free trial, please contact your local sales team: www.tandfebooks.com/page/sales

9 781138 184947